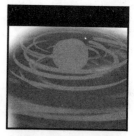

W9-BNQ-988

The NAT Handbook

Implementing and Managing Network Address Translation

Bill Dutcher

Wiley Computer Publishing

John Wiley & Sons, Inc.

NEW YORK · CHICHESTER · WEINHEIM · BRISBANE · SINGAPORE · TORONTO

Publisher: Robert Ipsen
Editor: Carol A. Long
Assistant Editor: Christina Berry
Managing Editor: Marnie Wielage
Text Design & Composition: Publishers' Design and Production Services, Inc.

Designations used by companies to distinguish their products are often claimed as trademarks. In all instances where John Wiley & Sons, Inc., is aware of a claim, the product names appear in initial capital or ALL CAPITAL LETTERS. Readers, however, should contact the appropriate companies for more complete information regarding trademarks and registration.

This book is printed on acid-free paper. ♾

This publication is designed to provide accurate and authoritative information in regard to the subject matter covered. It is sold with the understanding that the publisher is not engaged in professional services. If professional advice or other expert assistance is required, the services of a competent professional person should be sought.

Library of Congress Cataloging-in-Publication Data:

Dutcher, Bill, 1946–
      The NAT handbook : implementing and managing network address
      translation / Bill Dutcher.
          p. cm. — (Wiley Networking Council series)
      Includes index.
      ISBN 0-471-39089-5 (pbk. : alk. paper)
      1. Directory services (Computer network technology)   2. Internet
      addresses.   3. Computer networks—Security measures.   I. Title.   II. Series.
      TK5105.595 .D88 2000
      005.7'1369—dc21   00-061954

Printed in the United States of America

10 9 8 7 6 5 4 3 2 1

Wiley Networking Council Series

Series Editors:

Scott Bradner
Senior Technical Consultant, Harvard University

Vinton Cerf
Senior Vice President, MCI WorldCom

Lyman Chapin
Chief Scientist, BBN/GTE

Books in series:

- *ISP Survival Guide: Strategies for Running a Competitive ISP*
  Geoff Huston
  ISBN: 0-471-31499-4

- *Implementing IPsec: Making Security Work on VPN's, Intranets, and Extranets*
  Elizabeth Kaufman, Andrew Newman
  ISBN: 0-471-34467-2

- *Internet Performance Survival Guide: QoS Strategies for Multiservice Networks*
  Geoff Huston
  ISBN: 0-471-37808-9

- *ISP Liability Survival Guide: Strategies for Managing Copyright, Spam, Cache, and Privacy Regulations*
  Tim Casey
  ISBN: 0-471-37748-1

- *VPN Applications Guide: Real Solutions for Enterprise Networks*
  Dave McDysan
  ISBN: 0-471-37175-0

- *Converged Networks and Services: Internetworking IP and the PSTN*
  Igor Faynberg, Hui-Lan Lu, and Lawrence Gabuzda
  ISBN: 0-471-35644-1

Contents

Acknowledgments

The editor-in-chief at one of the big-time publishing houses (it may be bigger, but it is not as important as Wiley) once observed that editors toil in obscurity, even though they hardly deserve such a fate. Himself an experienced editor, Michael Korda observed, "Perhaps the first, and most important, thing I learned about editing is that the editor invariably neither takes nor gets any credit—his or her work is invisible, anonymous and unsung, and never more unsung than by those who need it most."

Speaking as one who has both needed and received the assistance of some excellent editors, I do not intend to repeat this transgression. My first and most important note of thanks goes to my technical reviewer, Scott Bradner, the chief technocrat of Harvard University's networks, who has either had a hand in or has been present at the creation of many of the complexities of the Internet. Scott had the unenviable task of reviewing my entire manuscript, then diplomatically pointing out (and correcting) each technical flaw, both flagrant and subtle. I could almost hear him groan each time he'd come across certain errors, only expressed differently each time, but he persevered. I learned a great deal about NAT, networking, and the mechanics of the Internet from Scott's edits, and I am deeply in his debt. I also discovered that Scott knows the differences among the different colors of Kryptonite, as well as its source, which heightened my esteem dramatically.

I am also indebted to Carol Long, my editor at Wiley, for convincing me to endure the struggle of writing another book, and for conceiving the idea for this book. It's good for the soul, she'd say, gently reminding me that I'd fallen behind the writing schedule once again, only to catch up in a burst of word-smithing. It was also Carol who brought in Scott as the technical reviewer, and who proposed this as a Wiley Networking Council book.

My thanks also go to the editorial and production team at Wiley—Christina Berry, Marnie Wielage, and Margaret Hendrey—who stayed with the project throughout. Theirs were the tasks of collecting and organizing the parts of the manuscript, matching figures with text, reviewing the text for an overall sense of completeness, and acting as goodwill ambassadors between myself and the Wiley production staff.

Last, I owe my greatest debt of thanks and appreciation to my family, including my parents, for instilling in me the sense that something worth doing is worth doing well, and my wife, Anne, and our son, Greg, for patiently bearing the exposure to considerably more than they ever wanted to know about network address translation.

August, 2000

Networking Council Foreword

The Networking Council Series was created in 1998 within Wiley's Computer Publishing group to fill an important gap in networking literature. Many current technical books are long on details but short on understanding. They do not give the reader a sense of where, in the universe of practical and theoretical knowledge, the technology might be useful in a particular organization. The Networking Council Series is concerned more with how to think clearly about networking issues than with promoting the virtues of a particular technology—how to relate new information to the rest of what the reader knows and needs, so the reader can develop a customized strategy for vendor and product selection, outsourcing, and design.

In *The NAT Handbook: Implementing and Managing Network Address Translation* by Bill Dutcher, you'll see the hallmarks of Networking Council books— examination of the advantages and disadvantages, strengths and weaknesses of market-ready technology, useful ways to think about options pragmatically, and direct links to business practices and needs. Disclosure of pertinent background issues needed to understand who supports a technology and how it was developed is another goal of all Networking Council books.

The Networking Council Series is aimed at satisfying the need for perspective in an evolving data and telecommunications world filled with hyperbole, speculation, and unearned optimism. In *The NAT Handbook*: *Implementing and Managing Network Address Translation*, you'll get clear information from experienced practitioners.

We hope you enjoy the read. Let us know what you think. Feel free to visit the Networking Council Web site at www.wiley.com/networkingcouncil.

Scott Bradner
Senior Technical Consultant, Harvard University

Vinton Cerf
Senior Vice President, MCI WorldCom

Lyman Chapin
Chief Scientist, BBN/GTE

Introduction

All communications on the Internet are rooted in a single concept—the IP address. Those long strings of numbers in an IP address can identify all manner of Internet objects, from users' PCs to host computers, mail servers, Web sites, communications circuits, router ports, and firewalls. Routers use IP addresses to determine how to send Internet communications to their destinations, firewalls judge the suitability of passing traffic to networks they protect by examining them, and Domain Name Services translate text URLs to IP addresses.

The IP address is the most ubiquitous concept in Internet communications, but sometimes a computer's IP address should not or may not be seen on the Internet. All IP addresses are equal, but some are more equal than others. Some network managers who are deeply concerned with security, for example, may want to hide the identity of their computers and systems on their networks. They may want to conceal both the real IP addresses and the text names of those hosts from anyone outside the organization's network.

Other network managers may have set up their companies' networks using private IP address space, numbering their networks and computers from IP addresses that won't work on the Internet. Traffic from computers that use these special IP addresses, intended to be used for experimental networks and applications, will be discarded summarily by Internet routers. These IP addresses brand the traffic as unroutable, to protect the Internet and other systems from potentially harmful or inadvertently confusing applications.

In another play on the security theme, other network managers may want to make it appear that all of their Internet traffic emanates from a single IP address or a small group of IP addresses. This "low-profile" strategy reduces a network's Internet security exposure, as a small number of IP addresses represents all of the users and devices on the network.

In each one of these cases, and in many more (as we will see), the addresses of computers and hosts on an organization's network must be changed, or translated, before reaching the Internet or some other external network. To achieve routability on the Internet, for example, IP addresses must frequently be translated or changed to other IP addresses before they leave a secure or confined network. The technique is called network address translation, or NAT. As we have mentioned, NAT is frequently a technique to achieve a greater goal, such as better security, or in the case of private IP addresses, routability.

In this book, we will examine all of the facets of network address translation, as well as its pitfalls and complications. Though it is simple on the surface, NAT can become, to paraphrase that old adage, as tangled as that web we weave when first we try to deceive. NAT is, at its root, deception. But it is deception with a legitimate purpose, such as security, routability, or making more efficient use of a shrinking pool of IP addresses.

The objective of this book is to explain the breadth of this topic and the underlying technology that supports it. In addition, it is also intended to give network managers, MIS managers, and IT executives a means to assess network address translation in the context of their networks and their situations. Network technicians, for example, may see NAT as a useful tool to achieve connectivity. IT executives, however, may view it as an unnecessary complication that makes their lives, and those of their network users, network managers, and business partners, more complicated than they really need to be.

Our purpose will be to understand NAT and its technological underpinnings, as well as its potential applications, but also to see its dark side clearly. Few things in networking are free, and as a general principle of behavior, deception and subterfuge are rarely free of costs and penalties, either in performance or maintenance. NAT carries with it all of those, and we will seek in this book to give everyone from IT executives to network technicians to your average how-do-you-turn-this-thing-on end user a comprehensive view of NAT.

The chapters of this book have been arranged to present an overview of network address translation and its application first, followed by chapters on implementing NAT and dealing with the complications it brings. Some of those complications are that certain types of applications won't work right with translated addresses. Finally, we'll look forward to the importance of NAT as a technique to allow the Internet to continue to expand and consider how NAT may be an invaluable tool for migrating networks to the next version of the IP protocol, IPv6.

Here's what's in each of the chapters of this book.

Chapter 1: What's NAT?

No network administrator would go to the trouble of changing or translating network addresses unless there were some terrifically good reason to do so. Network address translation can be a relatively simple process, but it can also be complicated. Sometimes, NAT can get downright messy, particularly if it makes things that used to be relatively simple become complex or makes things that used to work fine not work at all.

To start, we'll take a high-level view of network address translation, within the context of how companies and organizations might use it, as well as some of the most common reasons for NAT. We'll also look at the benefits and advantages of NAT, particularly in situations where NAT is the only solution for network or Internet connectivity. Finally, we'll introduce some of the pitfalls of NAT.

Our purpose in this chapter will be to introduce the concepts of NAT and to set an analytical tone for the IT manager or executive. NAT is a technique, but once it is installed, it becomes a way of life, and the IT manager needs a way to think about NAT to see if it's best for the organization.

Chapter 2: The Mechanics of NAT

With a framework for evaluating NAT, the next step is to understand exactly how NAT works. NAT is implemented in routers, firewalls, and proxies, which translate addresses from isolated "private" addressing domains to external "public" addressing domains. In doing so, NAT devices may also have to keep track of the "state" of communications between devices in the public and private addressing domains.

In this chapter, we will look at how the firewalls, routers, and proxies do network address translation and the considerations built into their NAT software modules. In some cases, NAT works at counter-purposes to those of the device itself. Furthermore, the network administrator may want NAT to be done only on certain addresses or address classes or only for certain networks or host addresses.

Last, we will look at some of the common scenarios in which NAT might be employed. A network in which security is a paramount concern comes to mind first, for example, but in other situations, NAT may be a necessity to translate private address space to public address space.

Chapter 3: NAT's Not for Everyone

Having made a good case for NAT in Chapter 2, we'll give equal time to the Loyal Opposition in Chapter 3. As innocent and well meaning as it might seem, and, in fact, essential for some network environments, NAT isn't for everyone. In some network environments, NAT might not work at all, or at a minimum, it might make for confusing Internet connectivity.

The most serious problem with NAT is that it has a way of interfering with some applications, to the point that they may not work at all. NAT may interfere with the smooth operation of even simple, widely used applications, like FTP. Worse, it may make other network management applications like the Simple Network Management Protocol (SNMP) not work either, blinding an essential network management system to what happens behind the NAT box.

Network managers and IT management must evaluate NAT carefully, with full awareness of its potential complications, before blindly plunging in. Of course, NAT can be a foregone conclusion if other decisions precede it, such as using private address space, which makes NAT essential for Internet connectivity.

Chapter 4: The Management Case for NAT

IT managers and network administrators who understand NAT and its implications fully can make intelligent and informed decisions about deploying it. They can also take steps to ensure connectivity with business partners and other organizations, if they know that NAT is being used to connect other systems to theirs. NAT is supposed to be transparent, but it is often helpful to know if NAT is being done, particularly if network management is part of network connectivity.

Network managers and IT executives must understand the networking environments in which NAT can and should be used, as well as its implications for connectivity. In this chapter, we will examine the management perspectives on NAT and the networking scenarios it implies. This includes using public and private address space, deploying proxies to manage and control network applications, managing networks and communications systems, and determining how NAT can affect other IT strategies.

In addition, we will look at the costs of NAT. The capability to translate network addresses is built into firewalls and routers, so a basic ability to do NAT isn't an extra cost item. NAT, however, implies administration, monitoring, and maintenance, all of which cost people time and add to the overhead costs of running a network.

Chapter 5: Dynamic and Static NAT

Having looked at the management view of NAT, in the next few chapters we'll return to examining the technology of NAT. Our view, as we stated before, will be not only to take a theoretical view of how NAT works, but at the same time to evaluate NAT technology in the context of running and managing real networks.

There are two general techniques for translating network addresses. The first is to use a fixed address to which a specific "inside" address will be translated. The second is to assign the "translate to" addresses dynamically, so that they may change each time NAT is invoked.

As you might imagine, both the former, which is called static NAT, and the latter, which is called dynamic NAT, have their own advantages and disadvantages. Depending on the network environment, either may meet IT needs for connectivity, security, and network performance, but one may be better than the other for the important issue of network management.

Chapter 6: Firewalls, Routers, and NAT

Routers, firewalls, and proxies are the "NAT boxes" that do the heavy lifting of translating network addresses. In this chapter, we will examine the differences among these devices and see how they are usually configured to do NAT. For most of them, NAT is an additional duty, a function ancillary to their main purpose in life, which may be routing IP traffic or examining traffic to fit security parameters. For NAT boxes, NAT is usually the equivalent of moonlighting, although it's a task they must do for certain addresses.

In this chapter, we will look at the hardware and software usually required of a device that is expected to translate network addresses. NAT can add a considerable amount of overhead and processing load to a firewall or a router, so it isn't the computer equivalent of falling off a log.

As we have done in previous chapters, we will look at these NAT boxes and how they do NAT from the perspective of the network managers and IT management who must acquire, size, configure, position, and maintain them.

Chapter 7: Making Applications Work with NAT

As the chapter title implies, there's more to NAT than dropping in a NAT box, translating IP addresses, and walking away. NAT is supposed to be transparent, working behind the scenes, unseen and unnoticed. In a perfect world, that would be true, but network managers and IT executives know that their worlds and networks are far from perfect.

In this chapter, we will examine the most common problem with many NAT configurations. The problem is that some applications don't work well when IP addresses are translated. It's not that the applications are at fault. It's just that they weren't designed with NAT in mind or that the way they operate can't tolerate the machinations of NAT.

Network managers and IT executives must be aware of the potential for application problems behind NAT boxes and prepare for those problems in rolling out a NAT strategy. They should also understand strategies and techniques to prevent these problems, or to minimize them if they do occur. We'll also examine the functions of application-level gateways (ALGs), which can make applications that run into problems with NAT work properly.

Chapter 8: NAT and DNS

One of the problems that NAT introduces to networks is that it breaks the end-to-end significance of IP addresses. Many network services, particularly the Domain Name Service (DNS), don't know that NAT exists, and therefore they don't recognize that the real end address of a host may not be what it appears to be.

DNS is one of those almost invisible network services that translates the text names of hosts to IP addresses. The problem is that DNS may have an IP address for a host that isn't its real address because its real address may be translated to something else by NAT. In some cases, applications won't work properly if DNS doesn't have an accurate address for a host.

In this chapter, we'll look at how DNS services are configured and the services they provide, in order to understand how NAT may affect the data maintained in the DNS resource records. There are ways around these problems with DNS application-level gateways, but in most cases, DNS and NAT work together quite successfully.

Chapter 9: Public and Private Addressing

We have tried not to cast NAT in a negative light because there are many circumstances when NAT is essential to achieving Internet connectivity. One of the most commonly employed solutions to the crisis in IP addressing (which will be examined in Chapter 12) is for an organization to use private IP addresses in its internal networks. These addresses won't be routed on the Internet unless they are translated to routable, public addresses.

For better or for worse, using private addresses implies using NAT. It's not a bad thing because NAT enables networks using private addresses to connect to the Internet as if they were using public addresses.

The task for network managers and for IT management is to make sure that NAT boxes have enough public IP address space to accommodate their needs. In addition, NAT boxes will have to be sized and configured for the number of devices for which NAT will have to be done.

Chapter 10: NAT and Routing

One of the primary reasons for using NAT is to give a company or organization that uses private addressing on its internal networks full connectivity to the Internet. Without the address transformation services of NAT, private addresses won't be routed by Internet routers because they're not supposed to be sent out of the private network addressing realm.

Internet connectivity is no longer a luxury, and in many businesses, it isn't an option, either. As a result, network managers and IT executives must be concerned with how NAT affects Internet routing. Routing information to external network routes, such as to networks on the Internet, may have to be passed back to routers on a private network, to advertise external routes. Conversely, some representation of internal routes may also have to be passed outside the private network, in order to achieve full Internet connectivity and routing.

Another issue that we will examine in this chapter is how NAT affects networks that have more than one Internet connection. Multihomed networks, as they are called, pose particularly thorny problems for any type of routing. NAT adds another complication for multihomed networks.

Chapter 11: Load Balancing and NAT

The volume of traffic to popular Web sites or FTP servers can quickly grow to such a level that it threatens to overwhelm a single server or host. One common solution to this problem is to distribute the load to the site across several hosts or servers in a server "pool." No matter how many servers are in the pool, to Internet users, they all appear to be a single same host.

There are a number of techniques to distribute traffic across several hosts or servers, one of which is NAT load balancing. A firewall or router can be configured to act as a load balancer, by using its NAT functions to readdress a sequence of incoming connections to the servers in the pool.

NAT isn't necessarily the best solution to the load balancing problem, though. In most cases, NAT doesn't necessarily make an intelligent decision about which server in the pool is best able to handle the request. It's really a load distributor because NAT doesn't necessarily know if the load is balanced across all the servers in the pool. It's a relatively simple solution to the load balancing problem that suits the requirements of many load balancing situations.

Chapter 12: The Crisis in IP Addressing

So far, we've discussed a great many of the problems that NAT may introduce, but in this chapter, we'll give NAT some credit. Many organizations use NAT because it gives them the freedom to use freely-available private IP address space on their networks. Those private addresses have to be translated by NAT to public, routable addresses before they reach the Internet.

As we discuss in Chapter 9, organizations that use private address space and NAT take pressure off the growing demand for the finite resource of public, routable address space. This forestalls the day when the Internet may run out of unique IP address space.

Of course, most network managers and IT executives don't have such altruistic goals when they choose to use private address space. Global address conservation isn't really one of network managers' primary concerns, but possibly IT executives may feel better knowing that in this case, NAT does help accomplish a greater good.

Chapter 13: NAT and Security

Just when we thought we were out of the woods with NAT and the problems it might create, along comes the vexing issue of security. Concerns about Internet security have heightened IT executives' and network managers' sensitivities to intruders and hackers. If you can't stop 'em, one line of thinking goes, maybe you can discourage them by obscuring the content of whatever they intercept.

Most network managers have introduced some type of security to their networks, in response to IT management policies about encrypting and securing transmitted data. The trouble is, as we will see in this chapter, that security schemes can interfere with NAT, as well as with network routing in general. Security techniques, such as encryption, can compound the problems that NAT may introduce.

We will also look at how NAT works into an organization's security plan. NAT is sometimes regarded as a security technique, but it's more appropriately regarded as a relatively minor aspect of a comprehensive security posture, not the centerpiece of a security strategy.

Chapter 14: NAT and Virtual Private Networks

One of the facets of the trend to try to use the Internet for everything is to use it as a substitute for leased lines or as an alternate way for remote users to connect back to a remote access server, instead of making a long-distance phone call. In both cases, the Internet is being used to create a virtual private network, or VPN. A VPN appears to be a private line, but it's actually being run over the shared Internet.

Most VPNs imply NAT, in order to provide an address management plan for VPN connections. In this chapter, we will look at how VPNs work, as well as some typical VPN configurations. We will also examine how NAT works in VPN environments, extending identities from a VPN address pool out to remote devices.

We will also look at VPN security and how NAT works with several VPN security techniques. Some types of VPNs imply different types of encryption, which may not be compatible with the address modifications that NAT does.

Chapter 15: Realm-Specific IP and NAT

As useful as NAT is for networks that use private addressing, concealing networks behind a firewall's external interface, or for load balancing, there are some barriers it can't scale. It still interferes with some applications, and some types of encryption can foil NAT's careful charade.

One of the proposals made by the Internet engineering community is a tactic to circumvent the problems that NAT may cause, yet still keep the same structure of NAT. This technique, called Realm Specific IP (RSIP) uses NAT, but it extends the outside addressing plan used by NAT all the way back to end users' PCs and application clients.

RSIP is still in the experimental stage, but it represents a technique that could solve some of the application and encryption problems that NAT can cause. It would also preserve the concept of NAT, as well as its utility for using private addressing on inside networks and for representing a large number of inside network addresses on a single external firewall or router interface.

Chapter 16: Planning for NAT

In addition to evaluating the suitability of NAT for an organization's networks, IT executives who decide that NAT is a suitable fit for their networks must also plan for its implementation. In this chapter, we will examine the process of planning to implement NAT, either in an existing network or in a new network.

As we have discussed in earlier chapters, introducing NAT may add complications to the network structure. It may also affect applications, and it may impact the performance of NAT boxes, such as routers and firewalls. This chapter will seek to give IT executives and network managers a framework for planning to implement NAT, as well as strategies for implementing NAT.

Chapter 17: Case Study: Moving to Private Addressing

This chapter and the following one are examples of how an organization might deploy NAT to meet different networking requirements. In this case study, the network managers and the IT executives have decided to use NAT to move their network to private addressing. In this case study, NAT will be implemented on a firewall, which hides the private addressing ranges and network identities of the systems on the company's network.

As we will see in this case study, there's more to securing a network than just hiding addresses behind NAT. Using private addressing behind NAT gives the network some measure of security, but carrying out IT network security policies may imply the coordination of a number of other systems and capabilities.

Chapter 18: Case Study: NAT Load Balancing

In the second case study, we will examine the implementation of NAT to balance the load on a number of Web servers on the internal network. As we will see, NAT can function as a technique to distribute the load on a group of servers or hosts. It's not as capable as some other types of load balancing or load distribution techniques, but it does work.

We will also see in this case study, in contrast to the first case study, how NAT can be deployed to translate only a limited number of internal network addresses. In this sense, NAT can be a "point solution" to a specific requirement, rather than apply to all traffic flowing into and out of the network.

Chapter 19: The Future of NAT

NAT was devised as an accommodation for the shortage of public address space, but also as a means to allow organizations to use private address space and yet still gain full Internet connectivity. The crisis in public address space, which we discussed in Chapter 12, is only going to get worse unless using private address space becomes much more widespread.

If the Internet did not threaten to grow both exponentially and infinitely, NAT could be the solution to the whole problem. Networks still need public, routable addresses, and those will eventually be exhausted. Before then, we hope, we will have successfully transitioned to the next generation of the IP protocol, IP Version 6. IPv6 would alleviate the addressing crisis because it has a 128-bit address field, which would give us trillions of additional addresses.

Even if it takes quite a while to get to implement IPv6, network managers and particularly IT executives need to understand the issues for IPv6, as well as the migration path to this new protocol and the obstacles they and the rest of the Internet would have to hurdle to get there.

What's NAT?

On the surface, translating IP addresses from one address to another doesn't make a whole lot of sense. After all, what matters in Internet communications is that you have an IP address, not necessarily what that address is. As long as the address is the appropriate length, and as long as routers on a network have some vague idea where the network to which that address belongs might be located, they will forward IP datagrams to the destination. The computer to which the address belongs might not be powered on, or it might be temporarily unreachable, or it might not exist at all, but IP addressing and IP routing will still work. One number is as good as another, right?

Well, yes, most IP addresses are as good as any other, but no, not all IP addresses are equal. Some fall into special categories, and some aren't intended to appear on the Internet at all. For Internet routing and applications on networks connected to the Internet to work properly, IP addresses must be the *right* kind of address, which means an address belonging to a *public* address range.

Some IP host addresses and network addresses might be used in more than one place on the Internet. It's not supposed to happen this way, but it does. It may be accidental, or it might be intentional. It might also be that instead of applying for or acquiring a unique IP network address, a network administrator has elected to set up a network using an IP address that he or she created.

The network may have run perfectly well with this made-up address because it was a valid IP address. Nobody may have thought anything of it. In fact, when the network administrator took a new job, everyone forgot it wasn't really their address at all because it had always worked just fine for internal network communications. But when the network was connected to the Internet, problems started because some other network had been assigned the IP address, with the understanding that it was unique to that network alone.

Other network administrators may have concerns about network security. The Internet is no longer a safe, protected world, where the greatest danger was accidentally stabbing yourself in the hand when reaching for that tiny screwdriver in your plastic pocket protector. Now we have cyber-terrorists, denial-of-service attackers, mail spammers, site hijackers, credit card record stealers, social engineers, and all manner of hackers, intruders, and computer miscreants on the Internet. It's no longer a safe place for an unprotected computer system.

In response to these threats, many network managers and IT executives have decided that one of the lines of defense they can erect is to conceal the existence of the hosts, PCs, and servers. Firewalls at the entrances to networks screen the existence of the systems behind them. Firewalls that do NAT hide both the existence of those systems, and, when they do communicate with other systems on the Internet, their real IP addresses with different addresses.

Other networks use IP addresses that can't be routed on the Internet. They are addresses from several special address ranges that have been set aside for use on private networks, which aren't intended to be connected to other networks. These network addresses must be changed by a firewall, router, or a NAT device before they ever reach the outside world.

What to Do?

What to do about these problems? Often the simplest solution, but, as we will see, not necessarily the most foolproof, is to substitute a different IP address for the address that was originally created in the IP datagram. It's sort of like posting an "in care of" address on an envelope, in that the person to whom the envelope is delivered knows to whom to forward the letter. The "in care of" person isn't the real addressee, but the letter gets delivered anyway, as long as he or she knows what to do with it.

IP address translation works the same way. For a variety of reasons that we will discuss shortly, the source or the destination IP address can be changed to another address. As long as the IP address is a valid one, and as long as routers in the Internet have an idea where the network that corresponds to that address might be located, they will forward the traffic to its destination.

IP ADDRESSES

IP datagrams, which are the basic unit of communications for IP networks and the Internet, bear two numeric IP addresses. One is the IP address of the system that originates the traffic, and the other is the IP address of the system to which the traffic is to be sent. The addresses are numbers that uniquely identify each system on a network or on the Internet. IP addresses are like telephone numbers or Social Security numbers, which also identify telephones or people uniquely.

Each IP address is a string of digits, separated by periods, as shown in Figure 1.1. Each IP address is actually a 32-bit binary number, but for our convenience, we express it as the decimal version of four eight-bit bytes. Instead of having to remember or type a sting of 32 ones and zeroes, we can type 26.5.0.2 or whatever the IP address is.

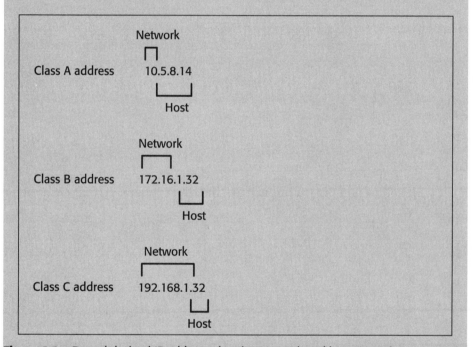

Figure 1.1   Dotted decimal IP address, showing network and host ID portion.

Each IP address has two parts—a network part and a host part. The former identifies a specific network, such as a local area network, and the latter identifies a computer on that network, such as a PC or a server. Special-purpose communications computers called "routers" use IP addresses to locate systems on networks and the Internet and to forward traffic to specific destinations.

Translation or Substitution?

This technique of IP address replacement is usually referred to as *network address translation*, or NAT. At its simplest level, NAT isn't translation at all, nor is it focused on network addresses. It is the substitution of one IP address for another, usually the substitution of a single host address or host addresses in a well-defined range of addresses, for one or more host addresses.

Because NAT substitutes host addresses, not network addresses, it might be called host address substitution. NAT usually replaces addresses from the host addresses within a specific range of network addresses. Those addresses usually belong within the range of addresses on a specific IP network. So, because NAT works on one or more host addresses in the range of addresses defined within a network, and even though it's address substitution, not translation, it's called NAT, not something else.

It's probably best to leave this hair-splitting to the number-of-angels-dancing-on-the-head-of-a-pin crowd, or to a presidential legal defense team. The key point is that at its root, NAT is substituting one IP address for another (usually the source IP address, but in special cases, the destination address) when IP datagrams leave one network to traverse the Internet, or some other network, to get to another.

This is not to say that NAT is necessarily foolproof. It can cause a number of problems, some of which are minor, and some of which are serious. One of the philosophical objections to NAT is that it breaks the end-to-end significance of IP addresses. IP addresses are supposed to identify uniquely the end-points of a network connection. If you throw NAT into the connection, that end-to-end significance of the IP address is broken.

And what difference does that make, you say? Maybe none, but network management systems, for instance, may want to know the real identity of the systems they are managing. Hackers and intruders like NAT because it can hide their real identities. And, as we will see, some applications and encryption schemes don't work well, or don't work at all, when NAT is interposed in the path between client and server. Frequently, a NAT device must translate well-known TCP port numbers, like HTTP's Port 80, to other port numbers, just to keep straight which client originated traffic. Even this relatively simple issue can become confusing, particularly when there are several servers using the same port numbers behind NAT.

The Reasons for NAT

You have to question why someone would want to change IP addresses, particularly if IP addresses are part of that largely hidden infrastructure of the Internet. For the most part, users never see IP addresses, except when they're poking around that Control Panels…Network icon on a Windows PC, or when an adventuresome, unique configuration-happy Unix user (by definition, aren't they all?) displays the system's etc/hosts file. Sometimes IP addresses of Web sites flash by in the Status Bar or Address Bar of a Web browser.

For the most part, though, IP addresses blend into that cosmic background noise of the Internet. Most users know they exist, but few users can tell you what his or her PC's IP address really is. In fact, techniques like the *Dynamic Host Configuration Protocol* (DHCP) can assign a different IP address to a PC each time it boots up, making IP addresses even more transient.

NAT definitely has a place in networking, and there are several well-established circumstances in which network managers might choose to deploy NAT. In fact, in several of these circumstances, it's essential.

Private Address Space

Many network managers view NAT as a security tool or an administrative device, unless they have networks that use private address space. Private address space, to be discussed more fully in Chapter 9, "Public and Private Addressing," designates specific ranges of IP addresses that have been set aside for use in experimental networks that don't connect with any other networks.

The experimental nature of this private addressing game preserve means that the addresses of computers within the private address range can't be

RFC 1918 ADDRESSES

RFC 1918 identifies three ranges of IP addresses that are to be used for private networks. There is one address range in each of the three Class A, B, and C address ranges. The private address space ranges are as follows:

Class A. 10.0.0.0 /8 (the entire Class A network 10.0.0.0; about 16 million host addresses).

Class B. 172.16.0.0 /12 (the 16 Class B networks from 172.16.0.0 through 172.31.0.0; about one million host addresses).

Class C. 192.168.0.0 /16 (the 255 Class C networks from 192.168.1.0 through 192.168.255.0; about 65,000 host addresses).

Even though these address ranges were set aside for experimental networks, any network may use them. RFC 1918 addresses, however, won't be routed by Internet routers because they are assumed to originate on isolated, experimental networks. That's why private addresses must be changed by NAT to routable, public addresses before they leave a network that uses private address space.

allowed out on the Internet. If IP datagrams that bear source IP addresses in the RFC 1918-defined address ranges are forwarded to Internet routers, they have been programmed to discard those datagrams. That router software convention ensures that unintended escapees from private address ranges won't get far from the border router of the private network.

A number of networks that aren't experimental do use private addresses. Private addressing frees an organization from the limits of having to get public addresses. Networks that use private addressing don't have a choice about NAT; they must use it to send traffic to the Internet.

In most cases, networks that use private address space will connect to the Internet through a firewall or a router that does NAT. The router or firewall NAT software module will substitute a routable, unique, public address for the unroutable private address in the source address field of the IP datagram. A response from an Internet server or host to the outgoing datagrams will arrive back at the router or firewall. There, the router or firewall will switch the destination address of the IP datagrams to that of the host that originated the request. The datagrams will now bear unroutable addresses, but they will traverse the private network, which can route them.

Connecting a network that uses private addressing to the Internet implies using NAT or some other technique to hide those unroutable source IP addresses. If they aren't changed to public addresses before leaving the private network, they'll never reach their destinations.

Avoiding Renumbering When Changing ISPs

Some people just don't like change. Among them are network administrators, for whom upgrading to a new version of an operating system, bigger and more feature-laden applications, or other software often means more problems than benefits. Another type of change those network administrators hate is changing IP addresses. There are perfectly good reasons for renumbering a network into different IP address space, but your average network administrator would probably take a root canal over changing the IP addresses on all of the computers and routers on the organization's network.

Sometimes, though, it might be necessary, particularly if the organization changes ISPs. These days, it's not uncommon for the IP addresses that an ISP's customers use to "belong" to that ISP. They're assigned to the organization's customers as part of the ISP's standard service. Larger organizations and companies may have their own, permanently-assigned address space, but not all do. In many cases, it's easier to get addresses assigned by the ISP.

The reason the addresses "belong" to ISPs is that doing so helps to perpetuate and preserve some measure of hierarchy in the IP addressing structure. With the Internet growing rapidly, ISPs are under a lot of pressure to keep Internet routing as simple as possible. One way to do this is for ISPs to aggregate addresses, which simplifies the routing tables maintained by other ISPs. Address aggregation means that a large group of numerically contiguous IP network addresses belongs to a single ISP, and it is advertised to other ISPs as a single block, rather than a large number of individual addresses. Address aggregation can be quite tricky for networks that have multiple connections to different ISPs, so sometimes ISPs can't control address aggregation as closely as they might like.

If the organization switches to another ISP—for better service, lower costs, or seats in the ISP's stadium skybox—the IP addresses that the organization uses on its internal networks don't necessarily stay with the organization. If the addresses belong to the ISP, the ISP may take them back and may not route Internet traffic back to those addresses if they're now reached through a different ISP.

What to do about this quandary? Many network managers solve the problem with NAT. They keep the old address space and translate network addresses to another block of public addresses assigned by the new, *gaining* ISP. An organization might do this even though eventually its old addresses might be reassigned by the *losing* ISP to another one of its customers.

Will NAT save the day and help the network manager avoid renumbering everything in the network? Yes, it will because using some other IP address space on a network isn't unlike using private address space, which we discussed earlier. The addresses on the internal network can stay unchanged, using NAT to translate them to and from other addresses through a firewall or a router.

In the long term, using public address space that an organization really doesn't own isn't such a good idea. Eventually, the organization should get its own address space, either by applying for it to the American Registry for Internet Numbers, ARIN (see Chapter 9, "Public and Private Addressing") or by getting it from the new ISP. It's bad form to use what could be someone else's address space, as it could escape into the Internet and confuse routing.

A better choice is private address space with NAT. It's cleaner, it's safer, and it's above reproach. And, if those internal addresses ever do escape into the Internet, the traffic will be thrown away harmlessly—unless it's your applications that are affected.

Load Distribution

Just a few years ago, back in Precambrian Internet time, many companies set up a single host to act as a Web server. When traffic loads were low, a single server might suffice. As traffic loads grew, that single server (and frequently its low-bandwidth Internet access line) was often overrun with traffic. The server bogged down, and response time grew. The best thing that could happen was that users trying to get into the site would lose interest and go somewhere else.

That's not an acceptable solution to high-traffic Web sites, online stock trading firms, and e-commerce sites. They have to be up all the time, and they have to scale their Web sites to meet the demand. And even though many high-traffic Web sites have expanded to try to match demand, we know from several well-publicized site outages that Web site traffic often tests the outer limits of Web site hardware and software.

One solution that many high-traffic Web sites have used is Web site load distribution, aided and abetted by NAT. Instead of a single server for a high-traffic Web site, there are two, three, five, or tens of servers, all acting as the same site, such as www.bigcompany.com. As shown in Figure 1.2, traffic to the Web site is distributed to each of the servers, either in a round-robin fashion or according to whichever server is least heavily loaded at the time. Some device, such as a specialized NAT box or a special load distribution system, makes the decision about which server will take each Web site request.

NAT is involved in this because while each of the Web servers has its own IP address, the Web site is known to the outside world by a single IP address and a single host name. The NAT box or load distributor changes the IP destination address of inbound traffic to one of the Web servers and forwards it to that host.

For example, let's say that the e-commerce site of BigCo, the world's largest online widget merchant, is reachable through www.bigco.com. There's a DNS entry that maps www.bigco.com to an IP address, such as 172.16.2.1. Inbound

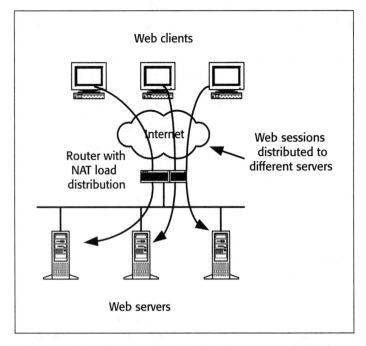

Figure 1.2   Load distribution, showing three servers behind a router with NAT with load balancing.

traffic will be routed to that address, but it's really a NAT box on the edge of the BigCo network. The NAT box changes the destination IP address to that of one of the Web servers under its control that has a copy of the www.bigco.com Web site files and forwards the traffic to that server. When the server responds, the source address is changed back to 172.16.2.1 and sent back to the originator of the transaction.

There's more to this, as we will see in Chapter 8, "NAT and DNS." Certain parts of other protocols must also be managed to make this work, but it's not terrifically complicated. This is a pure NAT play because it's a subterfuge for making an application or a site work better.

Overlapping Addresses

Many organizations have decided that even though it might seem a little strange, private addressing really isn't all that bad. Private addresses must be changed to public addresses to be routable on the Internet, which implies the use of NAT on networks that need Internet connectivity. As we discussed in the section in this chapter on private addressing, NAT works, and it shields those addresses from the outside world.

Aside from the requirement for NAT, one of the problems with private addressing schemes is that they tend to be repeated in many different organizations. If two different organizations both use private addressing, and from the same private address ranges, then NAT must be used twice, once on each side of the connection. This is frequently a problem when two companies that use private address space merge. Even with careful planning, some overlap may occur.

Take network 10.0.0.0, the Class A address reserved for private addressing by RFC 1918. Because its address space is so large, many organizations that want to use private address space choose to use 10.0.0.0. After all, if you're going to use private address space, why not use the biggest block available?

So, it's not uncommon for two organizations that communicate to have overlapping address space. Many companies that provide an information service or a common service point for electronic trading use private addressing space for their hosts and services. Networks that use the same private address space will need double address translation to communicate with this external service.

Security

Suppose a network manager or an IT executive is concerned about network security. We might define a smaller universe by saying that we should suppose a network manager or IT executive who isn't concerned about security. In short, few network managers or IT executives aren't concerned with network security. Most realize that if they aren't, they'll soon be looking for other jobs.

Many network managers use NAT as one of the weapons in their arsenal of security tools. In most cases, NAT is deployed as part of the security perimeter established in the firewall. NAT software in the firewall changes the source IP address in IP datagrams going through it to different addresses. The firewall may even change the source address of any traffic from any internal host to a single IP address. That single IP address might be the external network interface of the firewall, through which all traffic goes to the Internet.

The reason for doing this is to make it appear to the outside world (in other words, the Internet) that the organization's entire universe of Internet users is only one host. Moreover, that one host is actually the firewall. Unlike other host computers, the firewall understands security and runs application software to screen and filter all traffic that comes to it.

The screening and filtering power of the firewall, which appears to be the only host on the organization's networks that is visible from the outside, is only the first part of the NAT security justification. The second part is that whatever the identities are of other hosts inside the network, either by IP address or possibly by their text names (e.g., fileserver1.bigcompany.com), they can remain hidden behind the firewall. If the firewall and NAT and a few other things work right, their addresses and even their existence are never seen outside the organization's internal network. All that's ever seen is the firewall's external interface address, not the address of any of the hosts behind it.

It's another issue whether this really makes the network behind the firewall more secure. As we will see when we discuss how NAT can affect applications in Chapter 7, "Making Applications Work with NAT," some types of NAT still allow the identity of hosts (either the IP address or host name, or both) on a "screened" network to be visible to the outside world. NAT can be part of an overall security framework, but by itself, the security it affords is not impenetrable. In fact, most network security experts do not think that hiding addresses behind NAT is a particularly significant security measure. It helps, but it's not all that effective, particularly when compared to other security measures.

Transitioning to IPv6

NAT, private addressing, and other techniques have given us tools to cope with the IP address shortage problem. We are running out of IP address space, but facing up to the problem is still a few years away. At least that's the same thing people said about the Y2K problem in the mid-1990s.

Eventually, we may run out of IP addresses, or at the least, be constrained by the limitations of the current version of IP, which is IPv4. The next version of the IP protocol, IPv6, will solve the IP addressing problem by expanding the number of available addresses a million-fold. We'll address this more fully in Chapter 19, "The Future of NAT."

There will, however, be an uncomfortable and, most likely, prolonged transition period when both IPv4 and IPv6 addresses are running around the Internet. As we will see in Chapter 19, one of the techniques to achieve this transition without things getting too messy is NAT. Special NAT boxes can translate IPv4 addresses to IPv6 addresses, and vice-versa, providing that kind of seamless integration that software companies are forever promising.

Summary

Using NAT to help solve the IPv6 transition problem is an application for NAT that is out on the distant edge of the foreseeable future. It's not one of the more pressing, current-day issues for which NAT is a viable solution, such as security, using private addressing, overlapping addressing, and load balancing.

The are some circumstances in which NAT is an operational necessity, such as where private addressing has been used. Without NAT or some technique like it, a private addressing domain would forever be isolated from the Internet or be restricted to communicating only with partners that understood and accommodated its addressing problem.

In other circumstances, such as load balancing, NAT isn't necessarily an operational requirement, but it does simplify maintaining the illusion of a virtual host. Load balancing can be done by other techniques, such as having DNS return one of a set of IP addresses for a set of servers, but it's not as well controlled as it is with NAT.

Security, which is often cited as one of the most widely employed purposes for NAT, is improved by hiding addresses with NAT, but it's far from a foolproof technique. Just because NAT changes addresses doesn't mean they can't be discovered. Of course, whether this information is really of much use to a hacker is another matter.

In the next chapter, we'll look more closely at the *how* of NAT instead of the *why*. We'll examine how NAT works, and how NAT works in the typical scenarios in which NAT is employed, in order to build a framework for evaluating the suitability of NAT for various network environments.

CHAPTER

2

The Mechanics of NAT

Now that we have an idea of where network address translation fits into network operations, let's look at how NAT works. It certainly seems as though NAT is simple enough, as long as it just means translating one address to another. Its operation becomes more complex if changing and managing TCP port numbers is thrown into the mix.

How NAT operates usually depends on the software in firewalls, routers, and dedicated NAT devices, the capabilities and operation of which are determined by the vendors. Those functions can be tailored to meet different network environments, such as the address ranges in use and network security measures.

Some types of software, such as the firewall functions built into the Linux operating system, give a network administrator a greater degree of control over NAT functions than those found in firewalls and routers. For example, a sharp Linux wizard can develop customized address translation tables, port mappings, and other features, tailoring NAT to a specific network environment or set of security policies.

The other side of this rather sharp sword, as with any fully customizable software function, is the ability to disable the correct operation of NAT or to poke holes through a finely defined security screen. Sometimes the best intentions of programmers go awry when those intentions and a programmer's inexperience run head-on into the reality of network operations.

Finally, as we will see in this chapter, NAT imposes a performance penalty on network communications and on the devices that execute NAT. Translating network addresses isn't free—it does penalize network performance. There are also situations, such as in networks with multiple Internet connections, in which NAT requires both careful coordination between NAT devices and back-up of the NAT translation tables.

Looking for Mr. IP Address Field

The short answer to network address translation is that NAT substitutes one address for another, usually a routable, public IP address for an unroutable, private address. As with any communications technology, though, how NAT decides to make that substitution can be more important than the substitution itself. This is particularly true if you are a network manager or systems administrator trying to customize NAT or troubleshoot why an application no longer works after NAT has been put in place.

NAT is supposed to be transparent to devices on either side of the address translation process, so NAT functions are designed for speed and, if possible, simplicity. Let's look at a simple case of network address translation, then add progressively more complicated NAT scenarios.

At its simplest level, NAT means translating the source or destination IP address, or both, of the IP datagram, depending on which direction the traffic is going. The first problem that a NAT box must solve is to find the IP address field of an IP datagram. The IP datagram is the fundamental unit of Internet and TCP/IP communications. It packages the higher-level protocols that manage data delivery, such as TCP. Most important, the IP datagram is the wrapper around the user's file, Web page, DNS inquiry, or e-mail message, addressing it to and from its destination.

The IP datagram is illustrated in Figure 2.1.

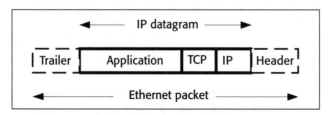

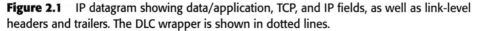

Figure 2.1 IP datagram showing data/application, TCP, and IP fields, as well as link-level headers and trailers. The DLC wrapper is shown in dotted lines.

Data Link Packaging

When it leaves a user's PC, the IP datagram is usually wrapped in a media access control (MAC) or data link control (DLC) header and trailer, illustrated in Figure 2.1 in dotted lines. The MAC layer is the technical term for the protocol that governs the structure of the Ethernet packet and defines the structure of the Ethernet addressing. The DLC layer is the technical term for other types of packaging and framing for IP and other protocols when they traverse other types of communications links.

For example, when IP datagrams go over a leased line that connects two routers in a TCP/IP network, such as the Internet, the IP datagrams must be packaged in a protocol that governs the flow of data over the link. IP isn't a link-level protocol. On LANs, it's usually Ethernet. On serial links like leased lines, it might be the High-Level Data Link Control protocol, which is HDLC. On a wide area network, it might be X.25 or ATM.

An IP datagram that traverses an Ethernet LAN, for example, bears an Ethernet address in the Ethernet packet header. The Ethernet address is completely separate from the IP address, as it determines only the destination on the Ethernet LAN, not on an IP network like the Internet. The Ethernet address isn't involved at all in NAT because the Ethernet address is dropped when an IP datagram leaves a LAN. The Ethernet address isn't valid for network-to-network addressing. It's valid only on an Ethernet. Only the IP address has relevance outside a LAN. Similarly, the addressing in X.25 packets isn't relevant to IP routers or hosts because it serves only to encapsulate the data for transmission over the link.

Data link-level packaging is always dropped whenever the IP datagram reaches a router, and it is created anew whenever the IP datagram traverses a link that uses a different protocol. MAC addresses are link-specific addresses, in that they are valid only for transmission across a specific link or network. For example, take a router that connects two Ethernets, one of which hosts the client and the other the server. TCP/IP traffic from the client to the server must cross the router. The client would package its IP datagrams in Ethernet packets, addressed to the Ethernet interface of the router on the client's Ethernet segment. After it made a routing decision on the IP datagram, the router would create a new Ethernet packet, addressed to the server's Ethernet interface. The link-level MAC packaging (the Ethernet packet framing) created by the client, the server, and the router would be valid only on a specific link.

The IP Header

When a computer creates TCP/IP or UDP/IP traffic, the sending system's IP protocol software creates the IP header. The IP header, the contents of which are shown in Figure 2.2, is tacked onto the other, higher-level headers created by TCP and an application-level protocol, such as HTTP. These, in turn, are attached to the data field, which is the payload of the datagram. The entire package—the data, the application-layer header, the TCP header, and the IP header—constitutes the IP datagram.

A firewall, router, or NAT box will have to perform surgery on at least the IP header to translate an address. As we will see, NAT operations aren't necessarily restricted to the IP header, so they may require more complicated surgery.

The primary purpose of the IP header, shown in Figure 2.2, is to indicate the source and destination IP addresses of the IP datagram. The source address is the IP address of the system that created the datagram. If NAT is applied, the source IP address is that of the apparent source of the datagram. The destination address is its ultimate destination. To be more accurate, the address is its apparent ultimate address. If NAT lies somewhere in the path, NAT might change the address, so the real "ultimate address" may not be apparent at all. Both source and destination addresses are standard 32-bit IP addresses.

The IP header has a number of other fields, only one of which, the checksum, is relevant to NAT. The other IP header fields are concerned with other facets of the IP protocol, such as tracking the parts of a datagram, in case it has to be fragmented and reassembled to get it across a data link.

The checksum in the IP header is the remainder of a mathematical calculation, based on all of the bits in the IP header. Routers and other hosts examine the checksum, then perform the same calculation to see if they get the same answer. If they do, they assume that the data in the IP header has arrived

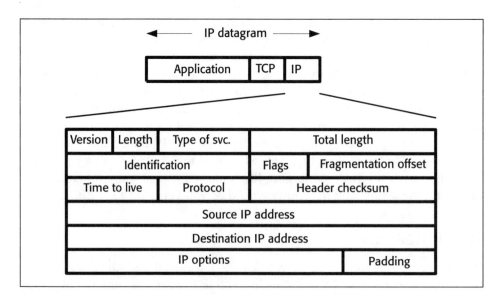

Figure 2.2 IP datagram showing fields.

correctly because the bits in a corrupted datagram wouldn't yield the same result.

As we will see, if NAT changes the source IP address in the IP header, it may change the value returned in the checksum calculation. This is only the first of what may be several implications and complications of using NAT.

TCP Header

The TCP header, which is depicted in Figure 2.3, has nothing to do with addressing, but it still may be modified by NAT. The TCP header's main function is to ensure that the data in the datagram payload is delivered reliably to the destination. In doing so, it also controls the flow of data between the sender and receiver, and it has its own checksum to ensure the integrity of the data in the header. TCP also identifies the application that created the data on the sending system, and to which the data is to be delivered at the destination.

Before any part of the data in a Web page, file, or e-mail message ever moves between a client and a server, TCP sets up a logical connection, or session, between the two. The TCP processes in the sending and receiving systems exchange a brief series of messages, each of which is packaged as an IP datagram, to establish the TCP session.

The TCP source and destination port fields link the application protocols and the data payload to an IP address on the sending and receiving systems. These fields, however, may be modified by NAT, so it's useful to understand how they're used.

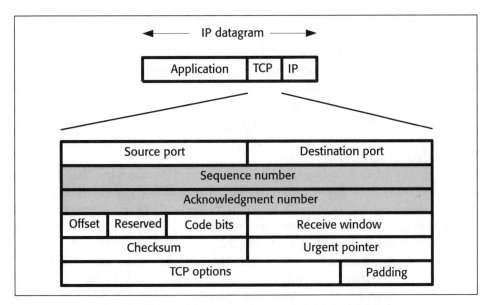

Figure 2.3   TCP header fields, with ports and Seq/Ack fields highlighted.

The IP Source and Destination addresses in the IP header indicate network interfaces somewhere on a network or on the Internet, but not the application that originated the data, nor for which application the data is intended. For example, a server on the Big Company network, using the IP address 172.168.1.1, could be running several applications. It could be the company's Web server, an e-mail gateway, and an anonymous FTP server. Each of these services might be advertised by the Big Company DNS as www.bigco.com, mx.bigco.com, and ftp.bigco.com, respectively. Whether it's good practice to have so many important and high-volume services running on the same server is another matter, but we'll ignore that detail for the sake of this example.

The TCP port field contains a number that identifies an application-level protocol. For example, HTTP is Port 80, and Telnet is Port 23. Some applications, such as FTP, use two or more TCP port numbers to identify different functions of the application. The TCP header has a field for both the source port and the destination port, not so much because client and server applications might be different (which is possible), but because the port numbers for client and server processes are different.

Server-side TCP port numbers are usually identified by "well-known" port numbers, which identify an application across most servers. For example, a Web server runs the HTTP server process, which is TCP port 80. So, an HTTP client (i.e., a Web browser) that sends a URL to the www.bigco.com server at 172.168.1.1 directs it to TCP port 80, which is the TCP port number for standard Web servers. Even though the server at 172.168.1.1 is running e-mail (SMTP) and FTP, its TCP process will send the request to the HTTP server.

On the client side, the TCP source port numbers may vary for each client and application. That's because the clients pick a number that is unique to them to identify the application that created the request. There are well-defined ranges for source port numbers, but in most cases, clients (or, more accurately, their TCP processes) don't use the same numbers. The TCP process on a PC will send a Web home page request to 172.168.1.1 at destination port 80 (HTTP), but that PC's TCP process might identify the source port as 3301. Another PC, also sending to the well-known HTTP port 80 on 172.168.1.1, might select its source port as 3107.

The reason for this incongruity is that the server customarily runs a common service to which many users may be connected, but the client could be a common host running many clients. All of those clients direct their application requests to the same service, identified by the well-known TCP port number of the service. The server-side TCP process, however, must be able to distinguish among separate clients, all of which could be running on the same machine.

In a PC environment, the source port usually maps back to the PC's single IP address. But on a Unix host, minicomputer, or mainframe (which was the client-side environment when TCP was devised in the early 1980s), there may be tens or hundreds of users, each of which is a different client. If even two clients on a multiuser system used the same source port number, how would the system know which one should get the response?

The client selects its TCP source port number and sends the request to the well-known port number for the application on the server. When the server responds to the client, such as when it returns the contents of a Web page, the server uses its well-known service port number as the source port and the client's original source port as the destination port. It also swaps the Source and Destination IP address fields from the IP header in the client's IP datagram, so that the response goes back to the correct address.

The reason for all this song and dance about TCP port numbers is that a NAT box, such as a firewall, may have to change the TCP source port numbers from clients on a network behind it, in addition to changing the IP address fields in the IP header. More complicated forms of NAT, which use a single external address for many internal addresses, must remap TCP source port numbers in order to keep track of which client sent which service request. This technique, sometimes called *port mapping*, is also known as network address port translation, or NAPT.

Getting back to the other relevant fields in the TCP header, the Sequence Number and Acknowledgment Number fields set up the TCP session and manage the flow of data between the client and the server. Like the client source port numbers, the Sequence and Acknowledgment number fields are values that are picked by the client and server. These numbers are incremented by the client and severs as they send and receive data, to track the number of bytes of data sent or received by either side.

Changing an address or a TCP port number with NAT may affect the values in the Sequence and Acknowledgment number fields. These two fields change according to the number of bytes in the data payload of the IP datagram, functioning as an acknowledgment/no acknowledgment (ACK/NACK) for data received. If there are IP addresses embedded in the data fields of IP datagrams, and if NAT changes those IP addresses to ones that are shorter or longer than the original addresses, the Sequence Number and Acknowledgment Number fields might be affected.

The last relevant field in the TCP header is the checksum. This is another error-detection mechanism, similar to the checksum in the IP header. The difference is that the TCP header checksum validates the integrity of the entire TCP frame, including the data payload field and the IP header. It's TCP's job to ensure that the data arrives intact, so the TCP checksum covers everything, including the IP header. Anything that changes the IP addresses (such as NAT) may affect the TCP checksum value, so NAT may have to recalculate the TCP checksum.

UDP

TCP implies a good bit of overhead to set up a logical connection between the sending and receiving systems, which are identified by the source and destination IP address fields in the IP header. The TCP session binds the TCP processes in each system together, so that they can keep track of the data they exchange.

Some applications don't need all that overhead because they aren't intended to be as reliable as file transfer or terminal sessions. For example, *ping* is intended to be a simple utility that might get a response, but might not, too. Many utilities employ the User Datagram Protocol, UDP, instead of the more reliable TCP. UDP, which could be called "TCP Lite" because it's less filling than TCP, doesn't set up a session at all, so it's "connectionless."

UDP-based protocols will work with NAT because UDP uses TCP ports, and UDP frames still need IP headers to navigate the routers in a network. There may be a slight performance hit for using NAT with UDP, but there may be a problem with NAT at the application level if the data field or the application field embeds IP addresses.

Having said all this, the point is that in addition to changing IP addresses, NAT implies changes in the IP header and the TCP header. For some applications, there may be a need for the NAT software to examine and change addresses embedded in the data field, too.

Changing Addresses

Now that we understand what's in the fields that NAT might change, let's take a look at how NAT would work in a simple address translation scenario.

Let's say that we've set up NAT as a means to translate the addresses in use on a company LAN from unroutable, private address space, to routable, public address space. If you remember, this is a situation where NAT is essential; Internet routers will discard datagrams with private addresses because they're not supposed to escape from private addressing domains. We'll use the private network address of 172.16.2.0 and assume that there are three PCs on the network, numbered from 172.16.2.1 to 172.16.2.3, one server, 172.16.2.4, and one router, with an inside address of 172.16.2.5. The network is shown in Figure 2.4.

We're going to use simple, one-to-one address translation, which will be done by the router. The router has two interfaces, one inside and one outside. The router's inside interface is 172.16.2.5, but its outside interface is

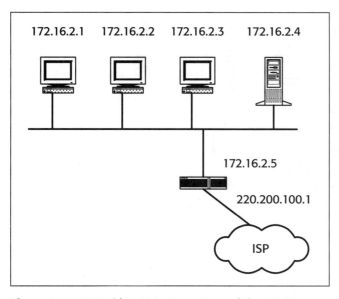

Figure 2.4   LAN with a server, a router, and three PCs.

220.200.100.1. Three other addresses from the 220.200.100.0 network have been assigned as a NAT pool to the router's external interface.

Let's say that the first of the PCs, 172.16.2.1, creates an HTTP request to a Web server on the Internet. The PC or a DNS resolves the Web server's text name in the URL to an IP address, which is 210.50.10.1. The PC creates an IP datagram with 210.50.10.1 as the destination IP address. The source IP address is the PC's IP address, 172.16.2.1, as depicted in Figure 2.5.

The IP datagram traverses the LAN and arrives at the router's inside interface. The datagram itself isn't addressed to the router's IP address, but the Ethernet packet that encapsulates the datagram is addressed to it. The router's inside Ethernet interface is the PC's default gateway, so the PC sends traffic destined outside the LAN, such as to the Internet, to the router.

The PC got the router's inside Ethernet address from its Address Resolution Protocol (ARP) table. This table maps a few important IP addresses to Ethernet addresses, such as that of the default gateway. Without knowing where to direct Ethernet traffic bound for addresses outside the LAN, the PC couldn't reach the Internet. The ARP table is one of those hidden parts of the connectivity infrastructure.

The datagram goes to the router, which removes the Ethernet framing, and examines the datagram to find its source and destination address. The router has been configured to route traffic between the LAN and the Internet, as well as to do NAT, but it's a router, so it does routing first and then NAT before it releases the datagram.

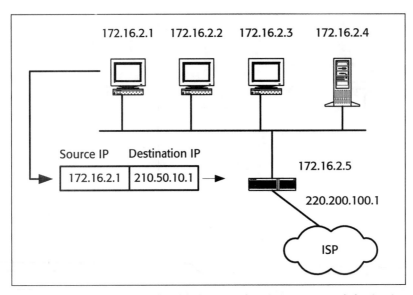

Figure 2.5   IP header on data leaving PC, showing source and destination address, but packaged in an Ethernet packet addressed to the router's inside interface.

The destination address, 210.50.10.1, or, from the router's perspective, a host on network 210.50.10.0 probably isn't in the router's routing table. There are too many Internet addresses in use for the router to know about all of them, so it may know about only a few, such as the two networks on its inside and outside interfaces. For all other addresses, it forwards the datagrams to its next higher router, which is probably the ISP's router on the other end of the 220.200.100.0 network.

The router queues the datagram to its external interface and prepares to package it in the data link protocol for the link. First, the router has to replace the unroutable source address with one of the routable addresses from its NAT pool.

The router picks the first address in the NAT pool, 220.200.100.2, and overwrites the source address with this new address. At the same time, the router copies the original source address, 172.16.2.1, and builds an entry in a translation table. The translation table maps the new source address, 220.200.100.2, to the old source address, 172.16.2.1, as depicted in Figure 2.6, and forwards the re-addressed datagram to the ISP.

The router's translation table is key to the operation of NAT. When the response comes back from the Web server, it will bear a destination address of 220.200.100.2, which will be one of several addresses on the router's external interface. The only way the router will know the address to which it should translate the destination address—or if it should do it at all—is to check its translation table. At this point, its only entry is the one mapping 220.200.100.2

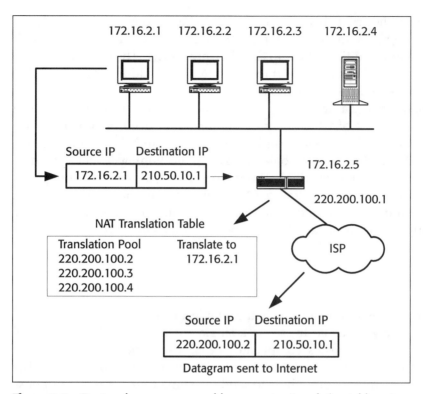

172.16.2.1   172.16.2.2   172.16.2.3   172.16.2.4

Source IP   Destination IP

172.16.2.1	210.50.10.1

172.16.2.5

220.200.100.1

NAT Translation Table

Translation Pool	Translate to
220.200.100.2	172.16.2.1
220.200.100.3	
220.200.100.4	

ISP

Source IP   Destination IP

220.200.100.2	210.50.10.1

Datagram sent to Internet

Figure 2.6   Router changes source address, creates translation table entry, and forwards datagram to ISP.

to 172.16.2.1. So, the router makes a routing decision and queues the datagram on its internal interface. Before releasing the datagram, it then translates the destination address back to the correct original source address and forwards it to the PC.

The router must do one other thing at the same time that it translates the address, in either the sending or receiving step. The IP header contains a checksum, to check that the contents of the IP header weren't corrupted en route. The checksum was calculated by the source PC, based on (among other things) the Source Address field being filled with the address 172.16.2.1. It's actually the binary representation of that address, but who's counting?

When the router changed the source address, it made the IP header checksum incorrect. The router must also recalculate the IP header checksum and rewrite the result in the checksum field. When traffic returns and the router replaces the substituted source address for the original source address, the checksum must be recalculated and replaced again.

The checksum is only one of the header fields that might be thrown off by NAT. The *Time to Live* (TTL) field, which is decremented by each router that routes the datagram, must also be adjusted. Routers normally do that anyway, though, when they route IP datagrams. That change, along with the recalculation of the IP checksum, is something that is done anyway by the router, so it doesn't add any additional load to the NAT processing. The checksum in the TCP header may also have been thrown off by the IP address change, so that may have to be recalculated as well.

As straightforward as this process may sound, NAT may run into additional complications, some of which may be unforeseen or even unknown. As we will see in Chapter 7, "Making Applications Work with NAT," some applications embed IP addresses in the data fields of application-level data. NAT may or may not know about how applications work. If it does, it may be configured with an application-level gateway (ALG), which can change IP addresses embedded in data fields. Encryption adds even more complexity, as it may encrypt application-level data that may be invalidated by NAT.

Port State

Translating addresses one-for-one is the simplest case of address translation. Translating many inside addresses to a single outside address, or to a small number of outside addresses, complicates the NAT scenario. The problem isn't so much translating the addresses on outgoing or incoming datagrams. The complication is figuring out where to send incoming traffic that is a response to a session that originated from inside the network. If all inbound responses are sent to the same IP address (i.e., the firewall or the outside address of the NAT box), the NAT box can't rely on the destination address of inbound traffic to determine how to translate the address to a unique inside address.

Instead, the NAT box must relay on some other indicator—possibly an artificial one that it creates itself—to map incoming traffic to inside addresses. Fortunately, there is something else that the NAT box can use to do this, but it isn't in the IP header. It's the TCP port number, but it's in the TCP header, at another protocol level. Translating inside IP addresses to a single public address or a small number of public addresses usually also means changing and tracking TCP port numbers too because they're the tags that can identify inside clients even if their external addresses appear to be the same.

This NAT technique goes by several names. It may be called port mapping, network address port translation (NAPT), or maintaining port state, but each is a variation on the same basic theme. The theme is changing the TCP source port numbers as well as the source IP addresses and using both to map returning traffic to inside IP addresses.

Clients that use the same application, such as HTTP, use the same port numbers in the TCP destination port fields in the TCP header. Users go to different Web sites, so the destination IP addresses on outgoing HTTP sessions will be different, but the destination TCP port numbers on all of their sessions will be the same. They will all be port 80, the standard, well-known port for HTTP. For the HTTP protocol, the only other variations for the TCP destination port would be an encrypted channel between a client and server running Secure HTTP (HTTP-S), which is port 443, or a special version of an HTTP service listening on another special, HTTP server port number.

Let's assume the standard HTTP port 80 is the destination port, so that won't help the NAT box distinguish the return traffic. The source TCP port numbers used by TCP clients will most likely be different, even if they come from different PCs or systems. If you recall from the discussion of TCP ports, the client usually selects its own source TCP port number. A multiuser system may have many clients, all of which will probably use the same source IP address. Using different TCP source ports, chosen from a range that can accommodate a large number of unique port numbers, identifies each client on a host uniquely, even if they all share the same IP source address and are using the same application-level protocol.

TCP source ports usually fall in the range from 4097 to 65535. The lower numbers, from 1 through 4096, are reserved as well-known server ports, on which servers "listen" for incoming requests for service. As we have noted, FTP listens for incoming client requests to establish control sessions on TCP port 21 and subsequently establishes a data connection on TCP port 20. HTTP uses port 80, Telnet servers listen on port 23, DNS listens on port 53, and so forth. RFC 1060 specifies the well-known port numbers used by TCP and UDP clients.

Let's say that a user of one of the PCs on the network depicted in Figure 2.4 sends an HTTP request to get to an Internet Web site. This PC uses one of the private addresses, 172.16.2.1, and, as in the earlier example, that address must be translated to a routable outside address. This time, let's replace the router in Figure 2.4 with a firewall that also does NAT, as shown in Figure 2.7.

In order to hide all of the addresses on the network from the Internet, this time there won't be a one-to-one correspondence of inside to outside addresses. Instead, all of the internal addresses will be translated to a single external address, which will be the external interface of the firewall (220.200.200.1). This means that all traffic originating on the internal network will appear to every system on the Internet as if it came from a single host.

This case will increase the processing load of the firewall because it will have to translate internal addresses to its single external address and manage a port translation table to keep track of which traffic "belongs" to which internal system. The port translation table is an extra step for NAT, but fortunately, it's built into most NAT software.

The TCP and IP headers of an HTTP request sent from the PC to an Internet Web server at 210.50.10.1 might look like those depicted in Figure 2.8.

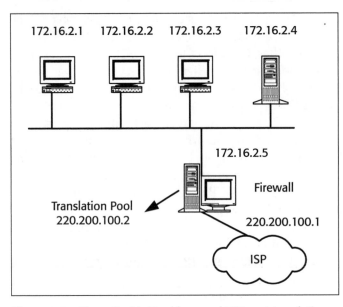

Figure 2.7 Firewall with IP address and TCP port translation.

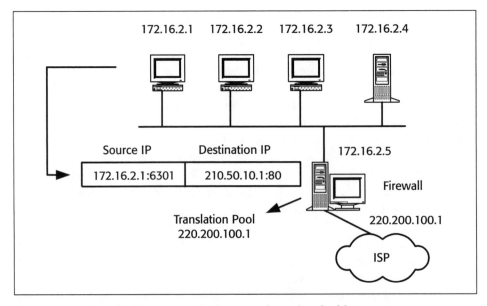

Figure 2.8 Firewall with NAT to a single external translated address.

The PC sends the datagram, encapsulated in Ethernet framing, across the LAN to the firewall, which is the default gateway to the Internet. The firewall receives the datagram and examines the destination IP address. It's a firewall, so first it checks its rulesets to see if this traffic clears its traffic screening rules. The firewall determines that the destination is an outside address, so it has to do some address translation before it can queue the datagram for its outside interface.

First, there's the problem of the outside address. The firewall represents all inside traffic as having originated on its outside address, so it changes the PC's source address, 172.16.2.1, to its own outside address, 220.200.100.1. The firewall also builds an entry in its address translation table, shown in Figure 2.9, to indicate that it's translated the source address.

Once the firewall has done its NAT trick, traffic from every system on the inside network will bear the same source address. The firewall will need something else to identify to which inside system the return traffic (such as the home page of the Web site the PC is trying to reach) should be readdressed. The key will be the TCP source port number. The destination port number will

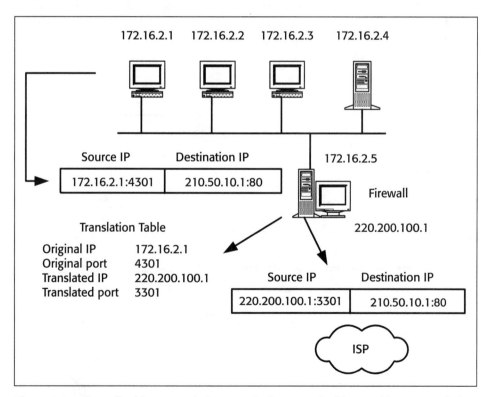

Figure 2.9 Firewall address translation to a single external address, with port translation.

be 80 (HTTP), but the PC client software picks a TCP source port number. In this case, let's say the PC's TCP software used 4301 as its source port.

The firewall builds another entry in its translation table for the PC's traffic, adding the number of the original source port, 4301, to its table row for the PC. Now, return traffic from the Web site will be directed to the firewall's outside address, but traffic for the PC will be directed to TCP destination port 4301. The firewall will look up that TCP port number in its translation table, to identify traffic for the PC.

The firewall's NAT software, however, may be programmed to translate the source port, too. There may be hundreds or thousands of inside systems and clients, all of which pick what they think are unique source ports. The firewall has no guarantee than every inside system will pick a unique source port number each time. In fact, it's likely that PCs running the same applications will pick the same source port numbers. On a multiuser system, the host operating system assigns different source port numbers, but PCs operate in blissful ignorance of other systems.

The firewall's NAT software usually translates the TCP source port as well, mapping the original source port back to a translated source port. When return traffic arrives at the firewall's outside interface, the NAT software uses the entries in its translation table to switch the destination IP address and the destination TCP port number back to their original values before forwarding the traffic back to the originator, as depicted in Figure 2.10.

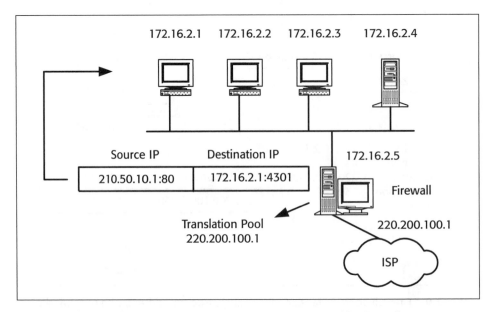

Figure 2.10   Original destination IP and TCP numbers restored by firewall.

Summary

As we will see in later chapters, there are a number of variations on the NAT theme, such as many-to-one translation, maintaining state information, and doing NAT twice between two addressing domains. Each fits a different type of networking environment, and each may impose certain limitations on network design and connectivity.

To preserve connectivity and interoperability, the network administrator may want NAT to be done on only certain addresses or address classes, or for certain networks or host addresses. The other complication that NAT adds is that certain applications may not work correctly because of the assumptions that some applications make about how they communicate with other systems.

Now that we have a grasp of the technology of NAT, in the next chapter, we'll take the perspective of the network manager or IT executive to evaluate NAT. NAT is a useful tool and, in some networking environments, an essential one. It's not for everyone, though, because of its drawbacks and complications.

NAT's Not for Everyone

As good a case as a network manager, systems designer, or worse, network consultant, may make for network address translation, it's not for everyone, nor for all networks. Even though it may seem to be that on the surface, NAT really isn't as simple and straightforward as it might seem.

The problem is that NAT adds a complication that IP networking wasn't intended to manage. You can call NAT address translation, but, as we saw in the last chapter on the mechanics of NAT, the translation extends to other protocol levels, such as TCP. As we will see in other chapters, NAT may also affect application-level protocols or even the data in the data payload of IP datagrams.

There are a number of network administrators, IT managers, and network engineers, including a substantial number of people in the Internet engineering community, who regard NAT as a cruel deception that should be banished from the earth. It's fair to say that NAT is not quite that bad. In fact, in some cases, it's essential. Like most statements that bracket the best and the worst of an issue, the truth is probably somewhere in between.

Opponents of NAT are quick to point out that NAT can complicate routing and connectivity and that its security benefits are specious, at best. It's fair to say that NAT isn't for everyone, even though NAT is a standard capability for network screening gear like firewalls and routers.

Network managers and IT management must evaluate NAT carefully, with full awareness of its potential complications, before committing to a NAT strategy. Of course, NAT can be a foregone conclusion if other decisions precede it, such as using private address space, which makes NAT essential for Internet connectivity. Given complete freedom of choice, or if there weren't such things as unroutable private IP addresses, it's fair to say that many network managers wouldn't even consider NAT. In some cases, though, it's unavoidable, but network managers must use NAT with the full realization of where its drawbacks outweigh its benefits.

Reasons Not to Do NAT

Some network managers and IT executives accept NAT as a fact of life in networking, and others approach it with trepidation. There are some situations in which NAT may be more trouble than it's worth, or just not worth the trouble at all. There are a number of valid reasons to use NAT, but also a number of reasons not to, which we'll examine in this section.

Just Say No

Let's take a look at some situations in which NAT might not be feasible, as well as some of the common reasons why NAT might be rejected, even though it may seem to be justified. Network managers, systems administrators, network analysts, and IT executives should consider these reasons carefully before implementing NAT. It isn't that NAT is as bad or as insidious as some in the Internet engineering community might have us believe. It simply has to be used with care, and after considering whether it can be supported adequately.

Simple Network with Not Much Support

You're running a small business or even a medium-sized one. You have a network in the office, providing access to file and print services and e-mail. Your Internet connection has become more important to you and your employees as you have expanded the role of your Web site to advertise, communicate with customers, and do business with vendors and suppliers.

Like most businesses, you've had a heck of a time trying to find, let alone hire, competent, experienced network support people. For lack of an experienced outside hire, your network administrator is the person who started out in shipping, but who liked to fool around with computers and who got to be known as the PC guru. He's pretty good, and he's been able to pick up quite a bit of knowledge about NT. Frankly, the network seems to work all right, but even he'd tell you he's no network genius, and quite a few things about networking beyond the rudiments of network administration are terra incognita. He's willing to learn, and those Microsoft wizards are a real help, but a lot of the details of network troubleshooting are beyond him.

So you want to throw NAT into this mix?

This situation, the blind-leading-the-blind network administration scene, applies to a lot of networks, both large and small. Even big companies with complicated networks and big IT budgets can't hire enough competent, experienced network professionals to support their networks. Even in big companies, frequently there are one or two key people to whom everyone else defers for networking expertise. If they jump ship, you've lost the rudder, and there better not be any big rocks nearby.

Running NAT implies that the organization's IT operation has a good grasp of how NAT works and precisely what device is doing what to translate those addresses. That box may be a router or a firewall, which implies that someone with some router or firewall configuration background or some network security experience is running the show. It's also helpful for that person or group to have a grasp of what NAT does, as well as precisely what addresses and ports it is translating.

If a problem with network or Internet connectivity occurs, without one or the other, or at worse, both, it's going to be difficult to develop a sound troubleshooting process. Even developing reasonable theories about what might be wrong, not to mention how to fix the problem, might be a substantial challenge. While NAT can operate transparently in many networking environments, NAT does add a complication to networking. Organizations that have little or no networking support are best advised to keep things simple, particularly if out-of-the-ordinary technologies or configurations have the potential to complicate network life unnecessarily. Even simple NAT configurations may affect the operation of certain applications, and determining just what might be wrong can be tricky indeed.

That's why many small companies and organizations find it easier to outsource as many network configuration issues to a third-party support organization or to an ISP. IP addresses usually come from ISPs, who assign them to their customers for use on their networks. ISPs may be in a better position to provide networking, security, and address management support than their customers are. Furthermore, ISPs usually have experienced support people who can configure network interfaces, as well as firewalls, routers, and NAT, correctly the first time. If an ISP doesn't have that type of support organization, maybe you should consider using another ISP.

The Not-Used-Here Syndrome

Dr. Argan, one of the characters in Moliere's play, *The Imaginary Invalid*, declines to listen to new musical compositions because, as he says, "I don't like music I haven't heard before." Some network managers and IT executives don't like NAT because they haven't used it before, either. Neither they nor their support organizations have any experience configuring or supporting NAT, so they don't want to use it because they don't configure it or support it.

This may sound like Catch 22-style circular logic, but it really isn't. Networking is complex enough already, and network managers and IT executives may have a point in resisting technologies and configurations that they feel may make their jobs more complicated or that may add unfamiliar support requirements.

Network managers and IT executives have every right to shut their minds to new and different technologies and techniques, particularly if they're unsure if they can support them properly. It's not unlike deciding not to upgrade to the newest and presumably improved version of a network operating system or to the latest and greatest (in terms of features and disk space consumed) version of a standard office application. If it hints at raising the bar on support requirements, do the benefits outweigh the costs?

For many networking environments, NAT doesn't have the same configuration and support implications as more exotic technologies, such as policy-based routing, reservation-based traffic management with Quality of Service, and level 3 switching. In addition, it isn't an application laden with so many network implications as desktop videoconferencing, streaming media, collaborative computing, or IP telephony. Still, NAT can make networking more complex. Needlessly complex, some network managers say, which is why they decline to use NAT even in situations where it's the best solution to a problem.

Networks that use private address space, for example, don't have many other options beyond NAT for certain types of connectivity. Those private addresses must be converted to public addresses before they reach the Internet, or they'll be discarded. In that case, something that does NAT, even if it's the ISP, will have to take on the task to ensure connectivity.

IT organizations that don't like supporting NAT will often be more receptive to using some other technique, such as a proxy server, to translate addresses. Most proxy servers are fairly straightforward devices, with user interfaces that maximize control and administrative simplicity. An IT organization that doesn't like NAT because it's NAT may find a proxy server an acceptable substitute. Although it is no less complicated than most any other NAT box, a proxy server is usually easier to understand, configure, and administer than other devices that do NAT. In addition, a proxy server isn't usually doing NAT in addition to its real responsibilities as a firewall or a router.

The IT organization that doesn't like NAT because it's never tried it before isn't necessarily rejecting NAT for any technical inadequacy, but simply to retain the consistency of its environment. NAT, like a number of other techniques, isn't in the same class as IP routing or firewall screening. There's no shame in not using something you don't think you can run properly or want to support.

You Could Drive a Truck through It

One of the most widely held beliefs about NAT is that it's a security measure. If outsiders don't know about the IP addresses in use on your network, the thinking goes, they won't be able to attack the systems that use those addresses. Better yet, the thinking goes, using private, nonroutable address space behind a NAT box makes for an even more secure network because those addresses might be used on a number of shielded, private-numbered networks throughout the Internet.

There is something to be said for NAT as a security technique, particularly because it hides the real IP address identity of systems behind a NAT box on a screened network. It's the equivalent of locking valuables in the trunk of a car. Every car trunk is like a different network. Every car trunk could hold valuables, but if you don't have any reason to differentiate one car from another, a thief will have to guess which ones contain valuables and which don't.

The truth is that by itself, NAT doesn't add much to the security of a network. Instead, NAT is more properly positioned as one of a number of measures that, taken as a whole, make up a coordinated and well-planned security framework of a network. To return to the packages-in-the-trunk analogy, relying on NAT alone to secure a network is like hiding valuables in the trunk of a car, but failing to lock the trunk. Hiding things in the trunk of a car works, but it's obviously not as reliable a security measure as, say, locking the trunk too or, better yet, not leaving valuables in the car in the first place.

The most insidious thing about using NAT alone as a security measure is that hiding addresses can give network administrators and network users a false sense of security, making them think that their network and their systems are secure when in reality, they aren't. After all, how big an obstacle can translated or hidden addresses be to a determined hacker?

For starters, a hacker assumes that he or she can't see most of the addresses on a network anyway, so that's not much of a problem. The real problem is getting inside the network, by breaking through a firewall or a screening router. That's the real challenge. Without another back-door route into the network, such as through a dial-up port or an otherwise unprotected connection, the real challenge is the firewall. The level of security the firewall actually affords, however, is a function of how well its screening rules have been written. Some, unfortunately, haven't been written too well, leaving huge holes that an intruder can penetrate.

The hacker's first step, once he or she has breached the firewall or screening router in front of the network (assuming one exists), is to find a system inside the network that can be used as a base of operations. Most any host will do, and if he or she is any kind of competent hacker, and there's no firewall, the hacker might be able to upload whatever software tools or utilities are needed.

If the hacker doesn't have a specific target in mind, he or she might want to roam around the network and discover what systems do exist there. At this point, that the network systems' addresses are translated to outside addresses by NAT is entirely beside the point. The hacker is inside the network and operating from one of those addresses.

From inside the network, the most convenient place to find out what hosts and systems are on the network, and what their real addresses are, is from the *Domain Name Service* (DNS). The DNS maps text names of hosts, such as www.xyzabc.com, to their corresponding IP addresses. There's probably an internal DNS to which systems on the network go to get the IP addresses of other systems on the network. The internal DNS usually passes requests for the IP addresses of Internet hosts to an external DNS, which may in turn pass the request to other DNS services.

The simplest way for the hacker to get a relatively complete list of real addresses of systems on the internal network is to take a copy of the DNS zone file from the internal DNS. Because it's the internal DNS, it's likely that only internal systems can talk to it. The DNS administrator probably hasn't taken any measures to prevent any system using one of the internal network IP addresses from taking a copy of the DNS zone file. The intruder is now using one of those addresses, so now he or she has the zone file.

The DNS zone file might list only the text host names and IP addresses of servers and multiuser systems on the network, instead of every PC and workstation. That's what the intruder probably wants because those hosts will be interesting targets for whatever mischief he or she has in mind next. Individual PCs and workstations aren't usually of much interest. At night and on weekends, they might be turned off, or at any time, they might be laptops that have been undocked. Besides, it's inefficient to attack individual PCs, particularly when an attack on a shared server or a host computer system could yield more fascinating information, such as customer records, payroll and personnel data, credit card numbers, and so forth. The DNS zone file will also list internal Web sites, which can be particularly interesting industrial espionage targets.

The point is that a determined, crafty hacker or intruder won't find NAT to be too significant an obstacle to some network second-story work. It is true that NAT will hide the network's internal addresses from the outside world, but that doesn't mean that they're not available or visible to an outsider. As we will see in the section of this chapter on applications and NAT, IP addresses and host names are sometimes embedded in the data fields of applications. Unless they are specially designed to do so, most NAT boxes don't change the contents of data fields, so they might be visible to a snooper as well.

Proponents of using private address space point out that it's more difficult for an intruder to launch an externally originated attack on a system that uses a private address space. First, if the private address is the destination address in the IP header of IP datagrams sent by the intruder, those datagrams will be discarded by Internet routers. Consequently, attacks on systems that are in private address space must be mounted from another device within the same private address space. As we have seen in the intrusion just described, that may not be all that difficult for a hacker to do.

The good thing about NAT as a security measure is that it is usually implemented by a device like a firewall, which incorporates a number of other, more effective and more reliable security measures. When considered together as a complete package of security measures, NAT can be one part of a comprehensive security perimeter, which might include some or all of these other measures or devices:

Intrusion detection system (IDS). An IDS watches all traffic going to and from the Internet, scanning for signs of known types of intruder attacks, suspicious traffic, or traffic originating from known intruders or from systems that should not be permitted to enter the network.

De-militarized zone (DMZ). The DMZ is a small network segment outside the network that all inbound and outbound traffic traverse, so that it can be scanned by the IDS, screened by a firewall, or subjected to other security measures.

Inside and outside Domain Name Service (DNS). As a security measure, many networks have an inside DNS, in which internal systems and a few outside systems are registered, and a separate outside DNS, which knows about only externally visible systems, like the public Web server. Outside DNS inquiries go to the outside DNS to protect the identity of inside systems.

In today's Internet, where hacking and intruding are often regarded as pranks rather than threats, having a little bit of security is essential, but having a lot of security is just common sense. If the hackers and intruders of the world would expend half as much programming energy on improving the performance of the Web as they do on hacking into computer systems, breaking into networks, and mangling Web sites, the world might be a better place. Besides, then they might be able to incorporate, do an IPO, and get rich, instead of just being a pain in the neck. But that's another story, as they say.

What Happened to Our Applications?

The most frequently cited reason for not doing NAT is that it can have a detrimental effect on some applications. In this case, "detrimental" means that some features or capabilities no longer work properly or worse, that some applications stop working completely. We'll explore these reasons, as well as what can be done about them, more extensively in Chapter 7, "Making Applications Work with NAT."

NAT does have this effect on certain applications, some of which are common, widely used applications, such as the *File Transfer Protocol* (FTP) and the *Simple Network Management Protocol* (SNMP). Other, newer applications, such as White Pine Software's CUseeMe, and videoconferencing applications that conform to the H.323 video image standards, also may not work properly. In some cases, whether an application works properly with NAT depends on how a specific vendor has implemented NAT software. Like a great many Internet protocol features and functions, NAT is described in an RFC (1631) and amplified and extended in a succession of other RFCs. Its actual implementation, though, is left to vendors, who may implement the basics of NAT, but either some or many of its other capabilities.

The problem that NAT boxes may have with some applications is that they may incorporate IP addresses in the data fields of the IP datagrams they create. A standard NAT box will translate the addresses in the IP headers and, in some cases, change inbound or outbound port numbers. Unless they are configured and capable of doing so, they may leave the embedded IP addresses in the data fields unchanged. Some applications embed host names, too. Embedded host names usually aren't a problem unless the application resolves host names to IP addresses through DNS and the DNS is outside the NAT device.

Because there are no standards that govern precisely how TCP/IP applications work, applications might work—or not work—in unexpected ways when they pass through NAT. There have been attempts to prescribe ways to make TCP/IP applications NAT-friendly, some of which are described in Chapter 7. TCP/IP applications, however, aren't governed by the same strict rules that govern the behavior of Windows or Macintosh applications. Some might argue that to do so might inhibit innovation or curb deploying new applications.

Even relatively simple applications can be affected by NAT. For example, certain modes of operation of FTP embed IP addresses in application data fields. The Simple Network Management Protocol does the same, in order to report back the IP address of the device that is reporting SNMP data back to a network management station.

That NAT can affect applications doesn't mean that it affects the applications in use on a particular network. The simple solution to the problem might be to determine what applications are being used on a network, then check with the vendor of whatever box is doing NAT to determine if a known applications problem exists.

Networks that use a variety of cutting-edge applications for streaming video and audio, videoconferencing, and IP telephony may not be the best places to deploy NAT, only because of NAT's well-known problems passing these applications transparently. There are solutions to NAT-related application problems, specifically application-level gateways, which will be discussed in more detail in Chapter 7. ALGs are NAT software capabilities that are specifically designed to handle the data field and addressing problems that NAT may introduce in the data streams of certain applications.

Unfortunately, as we will see in Chapter 7, many ALGs are vaporware, performance hogs, or available only in the text of an RFC. Few are real, operating products. This doesn't mean that they can't be real products, only that no one has seen the commercial appeal of building one.

Consequently, network managers and IT executives must look closely at the applications mix on their networks before committing to a network environment that implies NAT, such as using private addresses. Many organizations can do without those high-end video applications that are affected by NAT. There are others, however, such as SNMP, that may be essential to managing and monitoring the network.

Performance Hits

Anything that impedes the smooth flow of traffic from one network to another, particularly to and from a high-volume network like the Internet, assesses some kind of a performance penalty on its users. Vendors' claims to the contrary, firewall screening can be a drain on the performance of a network connection. It takes time and CPU cycles to examine every bit of traffic flowing through the firewall and to compare it to the firewall rulesets. That doesn't happen instantaneously, although efficient firewall software running on a fast NT or Unix box can take a heavy load before users see any performance degradation.

Throwing NAT on top of the firewall's already substantial burden can really kill firewall performance. It's one thing for the firewall to examine traffic and accept or reject it. It's quite another to have to examine that same traffic, then rewrite and recalculate header and datagram fields, and update its address and state translation tables before sending traffic on its way.

In terms of network performance, firewall screening isn't free, but NAT can be downright costly. The NAT functions that impose the most significant performance penalties, from the least to most severe, are these:

- Source address translation
- TCP source port translation
- Data field translation

The extent of the performance penalty will be influenced by the number of devices behind the firewall that use NAT services, the type of NAT required, and the processing power of the firewall. An approximate rule of thumb is that on an average firewall, every 100 users requiring NAT services can impose as much as a one-second delay on firewall performance. Imposing other loads on a firewall, such as outbound authentication and inbound *virtual private network* (VPN) authentication, can degrade its performance even more.

There is a tendency among network managers to assume that devices like firewalls and servers are fairly insensitive to loading. What's one more service on that server or one more function thrown on the firewall? Because NAT can impose such a burden on a firewall, it's best to consider its configuration. If NAT is necessary, the best thing to do is to use it as sparingly as possible on an already burdened device like a firewall. If NAT is added to an existing firewall, it's often helpful to move to a computer with a faster processor, to add more memory, or both, to help the firewall keep up with the added load.

The other option is to move NAT to another box entirely, such as a screening router with NAT or an application-level gateway. A network manager must be careful not to add NAT to a router that is also heavily loaded or that can be a single point of failure for an Internet connection. Given the cost of firewall hardware and software and the complexity of configuring and managing multipoint Internet connectivity, single points of failure are hard to avoid in many networks.

Anything but Readdressing

Some network managers use NAT as a subterfuge to avoid readdressing a network, even when circumstances indicate that it's time to do so. These circumstances may be that the company or organization has changed ISPs, and the address space they had been using was taken back by the ISP. Or, the company has decided to move from private address space into public address space, or it has merged with another company that already uses private addresses, but some devices that use private addresses can't be reconfigured easily with new addresses. The simplest thing is to leave them in private address space and change their addresses with NAT whenever they communicate with the outside world.

There are a number of other circumstances that usually imply renumbering a network. These circumstances include moving from unregistered but routable address space to registered address space, changing addresses to communicate with business partners, reorganizing address space to take advantage of more efficient routing, such as OSPF, and consolidating address space to use it more efficiently or to take advantage of route summarization for more efficient routing and subnetworking.

In any of these cases that indicate a need to renumber a network, network managers have a natural tendency to try to avoid renumbering the network. It's fair to say that most network managers embrace the task of renumbering with the same enthusiasm that they give to changing to a different operating system. It can be a lot of work, it can result in disruptions of the network, and users, hosts, servers, and routers can be put out of commission if things aren't done properly. Worse, communications both within the network and with the outside world (the Internet) may be disrupted if the addressing and routing plans aren't executed correctly.

Given the potential for problems readdressing a network, NAT looks like a great solution. It's true that NAT can eliminate the need to renumber a network. It's also true that NAT can give a network manager, as well as IT executives, an easy out to avoid renumbering networks, even when it might be better in the long run if they do.

Take, for example, a small company that changes ISPs. In recent years, IP address space has become a valuable property, and ISPs have to pay for the IP address space they use. Since 1997, the American Registry for Internet Numbers (ARIN) has assumed responsibility for assigning new IP address space. ARIN leases new IP address space to ISPs, who assign it to their customers. Because address space is now a cost item to many ISPs, they assign a relatively small number of IP addresses to each customer, expanding the number of assigned addresses if the customer requests them.

For example, an ISP customer who has 500 hosts on its network may be assigned the equivalent of two Class C network addresses, which would just be sufficient to assign an address to every host and network interface. If the customer requests more address space, the ISP may assign it for free or add a surcharge for the extra address space. Compared to their costs for phone lines, the fees that ARIN charges ISPs for IP address space are relatively minor, but it's still a cost item. The more important consideration for ISPs is not the cost of the addresses, but the pressure to aggregate addresses, to simplify Internet routing.

If the customer decides to switch to a different ISP, the original ISP may take back the IP address space and assign it to another customer. As part of its service agreement, the new ISP will assign IP addresses from its own address space to the customer and expect the customer to use those addresses.

Internet routing is the reason why switching address space may be necessary when switching ISPs. In order for their customers' networks to be reached from anywhere else on the Internet, ISPs must advertise the existence of the customer networks they serve. The ISP's routers advertise the networks they serve when they send routing table updates to other ISPs on the Internet. Generally speaking, it is simpler for an ISP to advertise a large block of network addresses as its own, so that other ISPs send all traffic for any of the networks in the block to that ISP. It's more work for an ISP to advertise "holes" or exceptions in its address blocks. These holes might represent networks that used to be served by network addresses in the ISP's address blocks, but that are now served by other ISPs. Furthermore, many ISPs see no benefit in advertising and aggregating address space from which they derive no customer revenue and that they must treat as an exception in their routing tables.

These large blocks of addresses, called CIDR blocks (for Classless Inter-Domain Routing) are contiguously numbered IP addresses, usually in groups of 64, 128, 256, or larger Class C equivalent network addresses. Internet routing, which isn't simple to begin with, is kept less complicated than it might become if most of the networks served by a single ISP are in compact CIDR blocks. There are many exceptions to this principle, but CIDR, along with other measures, has made it possible for larger, national, or international ISPs to maintain Internet routing and connectivity despite dramatic Internet growth.

The implication of CIDR blocks for ISPs is that they must keep their customers' network addresses within their CIDR blocks. If a customer leaves the ISP and goes to another ISP, the customer's networks should be numbered from networks in the new ISP's CIDR blocks.

From the network manager's perspective, the simple solution to the renumbering problem is not to renumber at all. Instead, the easy out is to keep the old ISP's addresses but translate them to the new ISP's addresses with NAT on a firewall or a border router. This will work because translating inside public addresses to outside public addresses with NAT is no different from translating inside private addresses to public addresses.

The only problem is that this is the easy way out. It will work as long as NAT and the border router tables have been configured to work properly, so that none of those inside addresses ever escapes to the outside world. If they were private addresses, traffic bearing them would be thrown away by Internet routers. They would be public addresses, however, and they may be used in two places on the Internet. This would cause Internet routing problems, which are considered extremely bad form among ISPs. Then there's the multihoming issue, which complicates matters even more because of routing and route advertisement considerations.

When an organization changes ISPs or reconfigures a network, *doing the right thing* frequently means readdressing instead of NAT. There are instances where a combination of both NAT and readdressing are appropriate, such as bringing a private address domain behind a screening firewall. Network managers and IT executives must evaluate all aspects of their networking circumstances to determine if NAT or readdressing, or both, are appropriate solutions.

Give Me Some Public Space, Man

There are those who would argue that private address space is another convenient dodge that really isn't worth the trouble. Their argument is that anything that private address space can do, public address space can do better. Why, their line of thinking goes, should a network use private address space, and therefore NAT, if there's plenty of public space to go around? All you have to do is ask for it or pay for it.

The counter to this argument is that there may be more public address space than there seems to be, but private space is abundant, it's immediately available, and it's free. Besides, the original purpose of RFC 1631, which describes the basics of NAT, was to establish a way to route traffic from private space over the public Internet. Private address space makes an organization independent of any ISP because internal addresses are always changed by NAT to whatever public addresses any ISP assigns.

Private address space is an appropriate choice for network managers and IT executives, provided they have a sound reason for using private addresses and they don't have operational or technical objections to NAT. There is a lot to be said for numbering all of the networks in a company or an organization from the 16 Class B equivalent addresses in the 172.16.0.0 /20 space or the entire Class A equivalent 10.0.0.0 /8 address space. Doing so allows an IT department to establish addressing consistency across a complex, multilocation network, without concerns about readdressing to change ISPs or running out of addresses.

The counter argument is that unless an organization is running an experimental or isolated network, the original justification for using private addressing (and therefore NAT) isn't there. Public perceptions about the shortage of IP address space notwithstanding, ARIN and other address delegation authorities are taking steps to conserve IP address space and to reclaim space that hasn't been used efficiently.

An IT operation that uses private address space, even one that uses it successfully, might be well advised to switch to public, routable addresses. There's no reason to do this for the fun of it, mostly because it won't be fun. But given a choice, public addresses are better than private ones, only because their uniqueness on the Internet is the basis for their routability.

Summary

NAT has its place in a variety of networking situations, but it does have its limitations. It's fair to say that because NAT is a form of translation, it causes something to be lost in the translation. That "something" is the end-to-end integrity of IP addressing, which is the foundation of Internet communications. IP addresses are supposed to identify end systems uniquely, wherever they are, and however they are connected.

Even though NAT trespasses on the concept of end-to-end IP address integrity, the fact of the matter is that NAT is both suitable for many networking environments and essential for others. For networks that use private addressing, networks for which readdressing would be problematic, or networks that show only a small group of addresses to the outside world, NAT is a suitable solution to addressing issues.

In the next chapter, we will take the perspective of IT management on NAT, examining the costs and complications that IT management may see in it. IT management will judge NAT on its suitability for a networking environment, as well as how it fits with the company's long-term strategic plans.

CHAPTER

4

The Management Case for NAT

Having just examined some of the reasons why NAT isn't appropriate for some network environments, we'll take the IT management view of NAT in this chapter. The IT organization and its leaders, such as the company's CIO, are responsible for developing the company's comprehensive information processing strategy, then executing it successfully. They're less concerned with bits and bytes than they are with direction and flexibility. Networking techniques like NAT aren't judged so much on how they work, but on how well they mesh with every other aspect of the company's IT strategy.

If it were up to network managers and administrators, there wouldn't be much question about whether NAT should or could be used in many network environments. Their view is that of the networking tactician: If it works, use it—because that's what matters.

The view of IT management has to be slightly different. Yes, technology must work, but that something works usually isn't enough justification to drop it into the network environment. IT management must take the strategic view of technology, evaluating its current and future fit into the network. IT management must also evaluate the strategic implications of technologies, as well as the costs of technologies and the things they imply or preclude.

IT management has to take the long view of technology. In this context, the *long view* means trying to predict the long-term effects of technology on the company's IT infrastructure and its information management strategies. Information technologies are changing so quickly that the strategic horizons that had been 10 years out a decade ago are now 5 years out, at most. In some industries, IT people who think they can foresee changes in information systems and customer markets 2 years ahead either are truly prescient or are deluding themselves.

Whatever the IT horizon may be, IT executives have to judge new technologies by many criteria. That something works today doesn't mean it will always work so smoothly. By nature, the strategic view is a suspicious view, inclined to place bets on relatively sure things. Bigger, better, faster, and cheaper technology is always part of the strategist's lexicon, but the key factor about a new technology or a different approach is whether it works reliably and still affords a good degree of long-term flexibility.

The work of IT executives and, by implication, the value of IT operations are judged on whether IT systems work reliably. They must work flawlessly to manage inventories, ship goods, and account for costs and revenue. Not coincidentally, those systems must also deliver information in useful formats that the company's executives need. Long-term strategic IT vision counts only in consultants' seminars. Most CEOs lack enough technical knowledge of IT to make technical judgments about IT operations. They want to know only that they work and how much they cost.

As a result, the IT executive's view of NAT might be whether NAT is one of those technologies that seems relatively benign but sets us on a path that's hard to leave in the future. Aside from its limitations and effects on applications, does it lock the company's IT systems into using it extensively? And what are its real life-cycle costs?

In this chapter we'll take the IT executive's view of NAT, answering the types of questions that IT executives may ask about NAT. For example, a CIO who understands something about NAT might want answers to the following questions.

Will NAT affect network connectivity?

The honest answer to this question is that yes, it might affect network connectivity, but it probably won't. As a general principle, anything inserted between the enterprise and the Internet, or between the enterprise and its subsidiaries, business partners, or service providers, can affect connectivity. But it depends on how you define "affecting" connectivity.

Certainly NAT changes network connectivity. Inside addresses are different to outside systems, but the latter do not know that they aren't the "real" addresses. If NAT is done by a firewall, inside system addresses may not be visible to outside systems at all, but they may be represented by the address of the firewall's external interface. Applications and systems that must see a system "real" address or that must identify the other system positively for security purposes will be affected by NAT. So, yes, NAT affects connectivity, but only if concealing a system's "real" address affects an application.

The IT organization's strategic viewpoint may be that imposing an interface or a screen between systems for specific purposes is permissible. It may be to improve usability, to ensure better security, to control access, or to enable more comprehensive management. Anything that impairs connectivity, without yielding a corresponding improvement in some other desirable objective, won't pass the test.

Judged on these factors, NAT may affect connectivity negatively, particularly in its effects on certain applications. As we have noted, NAT can impose a performance penalty on a firewall or router that does NAT in addition to traffic screening, routing, or both. For many networks, NAT's performance drag is likely to be the most serious consequence of using it.

Will NAT affect using new applications and new technology?

As we have already noted, NAT may affect applications, particularly ones that weren't developed with NAT in mind. Some applications assume the end-to-end significance of IP addresses, which means they may not work properly if the end addresses change. This isn't restricted to new Web-based applications, either. That old standby FTP, which works fine through NAT in a standard client/server file transfer, may not work properly if a more sophisticated user tries to redirect files to another host. Not that they are so significant in the corporate environment, but most NAT configurations prevent multiplayer games from working properly among players connected over the Internet. Then again, given the problems that corporations have had policing Internet use, that's a strong argument in favor of NAT.

Encryption can be another problem, but it's not restricted to NAT. Certain encryption methods, such as IP Secure, are notoriously NAT-unfriendly because they hide IP addresses that must be translated. It's usually not practical to allow a NAT device to decrypt data to do address translation. First, it's slow, and second, the decryption and subsequent reencryption may be detected by the destination decryption process as a security breach. Last, it may be a serious security breach to distribute encryption keys to anything but the source and destination of encrypted data.

NAT tries to be invisible, but that charade doesn't always work, particularly when it interferes with applications. The problem with NAT's transparency is that it could be located anywhere between the client and the server. If it's not on their end of the network, it's not necessarily clear to network troubleshooters precisely where the NAT is located, nor, for that matter, if NAT is the problem at all. That's not an argument against NAT, but a statement of the reality of networking. If a new application doesn't work properly, it may take an applications support team a while to determine what's wrong. The problem could be NAT if it's in the network path, although network troubleshooters often blame NAT or firewalls for mysterious application or communications ailments, whether they're to blame or not.

The answer is that yes, NAT may affect how applications and new technologies work. Any application that assumes the end-to-end significance of an IP address may be affected by NAT. Many of those applications may be ones that corporate IT managers don't want on their networks or that run afoul of network security measures. With the concerns over network security today, it's a given that there will be a firewall or a security barrier at the entrance to a network. Most firewalls translate inside addresses to a single outside address or to a small number of externally visible addresses. NAT on a firewall is a common network configuration, so many new network applications are designed with the assumption that NAT will be a part of the network environment.

Does NAT improve network security, or does it impose a security risk?

As we discussed in the last chapter, NAT is frequently regarded as a security measure, but there are many more effective security measures that should be deployed. By itself, NAT can shield the IP addresses of the systems on a network, but its defenses are weak and vulnerable to all but the most cursory attempts at discovery.

IT organizations cannot depend on NAT to provide security. Today, network security is such a pressing concern for companies, organizations, and government agencies worldwide that it is often handled by a separate operational unit within the IT organization. The reason for separating the security function from IT operations is that IT operations is frequently tempted to compromise security concerns in order to foster operations. It's not that IT operations can't be trusted with the responsibility for security; it's just that security sometimes runs at cross-purposes to operations' mission.

Security is always a compromise between availability and confidentiality. The security people in IT want to restrict access to the network and to information, while the operations people, who are usually part of the same IT operation, want to make information and systems accessible. Operations opens systems and information to the world, and security closes them down. A company's IT management usually stands between the two sides, using a security policy to manage the tug-of-war between the two.

The struggle of these two opposite sides sometimes results in some comical confrontations. In 1999, a large financial institution decided to open its internal network to its customers so they could access a new, online electronic banking system from the Internet. Security had been such an important concern for the company that until that time, its employees had not been allowed to access the Internet from their desktops. They couldn't even send e-mail from their internal e-mail system to Internet mailboxes.

The company designed its Internet gateway with three levels of firewalls and screening routers, plus an intrusion detection system. All internal addresses, which were public, routable addresses, were translated to a small number of different, publicly routable addresses by one of the firewalls. All incoming and outgoing transactions were proxied by one of the perimeter firewalls, so that neither inside nor outside users had direct access to anything. The intrusion detection system was set up to notify the firewalls of any suspicious activity in real time, so that access from the outside could be closed immediately, instead of after analysis by security system administrators.

When this complex but practically impenetrable security system was first brought online for a few test users, the triggers for the intrusion detection system were set so low that any actions by an external user to reach the internal online banking system caused the firewalls to cut off all outside access to the network. The system worked, but it worked too well. The system was certainly secure, but the security measures completely defeated the accessibility part of the equation.

Obviously, in this example, the security people had the upper hand in developing the network security perimeter and in implementing the network security policy. Even though the initial results were not practical, the company's security and IT operations people eventually reached a compromise that afforded more effective results.

In this case, NAT was part of the security system, but it was hardly the centerpiece of a security strategy. That's precisely the way it should be regarded by IT management. It's a tool that can be deployed as part of a fully coordinated security perimeter, but it's only the most rudimentary security device. NAT was never intended to be a security measure, even though some IT organizations think of it as such. It's one of those operational things, to translate private addresses into public addresses or to help manage traffic through a firewall's single outside interface.

Psychologists frequently ascribe human behavior and actions to left-brain and right-brain influences, dividing them between the creative and the analytical functions. To draw a parallel to IT management responsibilities, NAT is an operational side-of-the-brain issue, not a security side-of-the-brain issue.

The right way for IT management to think about NAT is in operations, not security.

Does NAT affect our ability to defend ourselves against attackers and intruders?

IT executives who consider the security implications of NAT usually focus on how NAT affects their own networks' security posture. As we have seen, NAT is a tool, albeit not a terrifically effective one, that may be one component of a comprehensive security perimeter.

What IT executives frequently miss about the security implications of NAT is how it may affect their ability to protect their networks from attack or intrusion. The most serious problem with NAT occurs when it's used by an attacker or intruder to hide his or her identity from the target. IT executives sometimes make the dangerous and naïve assumption that NAT is used exclusively by the Good Guys. The Bad Guys know that NAT is a poor man's substitute for address spoofing and not nearly as effective, but it can conceal an attacker's identity just as easily.

Let's say that one of the Bad Guys targets the XYZ Corporation's network. The intruder may not have any intention of deleting files, trashing the company's Web site, or stealing customer records. The intruder may be one of those inquisitive 12-year-olds who just wants to see what he or she can find on the network or, worse, one of those 21-year-old computer science majors with time on his or her hands and an Internet connection.

A sophisticated intruder might consider tinkering with the source IP address of his or her datagrams, in order to conceal the real source IP address identity. Changing the IP address of a PC is a simple matter of modifying the settings in the Control Panel/Network icon of a Windows PC. If the intruder changed the network part of the source IP address, the intruder's ISP wouldn't necessarily know how to route responses back to the intruder's network.

The intruder would have to resort to more sophisticated measures, such as setting up a system that can do routing and NAT. A dedicated router might be an expensive proposition, but an old Unix workstation, configured to do routing and NAT, might be readily available. This would conceal the real identity of the intruder, but the external NAT addresses would still have to be known to and routable by the ISP and traceable through a DNS or Whois lookup.

Internet routing issues foil most attempts by relatively inexperienced intruders to conceal their source addresses. Even if the intruder does change his or her source address and the attack is detected by an intrusion detection system, the target network's security administrators must still trace the intruder's address back to its source. They may not be able to trace the intrusion attempt, even though it has been concealed by NAT, any farther than the intruder's external interface to his or her ISP.

A sophisticated intruder would try to cover his or her tracks by breaking into and using a host on someone else's network as the source of the attack. He or she may have no way of guaranteeing this, but it would be even better if the network were fronted by a router or firewall that did NAT. In this case, the attack would appear to come from another network, with addresses changed by NAT.

The point is that NAT may affect the ability of the IT organization to protect its networks from attack if NAT is used by an attacker or intruder. NAT can help conceal the source addresses of traffic from the company's network, but it can also conceal the identity of an attacker, making it more difficult to pinpoint the source of an attack. NAT can become a two-edged sword when it is turned against the IT organization by an intruder, including ones who attack firewalls with NAT and use them as the jumping-off point for more wide-ranging attacks.

Does NAT affect our ability to manage our networks?

Network management has become one of the most important issues for IT executives. As networks have become more complex and businesses have become more dependent on continuous, reliable operation of their networks and information processing systems, IT managers and executives have overseen the installation of comprehensive systems to manage and control their networks. Passive trouble detection is a thing of the past because IT executives need automated systems to detect and solve network problems and to assess network reliability trends.

The primary data collection tool for most network management systems is the *Simple Network Management Protocol* (SNMP), an industry standard protocol for polling network devices and services by network management systems. As we have noted in previous chapters, NAT does not change anything in the management data in the SNMP data stream. The data field in the SNMP payload is called the SNMP object identifier. The object identifier contains embedded IP addresses to identify the device from which the data was sensed. In addition, proprietary or system-specific network management systems may also embed IP addresses and other identifiers in their data streams. New versions of SNMP, such as SNMP Version 3 (SNMPv3), incorporate security measures that make it impossible to manipulate IP addresses in SNMP data fields.

NAT may affect SNMP data, so the simple solution to avoiding this problem on a network that uses NAT is to position SNMP probes and data collection agents behind the firewalls or routers that are doing NAT. Unfortunately, that's not always possible. An organization that uses private addressing and manages the private addressing domains through virtual private networks tunneled across the Internet will still find that NAT doesn't change the SNMP data to report the "real" address. An IT organization that has outsourced network management to a third-party service bureau will encounter the same problems.

Managing the network also means managing changes to the network. Like any other special networking arrangement, such as a proxy server or a firewall, NAT may have to be changed periodically to accommodate changes in connectivity or addressing. NAT may affect Internet connectivity, applications, and network management, so it's best not to change it casually.

For example, any modification to firewall configurations, including changing NAT, should be done according to established change control procedures. IT change management procedures for modifying NAT may include some or all of the following steps:

- Describing the NAT change required
- Identifying parts of NAT configuration to be changed
- Recognizing effects of NAT configuration change on performance
- Creating documentation of before and after scenarios
- Specifying costs, resources, and equipment needed
- Implementing test and verification plans
- Setting up installation and change schedules
- Establishing installation control
- Preparing project documentation
- Monitoring network management system changes
- Documenting final NAT reconfiguration

Bringing a new application online that may be affected by NAT, such as Net-Show or VDOLive, will alter the cost and complexity of a change management scenario. Establishing a method to do DNS zone file transfers through a NAT box can require an even more complex change management scenario, and even greater costs.

The short answer to the network management and NAT issue is yes, NAT may affect an organization's network management capabilities adversely. Address translation is like any other part of the network infrastructure that can work flawlessly, as long as it's not changed. Changes to NAT, like changes to firewall rulesets or network routing, should be a managed, controlled change because it can affect basic network connectivity.

Is using private address space the wrong strategic decision?

IT people go back and forth on the private address space issue all the time. Private address space is always available, it's free, and the RFC 1918 Class A and Class B address spaces are large enough to accommodate all types of networks. But private addressing requires address translation to connect to other networks or to the Internet. Ten years ago, back when connecting a network to other networks over the Internet was the exception rather than the rule, private addressing could be justified easily.

Today, IT organizations may have a harder time justifying using private address space. If they were given a choice, most IT executives would elect to use public address space for their networks, even if they have to go to the trouble and expense of acquiring their own public address space. Companies and organizations can acquire their own address space. It is assigned by ARIN, the not-for-profit corporation set up by the U.S. government and Network Solutions, Inc. to manage IP address space and to control public address block assignments.

The other side of the private addressing issue is that it offers the organization a huge amount of flexibility. Using the 10.0.0.0 address space in a big corporation can free the IT organization from issues like conserving address space by using unnumbered links between routers, variable-length subnet masks, and strict controls on network growth. This is not to say that the IT organization won't have to exercise good network planning, but private address space can make the blank canvas of IP address space so large that most anything will work.

There is a crisis in IP addressing, in that the finite amount of unassigned address space is being exhausted at a rapid rate. With public, routable address space still available, most IT organizations have a hard time justifying using private address space. Unless a large enough block of public space isn't available, or an organization can't justify its request to its ISP, most organizations will choose not to use private address space. To the public-address-space-or-die crowd, NAT is an unnecessary complication. If you're going to screen addresses through a firewall, they argue, they'll be changed anyway to the firewall's external interface. It doesn't matter, therefore, if they're public or private addresses.

In the long run, which conforms to the strategic view that IT is supposed to be taking, what matters is low maintenance costs, flexibility, and stability. Private addresses always have to be changed to public ones to reach Internet resources, so they imply the maintenance and operational costs of NAT. Is private address space, and therefore NAT, the wrong strategic decision? The choice has to be based on whether the flexibility, availability, and range of private addressing meet the company's needs.

What will NAT cost?

The most dreaded IT exercise is the annual budgeting battle, in which IT expectations, technology, and objectives collide head-on with the costs of people, computers, and communications services. The outright cost of NAT may be buried in the purchase price and software license fees of router and firewall hardware and software, but its ongoing costs lie in the expense of an experienced technical staff to configure and support it. In addition, the IT organization must also budget for experienced systems analysts staff to track the ongoing performance of Internet paths on which NAT is being done and to troubleshoot applications and connectivity problems that NAT might have caused.

Once installed as part of the feature set of a router or firewall, NAT may be considered a sunk cost, with little or no ongoing maintenance costs aside from normal firewall ruleset maintenance and router configuration changes. Of course, the firewall and router people have to know how and where NAT is being done, and they need to have established a benchmark for its effects on firewall or router performance. It's also extremely helpful, and a highly worthwhile investment, if IT has mandated that the network managers document the host, interface, or network addresses that are being changed by NAT, as well as how those addresses appear outside the network.

NAT should require maintenance, and therefore incur maintenance costs, only if something changes. That "something" could be as simple as the addition of new hosts and networks that require NAT, a change in the firewall configuration, or the addition of a proxy server. It could also be something as complex as a change in the network security perimeter, adding a new application that doesn't work well with NAT, or establishing communications with a new business partner who uses NAT or private addressing, or both. It could also be changing ISPs, adding a substantial new number of users behind the NAT box, or changing the arrangement and relationship of inside and outside DNS servers.

Given the range of circumstances that might require NAT changes or maintenance, it's difficult to say exactly what the maintenance cost of NAT will be. It is safe to say that anything that affects the device that does NAT, such as a rearrangement of the firewall or security perimeter, may imply changes to

NAT. Those changes will have to be done methodically, just like any other system change.

Will NAT affect the company's ability to do mergers and acquisitions?

A company that is actively engaged in mergers and acquisitions may find that NAT is an effective tool to integrate acquired companies' networks quickly and easily. Instead of having to change addressing in a perimeter network in an acquired company, both companies can use NAT at the border routers where the two networks communicate, to isolate their networks from each other.

In a merger or acquisition situation, NAT lets the two networks communicate with each other, yet stay unchanged. That's a distinct advantage to both companies' IT organizations because the two companies can establish internetwork communications and consolidate access to common applications and data, without having to renumber either network in a common address space.

A basic assumption in each merger or acquisition scenario in which NAT fits is that one or both of the two networks use private address space somewhere in their networks or an overlap exists in their address spaces. It also may be that IT doesn't have the time or the resources to figure out a network consolidation plan before the merger is effective. Keeping the two networks separate may also conform to a business plan to hold an acquired company as a separate subsidiary, in order to spin it off or sell it to another company in the future.

As a network isolation technique, NAT is one of the tools that IT can use to manage and organize its networks for flexibility and change. It's not necessary for the networks of the acquiring and acquired companies to remain separate. In many cases, it's highly desirable that the networks be merged into a single network entity. NAT is one of the tactics that IT can use to make information systems conform to corporate business objectives.

Will NAT affect our users' ability to access the Internet?

Network address translation is supposed to be transparent to users and most network services, but it will affect some types of applications. It is also possible that it may affect Internet access, although probably not for most users. The key questions about whether NAT might affect Internet access are whether it has been configured to translate addresses correctly and whether those addresses can be resolved properly.

For example, the addresses of systems on a private network are usually translated to public addresses by a firewall or a router. For the sake of network security, not to mention routability, the firewall or router frequently advertises only a small number of external addresses. The firewall or router maps those addresses back to a larger number of internal addresses, translating addresses back and forth as appropriate.

This is not a hugely complicated affair, as long as the firewall or router outside address or addresses have been configured properly, and the firewall or router tracks address translation properly. The other issue is whether those addresses have been advertised and routed properly by the network's ISP. If they aren't, it will be evident soon enough, and it should be a relatively simple matter for the ISP to fix.

These types of technical problems, any of which might affect Internet access from an internal network, should not occur at all except when the network or NAT or the firewall is being set up. One ongoing effect of NAT on Internet connectivity might be the delay that users experience when their addresses are translated by an overloaded firewall. As we have already noted, NAT can add a significant amount of processing overhead, which translates into delay, to whatever device is doing NAT. Most firewalls can screen Internet traffic quickly and efficiently, so most users are unaware that a firewall has been inserted in the pathway between the network and the Internet.

Adding NAT to a firewall forces the firewall to change the traffic passing through it, instead of merely determining if it passes or fails its ruleset screen. Those changes take time and affect the ability of the firewall to act transparently and to handle as much traffic as it might without NAT. One solution to the firewall performance issue is to move the NAT function from the firewall and to place it on a less expensive device, such as a router, that can concentrate on NAT and routing, instead of firewall screening.

Assuming that NAT has been configured properly and that an ISP is doing its job properly, NAT should not prevent Internet connectivity, but it might affect it. The cause of delay in accessing Internet sites is usually difficult to identify because of the number of connections, routing points, and systems involved in Internet connectivity. Changing traffic is different from screening or routing, however, and NAT may impede Internet connectivity but not stop it.

Will NAT affect our relationships with ISPs and our business partners?

If it's properly configured, NAT won't affect relationships with ISPs and business partners at all. Remember that NAT isn't a "relationship" issue; it's a technical issue. If NAT is done right and the NAT task is performed by a device that can take the stress of NAT, NAT should be transparent to everyone external to the organization's network.

For that matter, ISPs and business partners themselves may be doing NAT as a means to shield their own internal addressing schemes from your network. If their NAT works properly and it's transparent to your routers, firewalls, and network, it won't affect your relationship with them either.

If both your network and that of a business partner are doing NAT, the managers of the respective networks may have to coordinate their address translation schemes. Sometimes a number of business partners that share a common information exchange network translate their internal addresses into a special network that uses private addressing. This technique is called *twice NAT*, and it helps to isolate the shared network from the members' networks.

What is the IT industry's view of NAT?

You might think that NAT would be viewed universally as a useful and beneficial technique for enabling communications from private addressing domains and to foster some level of security through external addresses from firewalls or screening routers. That's the widely held opinion, but there is a minority in the Internet engineering and technical community who regard NAT as a needless complication, particularly if it is a means to support private addressing, marring the end-to-end significance of IP addressing.

The biggest objection of the NAT-as-the-work-of-the-devil faction is that they think NAT complicates network operation and routing and that it interferes with public addressing schemes that work well for most networks. Why introduce NAT if you don't have to, they argue. The addressing crisis (to be covered in Chapter 12, "The Crisis in IP Addressing") isn't as much of a crisis as it's made out to be, they say, as there is plenty of public address space available, as long as we use what we have efficiently.

Most of the IT industry would acknowledge that in a perfect world, there would be no need to resort to private addressing. Private network addressing, however, gives network designers a great measure of freedom to configure network addressing plans to fit specific network circumstances.

Summary

Some IT managers may think it's somewhat presumptuous to believe that a networking technique like NAT should be part of the strategic thinking of the IT operation. The simple view of NAT is that it is only a way to allow different network addressing domains to communicate, without regard for the specifics of what could be conflicting or unroutable addresses.

NAT, however, can affect other, more important issues, such as how (or whether) certain applications work, network management capabilities, and network security. IT managers needn't know all of the details of configuring NAT and developing applications gateways. They do have to understand that what appears to be a simple issue of address translation may have other implications for network connectivity, and for network management and control. More important, NAT can give the corporation an extra measure of flexibility in acquiring or merging with other companies or maintaining a holding company structure over other parts of the corporation. NAT is just a tool for network connectivity, but IT management must have an understanding of its full implications for the corporation.

In the next chapter, we'll turn our attention back to the technology of NAT, examining static and dynamic address assignment by NAT. We'll see how the address ranges configured on the NAT device affect how NAT works and how outside devices see the effects of NAT. In some cases, the choice of static or dynamic NAT may be dictated by the devices behind the NAT device or by the applications supported by clients and servers on both sides of the NAT threshold.

Dynamic and Static NAT

The system that converts a network's inside addresses to outside addresses is the *NAT box*, which is the generic term we've used several times in previous chapters to describe a firewall or router that does address translation. The NAT box will be configured with specific addresses for translation. If we assume that the purpose of doing NAT is to gain connectivity to the Internet, then the outside addresses will be routable, public addresses. It doesn't matter what the inside addresses are because they will be translated by the NAT box before they reach the outside world.

The network administrator has a number of choices to make about precisely what the NAT box will do, particularly what those outside addresses will be. One of the first choices is whether the NAT box will assign those addresses dynamically or whether they will be assigned statically. That is, will the IP addresses of devices inside the network always be translated to the same outside addresses? Or, is it better to translate inside addresses to any of a number of outside addresses, with the address translation possibly changing each time an inside system establishes an outside connection?

On the surface, this choice may seem relatively simple. For that matter, it may not seem to make any difference at all if the same address or a different one is used to represent an inside address. In many network environments, though, it may matter what the external representation of an inside address is, for accountability, access control, security, or network management reasons. In this chapter, we will examine the issues involved in static versus dynamic address translation, as well as the considerations that the network administrator must make to configure an address translation scenario that makes sense for his or her network.

A Simple Plan

Static NAT is the simplest and most straightforward address translation technique. In static NAT, the NAT box translates the source addresses of inside systems to specific, fixed addresses. The outside addresses don't change from time to time, so there is a fixed relationship between inside and outside addresses. Static NAT also implies a one-to-one relationship between inside addresses and outside addresses, as each inside address corresponds to a specific outside address.

For example, let's take the network depicted in Figure 5.1. Each of the PCs, servers, and hosts on the inside network (only a few of which are depicted in the figure) uses its own address when communicating with any other system on the inside network. In this case, the inside network uses private addresses, taken from one of the RFC 1918 address blocks. In practice, the inside network

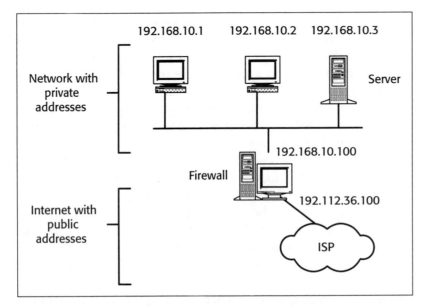

Figure 5.1   Network with private addresses connected to Internet, which uses public addresses.

could use addresses from any address range, including public address space. Whatever those inside addresses are, they must be translated to external addresses whenever they leave the network.

Let's say that the PC with the inside address of 192.168.10.1 sends traffic to an Internet Web site with an address of 140.49.10.1. The 140.49.10.1 address is a public, routable address, and it will be the destination address in the IP datagram created by the PC's Web browser. The source address of that datagram, however, will be 192.168.10.1. It's a private address, so it must be translated to a public, routable address before it leaves the network.

When the datagram, and every successive one after it, reaches the router, the router will replace the PC's source address with a predetermined outside address. For example, the network administrator may have configured the router's NAT software with the address translation table depicted in Figure 5.2. Note that the NAT table maps each inside address to a fixed outside address.

When the reply comes back from the Web site, the NAT router simply reverses the process. The router reads the destination address of the response from the Web site (140.49.10.1) and identifies the datagram as traffic that will be forwarded back to the inside network. Those addresses will have to be translated, so the router picks the original source address from the translation

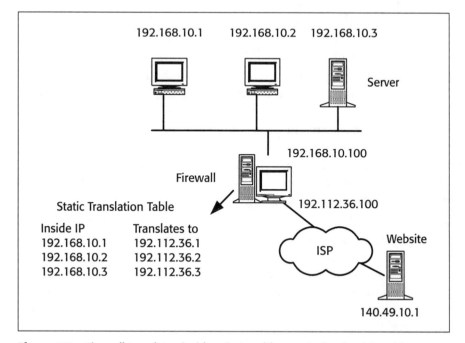

Figure 5.2 Firewall translates inside private addresses to fixed public addresses.

table, substitutes it for the destination address of the inbound traffic, and forwards the datagram to the inside network interface for delivery.

The Pros and Cons

Static address translation is simple and direct. Those are its greatest virtues, and in the computing universe, which is rife with technologies and techniques that are neither simple nor direct, those are good virtues to have. The simple case of static address translation, however, is not always the best case. Static address translation has a number of drawbacks that make it suitable for a limited number of circumstances. The disadvantages of static NAT include the following:

High maintenance. Static address mapping won't change automatically if either the internal or the external network addressing changes. This also happens to be one of those virtues we mentioned earlier, but it can also be a maintenance headache if there is a change to network addressing. Static addressing also means that for every inside system that is added or changed on the inside network, the network administrator may have to set up a new address translation table entry or change the old one. From sad experience, network administrators know that changing or adding addresses in an address translation table is another unfortunate opportunity to enter addresses incorrectly, transpose address digits, and make other mistakes in addressing tables.

High address usage. In a big network, the one-to-one addressing relationship of inside to outside addresses can consume a large number of external addresses in public address space. If there are hundreds or thousands of systems on an internal network that need address translation to communicate outside the network, each one will need its own external address. Because one of the purposes of NAT is to conserve public address space, static NAT on a large network runs contrary to the concept of public address space conservation.

Fixed routing. Static NAT may also imply some type of static routing for internal systems. That is, an internal system that utilizes static NAT will have to exit the network through the NAT box that maintains the static NAT table for that device. If the network is multihomed or if it has several connections to other networks, internal systems that use static NAT will have to go through specific NAT points for their addresses to be translated correctly.

Security. Fixed, one-to-one mapping between internal and external addresses is a flimsy security screen. Through careful traffic examination, an external observer might be able to determine which external address maps to which internal address. As we have noted in previous chapters, NAT really isn't much of a security measure in the first place. Network administrators who expect NAT to provide even the slightest pretense of security shouldn't use static NAT. It's too simple and too direct to be considered a security measure.

The disadvantages to static NAT do not mean that it is unsuitable for a modern network environment. As we will see in the next section of this chapter, dynamic NAT is more suitable for most network environments. What the disadvantages of static NAT do say is that static NAT is suitable for a small number of network environments. Those environments make the best use of the static NAT virtues of simplicity and directness. Some of the circumstances in which static NAT is useful are as follows:

Limited NAT requirements. In a network in which there is a limited number of systems that need NAT, static NAT can be an effective tool to control external access. Some networks have systems that use private addresses for internal communications and only occasionally need external network access. In that case, a small static NAT table may be an effective solution to the NAT requirement.

Network management. Many networks have requirements to manage external traffic or to identify which systems communicate externally. For example, network troubleshooting is easier and simpler if the addresses of inside systems can be tracked accurately when they communicate externally. Static NAT assigns a fixed address to traffic from each system or network interface, so that traffic can be tracked or traced reliably.

Applications compatibility. As we have noted, some applications embed IP addresses in data fields of IP datagrams. Not all NAT boxes examine those data fields, which means that some applications won't work properly through a NAT box. An application-level gateway, which changes embedded data, could be configured to examine traffic bearing static NAT addresses and "tag" them for examination by the application-level gateway.

Service requirements. Some network services, such as DNS, need fixed addresses so they can be found reliably by network services, systems, and other DNS servers. An internal network may have its own DNS that has been paired with an external DNS that is visible to the outside world. There may be a requirement for these two DNS servers to talk to each other, to forward recursive DNS inquiries, or to transfer zone files. The configuration files of the external DNS will list an IP address for the internal DNS, but that address can't change. A static mapping of the internal DNS's private address to a fixed public address is required. The static address to which the internal DNS's traffic is mapped will always match the external DNS's address for the internal DNS, even though it will be translated to its "real" address by the NAT box.

Traffic accounting. An e-commerce business with a number of Web servers that are identified by a common external address may want to use static NAT to maintain an accurate picture of server usage. For example, the Web site of eCommerceXYZ Corp., www.ecommercexyzcorp.com, may be a dozen servers, all of which are identified by a single DNS address. A firewall, router, or load-sharing system may direct inbound traffic to one of the 12 servers, depending on its availability, load, or other factors. In this scenario, the network administrator would probably want to use static NAT to track inside traffic reliably.

Multihoming. NAT can make it difficult to connect a network to more than one ISP. How NAT works with multiple network connections, or *multihoming*, can be a particularly thorny problem, as we will see in Chapter 10, "NAT and Routing." For example, say there are two network access points from a private network to the Internet, and private network addresses are changed to public network addresses by NAT at the access points. Each NAT device can translate addresses from a different NAT address pool, but once traffic goes out to the Internet, there's no guarantee that it will come back to the same NAT device so that it can be translated back properly.

Address utilization. Most NAT devices reuse addresses once the sessions for which they have been assigned have been terminated. Sometimes, it's not completely clear to the NAT device that a session has been terminated properly. Either the client or the server, for example, might have lost the connection, or timed out, or powered off. In none of these cases is the NAT device necessarily informed that the connection has been lost and the translated address returned to the available address pool. Most NAT implementations have a defined time, which can be quite long, for which the NAT device will wait for a connection to terminate before it decides to return the address to the NAT pool. If there isn't a large number of addresses in the NAT pool, addresses can be held hostage until the NAT device concludes that they can safely be reassigned.

NAT is one of those useful tools that is more suited to small networks or networks in which NAT applies only to a limited number of systems. As with the Dynamic Host Configuration Protocol (DHCP), by which network administrators assign IP addresses dynamically to PCs, DHCP isn't for every system. Servers and services are usually not assigned addresses with DHCP because they need fixed addresses. So, too, do some internal systems, for which static NAT is a practical solution to the NAT issue.

Doing It on the Fly

The other side of the NAT coin is dynamic NAT, in which those external addresses are assigned dynamically. That is, instead of a fixed, one-to-one relationship of internal addresses to external addresses, the NAT addresses may change from time to time. They may change each time an internal system establishes a connection to an outside system, or they may change periodically, such as each day or week.

Dynamic NAT is just like static NAT, only the outside addresses no longer map one-to-one to inside addresses. There may be just as many of them because all of the internal systems may have to communicate externally simultaneously. Dynamic NAT typically uses a smaller pool of external addresses because it offers the network administrator a significant virtue that static NAT does not: flexibility.

Dynamic NAT offers flexibility because it removes the one-to-one relationship between inside and outside addresses. Not only need there not be a fixed, corresponding outside address for each inside address, but there may not even be a need for as many outside addresses as there are inside addresses. Dynamic NAT scenarios may need only as many outside addresses as there are simultaneous connections from inside systems to outside systems, instead of as many outside addresses as there are inside systems.

As its name implies, dynamic NAT replaces the source addresses of traffic from inside systems with routable outside addresses that are taken from a pool of addresses. As long as the NAT box keeps track of which outside address has been assigned to which inside system, the system works transparently to inside and outside systems.

For example, let's take the network that we used to illustrate static NAT earlier in this chapter and expand the number of inside systems somewhat. The network, shown in Figure 5.3, uses the same inside and outside address ranges, but we've depicted a few more inside systems on the network. This time we'll use dynamic NAT to change the inside addresses to outside addresses.

Let's say that the PC with the inside address 192.168.10.3 initiates an HTTP session with an Internet Web site at 140.49.10.1. When the NAT router receives each of the IP datagrams in the data stream from the PC, it takes one of the outside addresses from its pool of external addresses (192.112.36.1, 192.112.36.2, and 192.112.36.3) and replaces the source address with the external address. At the same time, the NAT router builds a translation table entry, just as it did when translating addresses statically, to map the inside address to the corresponding outside address. The translation table is depicted in Figure 5.4.

Datagrams from the second PC that sends traffic to another external site will be handled similarly by the NAT router. For example, the NAT router might translate the source IP addresses in the IP headers of an outbound FTP session

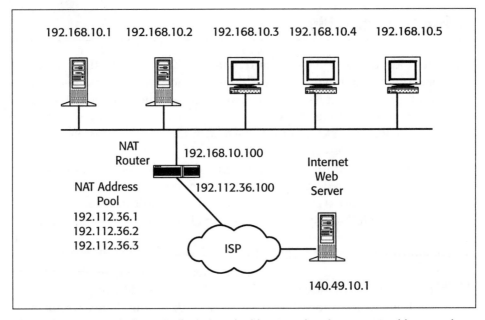

Figure 5.3 NAT with dynamically-assigned addresses taken from a NAT address pool.

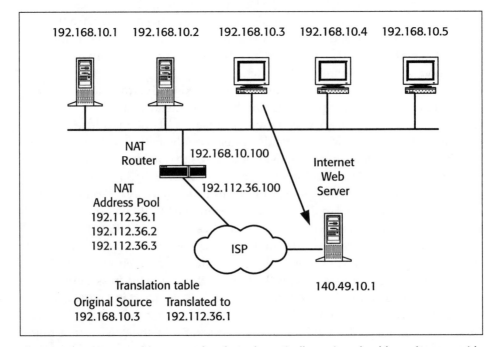

Figure 5.4 Source address translated to dynamically assigned address from outside address translation pool.

from the PC at 192.168.10.4 to the next address in the outside address pool, 192.112.36.2. A third session initiated by an inside host with the inside address of 192.168.10.5 might take the last available external address in the pool, 192.112.36.3, as shown in Figure 5.5.

When each of the PCs terminates its session with the external site, the NAT router returns the external address to the NAT pool. It does so after waiting the configured time for the address to be safely reused. As each of these "empties" is returned to the NAT pool, they become available for reassignment as the source addresses for subsequent sessions from inside systems. The same address might be assigned again to an inside system, or it could be a different address. It wouldn't matter, as long as the NAT box maintained the inside-to-outside address mapping, substituting inside for outside addresses as appropriate.

Making Do with Less

We purposely used a small NAT pool of only three external addresses in the example of dynamic NAT because that's how it is typically deployed. That is, the network administrator can create a NAT pool that is only large enough to

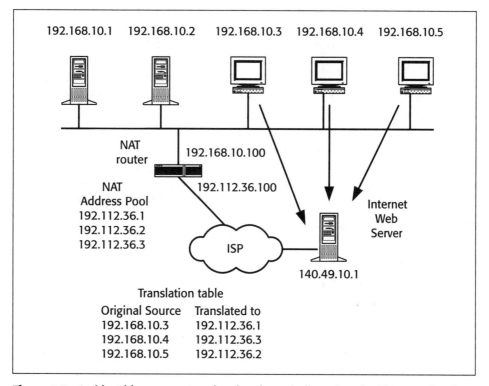

Figure 5.5   Inside addresses are translated to dynamically-assigned addresses taken from address translation pool.

accommodate as many systems as will be communicating through the NAT box simultaneously, instead of a NAT pool large enough to accommodate the total number of inside systems that will even communicate externally. As long as the number of external addresses in the NAT pool is sufficient for however many systems communicate externally, there needn't be enough external addresses for every inside system. There only need to be as many external systems as there are simultaneous external connections from inside systems.

For the network administrator, the trick is determining just how big that dynamic NAT address pool must be, if it won't be large enough to accommodate all systems simultaneously. The first thing the network administrator must do is determine if a smaller address pool will be sufficient. Networks with requirements for high external traffic loads or high-traffic e-commerce networks may not be suitable candidates for using a limited number of external addresses.

In a typical network of client PCs, the network administrator may be able to use a traffic monitoring or traffic logging system to analyze external traffic patterns. In a network of 1000 PCs, for example, 75 percent may access the Web or some other external site during the day. The other 25 percent of the PCs might not be powered on or in use during a typical day, if their users are on the road or out of the office. Even at peak times, such as midmorning and midafternoon, only half of the 75 percent might be online. Using this data, the network administrator might configure an external address pool of 500 addresses, which would allow enough dynamically assigned addresses for peak usage, plus some additional room for usage spikes.

This ratio wouldn't be applicable to networks that use proxy servers. The proxy server would get a single address from the NAT device. All connections that are proxied through the proxy server appear to come from a single address, which is that of the proxy server.

The guess about the size of the address pool may be sufficient, or it may prove to be hopelessly inadequate. It may also change over time if usage changes. Assuming the network administrator has enough external addresses to cover peak loads and unusual traffic spikes, the address pool may not have to be adjusted except to accommodate network growth.

The Good and the Bad

Given a choice between static and dynamic NAT, most network administrators would choose the latter unless they have requirements for traffic accountability and control, or unless their networks consist of a relatively small number of systems that require NAT. Dynamic NAT has a number of advantages that recommend it strongly, including the following:

Flexibility. Dynamic NAT offers network administrators more latitude in how they manage external address mappings, by removing the requirement for one-to-one address translations. If the organization changes ISPs, renumbers external interfaces, or reconfigures a firewall or router perimeter, the network administrator may also change the address range of the outside addresses without affecting a static address translation table.

Low maintenance. Because dynamic NAT doesn't maintain a fixed mapping between inside addresses and specific outside addresses, there's no need for the network administrator to update the NAT mapping because it changes from time to time. Unless there's some need to track traffic from specific IP addresses, it really doesn't matter what address the NAT box uses for its translation. Even with dynamic NAT, there may still be some need for a small static NAT table if there are a number of systems that can't have dynamic NAT addresses, such as DNS servers, Web servers, and the like. Dynamic NAT isn't necessarily maintenance-free, but it does get the network administrator out of the game of maintaining address translation tables for most of the run-of-the-mill user PCs.

Lower address usage. Given the constraints on getting new blocks of public IP address space, which will be covered in more depth in Chapter 12, "The Crisis in IP Addressing," dynamic NAT can relieve some of the demand on new public address space. Because there needn't be a one-to-one mapping of inside to outside addresses with dynamic NAT, it may require a smaller number of outside addresses than static NAT would require. ISPs are under pressure to justify and manage their use of routable address space closely. Some organizations may find that their ISPs want to impose an additional charge for public address space beyond a standard allocation given to a new ISP customer.

On the downside, dynamic NAT has many of the disadvantages of any address translation scheme, including the following:

Adequate address ranges. If the network administrator configures a NAT address pool of fewer addresses than there are inside systems, he or she is gambling that the outside address pool will be sufficient for normal and peak usage. It may not be adequate for unusual traffic spikes, but as with any network configuration issue, the network administrator must balance the prospect of unusual demands against the resources that are available.

Reclaiming unused session addresses. The NAT box will hold a dynamically assigned outside address for an inside system for as long as it has an open session. A single inside system may have several outside sessions going at the same time, such as an HTTP and an FTP session, both of which will use the same outside address. If all of the outside sessions end, the NAT box can return the outside address to the address pool. The problem, as we noted earlier, is determining when or if those sessions end. Many Windows users open sessions, and then minimize them. This leaves the session active, but it may be forgotten or not maximized for hours. A typical solution is to set the NAT box to set a time-out on unused or abandoned sessions, so that the outside addresses can be reclaimed and returned to the NAT pool. To be safe, the time-out may have to be hours long, to prevent cutting off sessions that are still alive but not terrifically active.

Taking It to Extremes

As we have noted, one of the advantages of using dynamic NAT is that the network administrator doesn't need to have enough external addresses for every inside system. There need to be only enough external addresses to handle however many inside systems communicate externally at the same time.

For security reasons, it may be desirable to have as few externally visible addresses as possible. The idea is that an external observer may be able to estimate the number of inside systems by counting the number of external addresses used. Further, that intruder may even be able to determine the real, inside addresses of those systems if he or she is able to intercept traffic and examine application data fields that may contain those inside addresses.

Firewalls usually incorporate NAT capabilities so that the addresses of most internal systems can be translated to a single external address. In a way, that's taking the external address reduction logic of dynamic NAT to an extreme degree, but it's a useful way to employ NAT for security purposes. For this everything-as-one-address technique to work, the firewall must also use other methods to track which incoming traffic belongs to which inside address. We'll look at how the firewall does this in the next chapter.

The Management View

Is there a clear choice that IT management should make between static and dynamic NAT? Common sense seems to point to dynamic NAT because of its reduced maintenance and support requirements and because it may require fewer external addresses. But even with dynamic NAT, there are usually a few systems that will need static address mapping because they have to be accessible reliably and continually by the same address.

The right choice might be to use dynamic NAT for most of the inside systems, particularly PCs, whose external addresses really don't matter, but static NAT for those few systems that need fixed addresses, such as servers and DNS services. Dynamic NAT does have quite a few things going for it, not the least of which is low maintenance; it is also able to accommodate changes in the network's internal structure and addressing without affecting external addressing.

Summary

It's not hard to draw the line between static and dynamic NAT, placing static NAT in the "more difficult" category and dynamic NAT in the "much easier" category. That view, though, may be prejudiced by the notion that static NAT can't adapt easily to change, while dynamic NAT, by its very nature, implies changing addresses translation all the time.

In reality, the choice between the two is determined by network circumstances. Are there just a few systems that need NAT, and is there a requirement that they be known and managed carefully? If so, static NAT is a perfectly adequate choice. In that situation, dynamic NAT introduces variability that isn't needed and interferes with the certainty that static NAT provides.

Does the network have a large number of clients, only some of which need external access at the same time? If so, dynamic NAT is a more logical choice. It offers fewer maintenance and system configuration requirements, but external traffic may be harder to track and manage. But then, maybe that's not as important as simply making it possible for inside systems to get to the outside world.

Neither approach has much to recommend it to security people, who prefer that as few inside network addresses as possible are ever visible to the outside world. In the next chapter, we will look at how firewalls, routers, and proxy servers translate many inside addresses to a single outside address, or to a small number of outside interface addresses, to achieve a security objective that neither static nor dynamic NAT considers.

Firewalls, Routers, and NAT

Several types of devices can act as the *NAT box* we've referenced several times in this book, including routers, firewalls, and proxy servers. With the current and well-justified interest in network security, however, the NAT task is often given to a firewall, instead of to a router.

Many security experts argue that the firewall is the right place to do NAT because it complements the other security screening tasks of the firewall. The router is a communications device that should be dedicated to that task and not burdened with chores like NAT.

In this chapter, we will look at how firewalls do NAT, as well as how they implement network security through NAT. As we will see, firewalls take the concept of dynamic NAT to its extreme, translating most all inside addresses either to a single external address or to a small number of externally visible addresses. As a security device, the firewall is concerned first with controlling traffic into and out of the network. One of the techniques that it employs to enhance network security is to shield the identities of inside systems. By translating most or all inside addresses to a single external address, firewalls give inside systems a measure of anonymity, thereby adding to the security of the network.

The anonymity of NAT doesn't come without a cost. As we will see in this chapter, and as we have noted in previous chapters, doing NAT on the firewall can affect the performance of the firewall significantly, depending on the number of systems communicating through the firewall. From a security perspective, the firewall is the right place to do NAT, but from a performance perspective, it might best be left to another device, such as a router whose job is screening, instead of routing, to reduce the performance hit of NAT.

The Good Old Days

As short a time as 10 to 15 years ago, which is eons in Internet time, network security was a luxury for the paranoid instead of a necessity of standard operation. Back then, network security was a relatively simple thing. Network security meant using passwords and user IDs, and controlling file and directory access rights. The Internet, as it existed then, was a kinder, gentler place, where camaraderie, instead of criminal intent, was the motivation for roaming around from system to system on the network. Hacking was considered a relatively harmless recreational sport among the computer nerd set, and intrusion was the exercise of a healthy curiosity.

Incidents of malicious intrusion were not unknown on the Internet 10 to 15 years ago. Most of the energy of the Legion of Doom, the Masters of Deception, and other bands of computer pranksters was devoted to fooling telephone systems into allowing intruders to make free long-distance calls. The "2600" group of telephone system hackers ("phone phreaks," in their argot), named after the 2600 Hertz tone used by telephone switches to send control information from switch to switch, got their jollies by browsing around phone company computer systems, fooling telephone switches into allowing them to place long-distance phone calls, and making the occasional run at a university or Department of Defense computer system. The average 12-year-old with a TRS-80, a modem, and a rudimentary understanding of Telnet, or a 24-year-old graduate student with a university time-sharing account and too much time on his or her hands, might have presented just as much a threat as any of the recreational hackers.

Back then, no one paid much attention to network security. For one thing, most computer systems were mainframes or minicomputers, and they weren't connected to other computer systems. Their chief vulnerabilities lay in dial-in ports or, worse, a hacker who was a user or system administrator who had direct access to the system.

The Internet, of course, changed all that. Today, with a huge and ever-increasing number of systems interconnected over the Internet, security has become a paramount concern. Network security is no longer just something that the network manager worries about. It has become a serious issue at the IT executive level, as the IT organization is responsible for all aspects of network performance, including network security, availability, and management.

The hacker community has proven to be remarkably inventive, shifting its focus from target to target, each time with more clever and even more devious tactics. If they are denied access to the files stored directly on a computer system, they might compromise on a denial-of-service attack, keeping everyone, including legitimate users, out of the system. The denial-of-service attacks on major Internet e-commerce, online brokerage, and information sites in February 2000, which were staged from a number of computers that had been commandeered with attack programs, took hacking another step up the food chain. It also showed that anyone could be victimized by certain types of security threats.

NAT on the Firewall

No IT executive in his or her right mind, or who wants to keep his or her job, would consider having an organization's Internet-connected networks unprotected by some type of security system. The most commonly used security system is a firewall, which screens traffic going to and from a system or a network. Often the firewall is just one part of a more comprehensive security perimeter, which might be composed of a firewall, an intrusion detection system, a screening router, or other security devices. Some networks are configured with double firewalls to add an extra measure of filtering on the network perimeter.

Firewalls, like their identically named counterparts in the construction industry that stop fires from spreading to adjacent buildings, isolate networks and systems from other networks. They are computer systems that are specially designed to examine all traffic that passes through them, evaluating the traffic against a set of rules that establish if that traffic should be allowed to pass, generate an alert and be logged, or denied access, either into or out of the network.

As part of a comprehensive security architecture, firewalls may also translate the source addresses of systems on the networks behind them, in order to conceal the addresses, identities, and, if possible, the existence of those systems. As we have already noted, NAT is only a security technique, not a security screen in itself. NAT address modification must be used as one part of a comprehensive security strategy, not the sole security stratagem.

For that matter, translating addresses of inside systems to externally visible addresses really isn't much more than extra insurance, as far as security is concerned. To a determined and skilled hacker, NAT is only one of those annoying speed bumps on the road to breaking and entering. It's the firewall itself that provides the real security, screening and examining traffic going to and from the network. NAT is only one of the tools the firewall employs, but it's still a useful screen as part of the firewall's comprehensive defense lines.

Whether or not it does NAT, a firewall is only as good as the rules the firewall administrator deploys to screen traffic. Furthermore, firewalls don't do anything about internal threats, which may be more destructive and more insidious than any external threat. Firewalls trust few things outside the firewall, but most firewalls implicitly trust anything behind them. That's why whoever designs a security perimeter must consider both inside and outside threats.

The Enigma Effect

If NAT isn't a particularly powerful security mechanism, why does the firewall use it at all? The reason is that by hiding inside addresses, the firewall adds an important part of its defenses: the Enigma Effect. The firewall's most important role is screening, controlling, and blocking traffic into and out of the network. As part of this role, it also attempts to protect the network from various types of attacks, including denial-of-service attacks.

The firewall's other role is to conceal not only the identities of the systems on the network behind it, but also the very existence of those systems. That's the reason for using NAT on the firewall. If it has been configured to do NAT (and not all firewalls are), the firewall will give the impression that there are relatively few systems behind it.

For that matter, the firewall may be able to shield the identities of the networks behind it. Routing information advertisements and DNS records, though, may reveal more about the networks and systems behind the firewall than the firewall can conceal.

From Many, There Shall Be One

The most common firewall address translation technique is for the firewall to translate practically all of the inside addresses to a single outside address. The effect is to make it appear that the entire network consists of only a single system, which communicates with the outside world from a single network interface. That network interface is the single external interface of the firewall, as shown in Figure 6.1.

This charade is not as transparent as it might seem. To the outside world, the firewall's outside interface seems to be the network interface of a multiuser computer system. A multiuser system hosts tens or hundreds of users, all of which may be running a number of different client processes. To an external observer, who sees identical source addresses on all of the client processes, the firewall looks like a typical large multiuser system. The only difference is that it looks like a multiuser system that appears to be noticeably unresponsive to

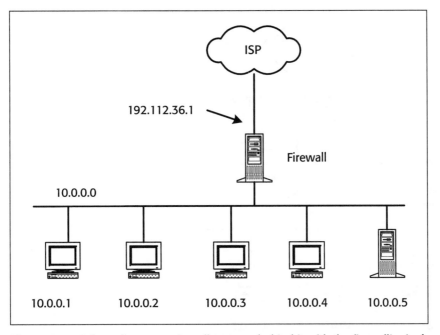

Figure 6.1 A firewall representing all systems behind it with the firewall's single external interface address.

requests to honor service requests from an external client. Obviously, that's the firewall just doing its thing—it's probably running rulesets that prohibit external client requests from reaching behind the firewall.

Translating the Ports

If the firewall translates most or all of the addresses of systems behind it to a single external address, the real trick in firewall NAT is figuring out which system gets which reply from an external host. We've touched on this problem in Chapter 2, "The Mechanics of NAT," but now we should look at how the firewall keeps track of all of these seemingly disassociated incoming replies. Remember that all of them bear the same source address, so all of them will be directed back to the same destination address.

Let's say we have a simple network with only three hosts, which use the firewall as their default gateway to the Internet. The sample network, which includes a router outside the firewall, is depicted in Figure 6.2.

When any of the PCs on the internal network sends traffic to the Internet, the firewall translates the source IP address of the outgoing traffic to its own external interface address. This works fine, but when a Web server on the

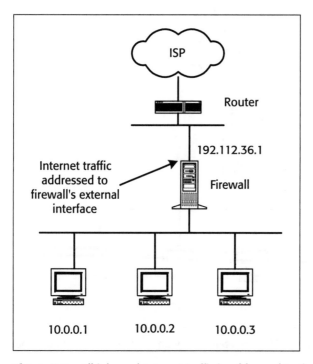

Internet traffic addressed to firewall's external interface

ISP

Router

192.112.36.1

Firewall

10.0.0.1   10.0.0.2   10.0.0.3

Figure 6.2   All inbound Internet traffic is addressed to the firewall's external address.

Internet sends back a home page to an HTTP client behind the firewall, the IP datagram will be addressed to the firewall's external interface. For that matter, datagrams from any Internet host will be addressed to the firewall's external interface, no matter which of the systems behind the firewall originated the exchange.

As we discussed in Chapter 2, the firewall keeps things straight by maintaining state on each of the connections from inside to outside systems. The firewall also does the same thing for connections initiated from outside the firewall—if the firewall's rulesets allow connections to be initiated from clients outside the firewall.

Using the TCP Ports

The key to maintaining "state" is changing the TCP source port numbers in IP datagrams from inside and outside clients. The firewall changes both the source IP address and, if necessary, the TCP source port, to track which traffic goes to which host.

For example, let's take our sample network in Figure 6.2. IP datagrams from one of the PCs on the inside network that are addressed to a Web site somewhere on the Internet bear the PC's source IP address, 10.0.0.1. It's a private address, so it must be translated to a routable address before it can go to the Internet. The address to which the source address will be translated is the firewall's external address, which is 192.112.36.1.

In addition to translating the source IP address, the firewall's NAT software will also translate the TCP source port number. By translating the source port number as well as the source IP address, the firewall will be able to map replies from Internet hosts back to the system that originated the transaction. Different PCs and hosts are likely to use the same source port numbers because the TCP source port is supposed to be a system's way of tracking the application to which return traffic is to be directed.

Although the source port numbers will most likely be different, PCs and hosts will definitely use the same TCP destination port numbers. Standard applications, such as FTP, HTTP, Telnet, and so forth, are assigned "well-known" port numbers. Hosts running the server-side processes for these applications "listen" on these well-known ports, just as clients "listen" for replies on whatever source port they've selected. It's more important that the servers have well-known ports than the clients, so that all clients, for example, know that a Web server will "listen" for home page requests on the standard HTTP destination port, which is port 80, as illustrated in Figure 6.3.

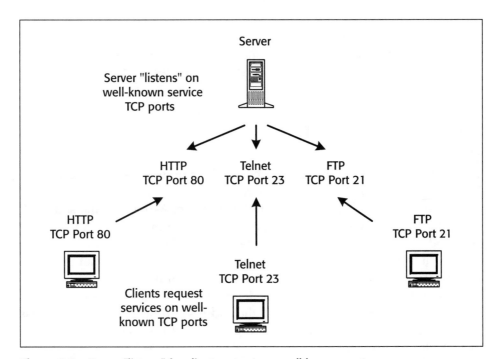

Figure 6.3   Server "listens" for client requests on well-known ports.

It doesn't matter which TCP port the firewall uses for the TCP source port, as long as it is unique to the firewall. The firewall, however, will have to record the PC's original source port, as well as the one to which it has translated the original port, in its source port and source address mapping table.

Changing the Checksums

NAT would be a simple and a relatively speedy process if all of the translation work stopped there, but it doesn't. Both the TCP header and the IP header have checksum fields, which are calculated for error detection. Those checksums are calculated and created by the system that originates the traffic. Consequently, the checksums are valid for the values of the original TCP source and destination port numbers and source IP address, not whatever source port and source address to which the NAT box changes them.

The IP header checksum applies to, and is calculated on the contents of, only the IP header. TCP is responsible for ensuring reliable delivery of data, so the TCP header applies to the TCP header and to all of the other fields behind it. The TCP checksum takes into consideration not only the contents of the TCP header, but also the application-level protocol header (if there is one), as well as the data payload and the source and destination IP addresses.

Changing either or both the TCP source port and the source IP address means the original checksums will no longer be valid. The NAT box must also recalculate the checksum field or fields and rewrite them, too. An application-level gateway may also have to recalculate checksums in data fields and other headers, if they exist, in addition to changing addresses in the payload of each datagram.

Translating the Reply

The server's response to the client's request for a network service, such as an HTTP request for a Web page, will contain whatever source port and IP address the NAT box used on the outgoing traffic. As long as the source IP address is a valid, routable address, and as long as a route to that address can be found by network routers, responses will be delivered to the firewall's external interface. Routing back to that firewall interface is another issue, which will be covered in Chapter 10, "NAT and Routing."

As far as the Web server is concerned, the firewall is the client—but it really isn't. The firewall will have to reverse the address and port translation to pass the traffic back to the real client, referring to its port translation table to complete the translation request.

To handle outgoing traffic, the firewall had already built an address translation table in memory, which was depicted in Figure 5.5 in Chapter 5. The firewall will refer to the same table to translate TCP ports and addresses back to their original values, before passing the traffic back into the internal network. All of the incoming traffic will be addressed to the same address, so the firewall will rely on the TCP destination port number to determine where to re-address the datagram.

If the NAT box is a firewall, the incoming traffic will also have to pass the firewall ruleset screen before it passes the traffic through to its inside network interface for delivery to the protected, interior network. Processing the traffic through the firewall's rulesets and handling the address translation and checksum recalculation steps may add a delay of a few milliseconds to the response time.

Border Guard or Traffic Cop?

Routers can do NAT, too, and their methods of handling address translation are similar to those of firewalls. The only significant difference is that a firewall, unlike a router, doesn't consider routing traffic through to different interfaces to be its first priority. The firewall is a border guard who stops everyone and checks their papers; the router is a traffic cop, more interested in keeping traffic flowing than stopping a motorist for an occasional infraction. Lest the router people unleash a torrent of hate mail my way, let's say that the analogy is a bit unfair to the router, but with the router, passing traffic speedily is a genetic thing. It's a router, even if it does use a traffic filter to screen traffic.

The router isn't intended to be as picky as the firewall might be in screening traffic or in controlling traffic on as many different criteria. The firewall's rulesets, for instance, may specify that it should allow or disallow traffic based on source or destination IP address, TCP ports, application, or some combination of those criteria. The firewall may also do an extensive amount of traffic logging, creating files that summarize the results of its traffic screening operations, logging which traffic was rejected and which traffic was passed successfully, and other results. It is only after making its value judgment on each datagram that the firewall passes traffic to another interface for delivery.

The router's traffic screening filters, or *access control lists* (ACLs), are similar to a firewall's rulesets. Router filters, however, may be less comprehensive, and potentially less restrictive, than firewall rulesets. Although such a generalization may be both dangerous and unfair, it is usually the case that routers will allow everything that is not specifically prohibited and that a firewall will prohibit everything that is not specifically allowed.

This is not an entirely accurate statement because whether a firewall or a router permits or denies traffic really depends on what is in its access control list or its firewall rulesets. Typically, a firewall's last rule prohibits everything that has not been specifically allowed by previous rules. A router is primarily a router, so anything that isn't filtered out by its access control list or traffic filters will be permitted to pass and be routed.

This is not to say that router filters and access control lists can't be configured to be more restrictive than firewalls. If they can be configured to filter and control traffic in similar ways, the differences between the two can be more semantic than real. Because the primary function of a router is doing IP routing, not traffic screening, routers tend to be deployed as routers, with traffic filtering a secondary consideration. Firewalls, on the other hand, are not intended to be traffic routers, although they may be required to do some IP routing, particularly if they manage traffic flows among several interfaces.

As far as NAT is concerned, there aren't any significant differences between how a router and how a firewall do NAT. The issue is more one of positioning the NAT task on a device that will be affected least by the overhead penalty that NAT can impose. It's not necessarily a burden that a router at a key network intersection should bear. NAT should also not be imposed on a firewall at the entrance to a high-traffic network that hosts a heavily used Web site, either.

Addressing on Proxy Servers

The other network device that may do NAT is a proxy server. A proxy server usually doesn't sit on the network perimeter, so it's not considered a NAT device in the same sense as a router or a firewall. Technically, a proxy server may not translate addresses at all, as its customary function is to substitute complete sessions instead of simply replace source or destination addresses. The reason a proxy server is even mentioned in a discussion of NAT is that a proxy server creates many of the same results as a NAT box, without performing the same type of on-the-fly address translation.

A proxy server is more of a control and security device than an address translation service. Its real purpose is to give a network administrator a method to control how users and systems on the internal network access external Web sites and hosts. In doing so, the proxy server also conceals the existence of internal network hosts and workstations because all internal traffic appears to come from a single system, which is the proxy server.

A proxy server acts as an intermediary between clients and servers, accepting requests for connections from clients and setting up separate connections for clients from the proxy server itself to servers, as illustrated in Figure 6.4. The client directs its request for a connection to an outside server to the proxy server. The proxy server acts as the target server, responding to the client as if it were the real server. In order to get real responses back from the target server, the proxy server sets up a second, completely separate connection to the external server and acts as if it were the real client.

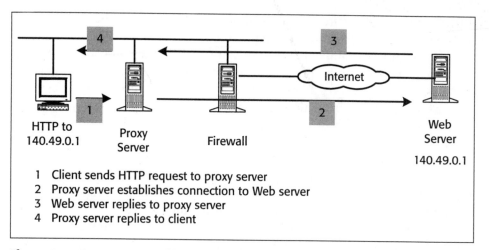

1   Client sends HTTP request to proxy server
2   Proxy server establishes connection to Web server
3   Web server replies to proxy server
4   Proxy server replies to client

Figure 6.4   Proxy server establishes separate connections to outside network servers on behalf of inside network clients.

The proxy server runs two linked sessions, one from the client or the proxy server and the other from the proxy server to the network service. The two connections are completely separate transactions, although the internal network client and the external network server don't realize that they're not really talking to each other directly, but through the proxy server. The client thinks that the proxy server is the server process, and the server process thinks the proxy is the client. As long as the proxy server successfully juggles the two independent sessions and passes traffic reliably from one connection to the other, neither the client nor the server will be aware of the existence of the proxy server.

A proxy server adds a measure of security to a network because the inside network addresses of clients that go through the proxy server are hidden from outside services. The client and server connections don't necessarily have to be from internal network clients to external network or Internet servers, but they usually are. All traffic that goes through the proxy server bears the source address of the proxy server, not the real client. The proxy server must maintain a table that links a client session with an external server session, so that it can pass traffic between the two. The proxy server uses its own "outside" interface address as the source address of communications with network services. The proxy server isn't doing NAT, however, because it's not translating addresses. Instead, the proxy server sets up completely separate sessions on behalf of clients, and those sessions bear the proxy server's source address, not the clients' addresses.

The greatest advantage of a proxy server isn't security, but the control it gives a network administrator. It lets the network administrator regulate users' access to outside services, it can block access to specific Web sites and hosts the network administrator deems inappropriate, and it can log detailed network usage. For example, a firewall protecting a network that doesn't have a Web server may be configured to allow outbound HTTP sessions, but prohibit any externally initiated HTTP. In that case, the firewall could be configured to allow only outbound traffic originating from the proxy server's IP address. That would force all internal network clients to go through the proxy server for any HTTP connections.

The second benefit of using the proxy server is that it can permit the network administrator to control which inside clients can access external services, as well as restrict access to certain Web sites or servers. The firewall or a screening router does the same thing. The benefit of this dual control mechanism is that the network administrator can control access through the proxy server, without affecting or possibly misconfiguring the firewall's rulesets. Proxy server controls may be more restrictive than those on the firewall, as proxy servers may restrict access to nonbusiness Web sites or services or control Web or service access at certain times or on certain days.

The IT Perspective

If the IT organization has made the decision to use an addressing scheme that requires NAT, such as RFC 1918 private addressing, one of its other decisions must be where to place the NAT function. As we have seen, there's no substantive difference between the way that a router or a firewall translates addresses. Either one will translate source and destination addresses, and either one can also map and change TCP port numbers.

Because its role is different from that of a router, a firewall may take on additional tasks that are related to NAT, such as acting as an application-level gateway. A firewall may be able to look into the data payload of IP datagrams and change addressing and protocol information embedded in data fields. Routers could do the same thing, but modifying application data isn't the type of task for which routers are designed. It's not that they couldn't do it, but routers are optimized to route datagrams and to do other tasks, such as NAT and screening traffic, on the side.

Performance is the other IT consideration in positioning the NAT task. As we have discussed in previous chapters, NAT may place a performance penalty on any device that translates addresses, and translating addresses and TCP ports and recalculating checksums can throttle traffic flow through the box. If there are a substantial number of systems for which NAT will have to be done, the NAT task will have to be placed in a device that won't restrict traffic any more than necessary.

It may even be wise for IT to put the NAT task on a router that doesn't do any more complicated routing than pass traffic between an inside and an outside interface, as illustrated in Figure 6.5. This may seem like an extravagant

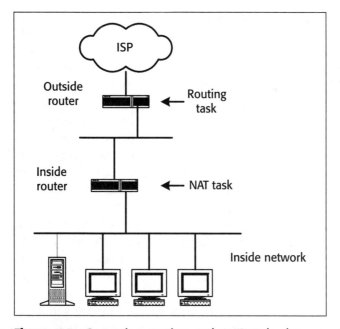

Figure 6.5 Separating routing and NAT tasks between two routers to improve performance.

waste of a router, but it would allow the router to use most of its resources on NAT, and not on routing. Network routing would be handled by another router upstream from it, which wouldn't have to do NAT at all.

Some IT departments have a philosophical objection to proxy servers because they split control of external access between the proxy server and a firewall or screening router. IT organizations that frown on proxy servers because they feel they dilute control over security are missing an opportunity to simplify their lives. Remember that a proxy server doesn't really do NAT, so there's no operational address translation issue of which IT loses control. Instead, IT can control external access, restricting the firewall or router screen to specific protocols and networks. Meanwhile, the network administrator, who has no access to the firewall rulesets or the router filters, can restrict access to certain Web sites or network services and control which users can access them. IT has the high-level control, and the network administrator has lower-level control, but IT still retains control of overall network security.

Summary

For the most part, NAT is NAT, whether it's done by a router or a firewall. As long as we're not expecting the NAT box to do anything terrifically exotic—

that is, anything beyond swapping one source IP address for another and recalculating header checksums—either a router or a firewall should be able to handle the task. Translating TCP ports in addition to IP addresses makes for a more complex NAT task, but both firewalls and routers with sufficient memory and processor speed should be up to the task.

The difference between router NAT and firewall NAT is mostly a difference of intent, processing power, and capability. Firewalls are intended to be security devices, which screen all traffic with the intent of blocking everything that's not supposed to pass. A router, though, is a traffic handler, designed to pass as much traffic as possible, and as fast as possible. The router may have a filter table, but router filters are usually designed to allow most traffic except what has it has specifically been told to deny.

In the next chapter, we will move up the scale of NAT box complexity and look at how NAT can affect the operation of the application-level protocols. To this point, we've looked mostly at how NAT affects the transport- and network-level protocols, TCP, and most importantly, IP. Most application-level protocols are unaware of what lower-level protocols like TCP and IP are doing. In a layered or modular protocol architecture, that's the way things are supposed to work. A normal NAT box may be oblivious to whether an application passes an IP address and TCP port number in the data stream. If those addresses and ports aren't translated in the same way as parts of the TCP and IP headers, the application won't work. In the next chapter, we'll look at what applications may be affected by NAT, as well as some potential solutions to those problems.

CHAPTER 7

Making Applications Work with NAT

As the chapter title implies, there's more to NAT than dropping in a NAT box, translating IP addresses, and walking away. NAT is supposed to be transparent, working behind the scenes, unseen and unnoticed. In a perfect world, that would be true, but network managers and IT executives know that their worlds and networks are far from perfect.

In this chapter, we will examine the most common problem with many NAT configurations. The problem is that there are some applications that don't work well when IP addresses are translated. It's not that the applications are at fault. It's just that they weren't designed with NAT in mind, or the way they operate can't tolerate the machinations of NAT. For example, with some applications, simply translating addresses in the IP header isn't necessarily enough to get them to work with NAT. Some applications open up connections on a random set of TCP ports, which can stymie NAT's attempts to track sessions by port numbers.

In this chapter, we will look at the internal workings of a number of applications to see how NAT works with them. In some cases, NAT must manipulate not only IP addresses, but also TCP port numbers, to translate addresses cleanly and to maintain traffic flow. The combination of applications and NAT is not a marriage made in heaven, as there are some applications that NAT can't deal with cleanly. For those, the solution is often an *application-level gateway* (ALG), which extends NAT down into the application's data payloads.

Network managers and IT executives must be aware of the potential for application problems behind NAT boxes and prepare for those problems in rolling out a NAT strategy. They should also understand strategies and techniques to prevent these problems or to minimize them if they do occur. In some cases, the mix of applications used on a network may make deploying NAT difficult, if it is even possible at all.

It's Like Kryptonite

Even Superman had his weaknesses. In the presence of that rare substance, kyptonite, Superman lost most of his super powers. NAT is no Superman, but NAT too loses some of its superhuman powers, such as the ability to translate IP addresses in a single bound, in the presence of some applications. It's not necessarily NAT's fault that this happens. It's just that certain applications don't play ball NAT's way.

The nub of the application issue is that some applications use IP addresses inside the data payloads of the application. As far as NAT is concerned, application payloads are just so much extra baggage in the data stream. NAT works at the IP level, translating addresses in the IP header, although it also understands enough about the TCP level to track and, if necessary, change TCP port numbers.

For instance, the File Transfer Protocol (FTP) is the best example of a widely used protocol that can, in certain circumstances, use IP addresses in the FTP data payload. Not only can FTP embed IP addresses, but those addresses include TCP port numbers, and the whole shebang is in ASCII text. We'll look in detail at how FTP works in this chapter, to illustrate the complexities of applications and how NAT can and can't work with them. Other applications, such as the Domain Name Service (DNS), put IP addresses in data fields all the time because that's what DNS does.

To NAT or to ALG, That Is the Question

The usual solution to the application payload problem is an application-level gateway, or ALG. An ALG is software, usually implemented with NAT, that can do what standard NAT cannot. ALG software is specific to an application, in that it understands how the application works and the format of the data in the application payload. The ALG is configured to identify IP addresses or TCP port numbers in application payloads and to change them to whatever is their correct representation, either to inside or to outside hosts.

In most cases, NAT and an ALG are implemented together, although they are not halves of the same split personality. Rather, an ALG is a separate function that augments the operation of NAT, for handling the details of a specific application. A NAT device may have several ALGs implemented with it, each designed to handle a specific application. NAT and ALGs usually have to be implemented together because an ALG must be aware of what NAT has decided is the correct translation of addresses and port numbers. The significant differences are the levels at which NAT and ALGs operate and the types of data they change.

The problem with ALGs is that they can be tricky to configure, and they can have a serious effect on network throughput and performance. The other issue is that for some applications, such as DNS, they won't work properly on all kinds of transactions. A DNS ALG is usually incapable of handling a DNS zone transfer, for instance, because of the number of addresses involved and because the translated addresses may not be known. Encrypted data is another problem because the ALG doesn't necessarily have the encryption key. Even if it did, and even if it translated and changed the data, it would modify the encryption checksum, leading the recipient to believe the data had been tampered with along the way.

The science of ALGs is not perfect. It's fairly good for those ALGs that exist, but then, there aren't a whole lot of them because they must be developed and implemented one application at a time. Generally speaking, some ALGs have been developed for major applications, but they aren't widely available. Some networking professionals consider the lack of ALGs to be evidence that NAT should be avoided if possible. That argument overlooks the advantages of NAT, but it recognizes some of the issues that NAT raises. In any case, that argument must be considered by network managers and IT executives who are considering NAT or who have already implemented NAT.

FTP and NAT

The File Transfer Protocol (FTP) is one of those TCP/IP application protocols that can run afoul of NAT. That is, there are some modes of FTP operation for which NAT software must make some special accommodation. The problem is that unlike other application-level protocols, the FTP protocol can embed IP addresses and TCP port numbers inside the data field of the FTP frame. If NAT looks only at IP addresses in the IP header and TCP ports in the TCP header, it might miss addresses and ports embedded in the FTP data field and drop the ball on the elaborate charade of NAT.

Fortunately, the problem is confined to only two types of FTP operations, which are controlled by the FTP PORT and PASV commands. To understand how these commands work, it's useful to understand the rudiments of how FTP works.

FTP is unlike most other application-level protocols, which set up a connection, then transfer data over that connection. Most TCP/IP applications are simple, one-client-port-to-one-server-port protocols, but FTP isn't. FTP uses two TCP ports and sets up two different TCP connections. The first connection is a control TCP connection to the FTP server on TCP port 21. The client uses this connection to send the FTP server a user ID and password, as well as commands to navigate around the FTP server file system, such as "list", "pwd", and the "cd" commands. The FTP commands to move files, "put" and "get", are also directed to the server's control port 21.

In response to a PUT or a GET, however, the FTP client and server set up a second TCP connection, using TCP port 20 on the FTP server. On the client end, it's a random source port number, chosen by the client. This is the data channel, over which the client and server actually transfer a file. The difference between this connection and the control channel connection is that the data channel connection is initiated by the server, not the client. Consequently, in the second phase of the FTP connection, the server acts as the client, and the client acts as the server. The reason for this role reversal is that the server, which is either receiving or sending the file, is in control of the data transfer, so it acts as the client for the file transfer phase.

Note the use of the singular "file" with reference to the data connection. When FTP has finished transferring a file, the client and server close the data connection. If additional files are to be transferred, the client and server open a new, separate connection on port 20 for each file, closing the connection after each file has been transferred and opening a new connection for each new file. FTP keeps the TCP control connection alive as long as the user is logged into the FTP server, but it opens and closes the TCP data connection for each file.

FTP and IP Addresses

When an FTP client asks for a file from an FTP server, the client tells the server where the file is to be sent, specifying the IP address of a host and the TCP port on which that host is prepared to be listening for the connection. The address and port don't necessarily have to be the same as those of the client that requests the file transfer. That may sound odd in today's PC-centric world, but remember that FTP was devised more than two decades ago, originally for use in a world of multiuser hosts. Users frequently started FTP clients on one system, then directed an FTP server on a second to transfer files to a third system. The convention persists today, even though the client environment has changed substantially.

The IP address and TCP port number of the system to which the file should be directed are embedded in the data fields of IP datagrams, as illustrated in

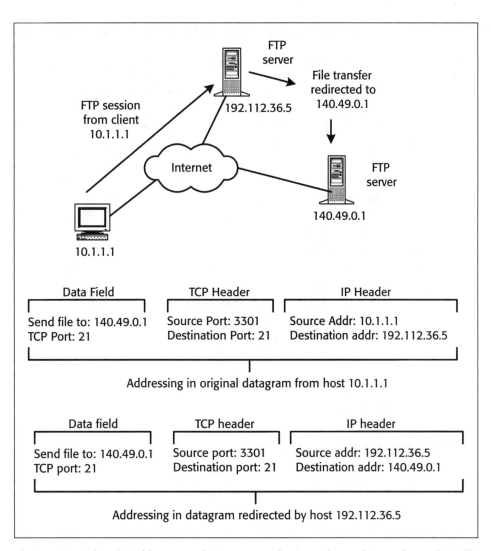

Figure 7.1 IP header addresses and TCP port numbers are changed in a redirected FTP file transfer.

Figure 7.1. The addresses and port numbers in the IP and TCP headers, and those in the data field, are usually, but not necessarily, the same.

The Internet hacker community has seized on this address and port specification characteristic of FTP as a means to cause mischief on the Internet. As far as the FTP server is concerned, it's just sending a file to the target system. The target system, however, may not think it's FTP. For example, an Internet junk mailer could upload a file that contains junk mail messages to an FTP server. The junk mailer could then request that the files be sent to another host. If the

HTTP SESSIONS

FTP sessions, which maintain separate control and data channels and open and close a TCP session for each file transferred, are the exception, rather than the rule, in TCP-based applications. The HyperText Transfer Protocol (HTTP), the client and server-side protocol for Web server access, is a simpler and cleaner protocol. HTTP is, at heart, a file transfer protocol, managing the transfer of HTML files (Web pages) from the Web server to the client, in response to URLs, which are like command-line arguments.

HTTP works like most TCP-based protocols, in that it opens a TCP session between the client and the server for each new URL. Control information (the URL) goes to the Web server, and files (Web pages, images, and other content) come back to the client. HTTP was designed as a simpler protocol than FTP because of the need for efficiency and speed in accessing Web sites. It's a good thing, too, given Web surfers' tendencies to click through Web pages rapidly, even before they've finished loading. HTTP handles each URL as a separate session, so a Web surfer doesn't have to wait for each Web page transfer to complete before clicking on a new link.

second target host were an SMTP server, it might accept the messages and forward them as Internet junk mail.

Redirecting Files to Another Server

Most users of FTP know little beyond FTP's simple OPEN, PUT, GET, and END commands. One of the less well-known commands is the FTP PORT command. PORT is a control channel command that directs an FTP server to transfer a file to a third FTP system. This capability may seem odd today because we are accustomed to doing FTP directly from a client to a server. Redirecting files to a different FTP server isn't widely used today, but it's frequently cited as a problem with FTP and NAT, and the PORT command is still part of FTP. In the days when most everything was a multiuser mainframe or minicomputer, it was common to log into one host computer, set up an FTP session with a host running an FTP server, and then transfer files from the first FTP server to a second.

Today, the FTP PORT command is both a NAT issue and a security issue. The NAT issue is that the data field of the FTP frame containing the PORT command also has two other arguments to FTP in it: the IP address of the destination system and the port to which it should open the connection. Normally, this would not be a problem because the IP address would be known to the client requesting the file transfer. The third system, however, might be screened behind a firewall and known to the outside world by the single external address of the firewall, on which inside addresses are changed by NAT. Or, the third system might be on an isolated network using private addresses, which must not be seen by the outside world.

As a result, NAT might change the source IP address in the IP header, but not change the IP address embedded in the data field of the FTP frame (assuming the PORT command were used). The FTP server that received the PORT file transfer command might use the IP address in the data field, but it might not work. If it were the external address of the firewall, how would the firewall know what to do with it?

The security issue is that a hacker might be able to penetrate a protected network, set up an FTP session to an FTP server on the network, and then upload a Trojan horse program or a virus to the FTP server. Then, using the FTP PORT command, the hacker could transfer the virus or worm program to another FTP server on another network. It would appear that the file originated from a safe system on a friendly network.

As a side note, some FTP servers, such as the Microsoft FTP server, require that the IP address in the PORT command match the original IP address provided by the client to set up the connection on the FTP control channel. This would prevent the FTP server from being hijacked by an intruder because the client-side address and the hijacked server's address wouldn't match.

PASV Mode

The other mode of FTP that may affect how the protocol works behind a NAT box is the passive FTP mode. It's referred to by the abbreviated PASV command, by which the client invokes it. As we have said, FTP uses two TCP connections, a command connection and a data connection. The client initiates the former, and the server initiates the latter. It's unusual to have a server initiate a connection to a client, but that makes it possible for a client to "redirect" FTP between servers.

The FTP PASV mode reverses this process, so that the client initiates the FTP data connection instead of the server. The server transfers the file over the data connection (as with normal FTP, over TCP port 21), but the session is opened and closed by the client, not the server.

So, what's the big deal, and why isn't this done all the time? Maybe it should be done this way, except for those server redirects to other FTP servers. The reason, though, is that at the entrance point to networks, there is usually a firewall that screens all traffic entering or leaving the network. The firewall will usually permit FTP sessions to go through it if they are initiated by clients behind the firewall, but not if they are initiated by external systems and destined for systems behind the firewall. The PASV mode, initiated by the client, tells the server that the client will initiate the data session, so that it will be initiated from the correct side of the firewall.

In today's hyper-sensitive security environment (a sensitivity that is, unfortunately, quite necessary), most firewalls don't allow PASV mode connections, period. Most firewalls today can be configured to watch traffic closely enough and maintain "state" information about connections, so that they are aware of and watch the "reverse" data connection from a normal FTP session. That is, they will allow FTP data connections from outside the firewall as long as they can match those connections to an existing control channel from a client behind the firewall.

There's also a NAT implication for the PASV mode. As with a standard FTP data connection, the client may specify that the file be redirected to another host. If that's the case, the client, which is initiating the data connection, may embed an IP address and port number in the data stream. If a NAT box is in the path between the server and the client, it will have to be able to read and, if necessary, change the contents of the data field, as well as the TCP and IP headers.

Voice and Video Applications

Because FTP is so widely used, it can be the source of the most common NAT problems. There's a whole class of new applications for voice and video services, though, that may also embed IP addresses in application data. Those applications too may be completely stopped, or at least slowed down considerably, by a NAT box at the entrance or the exit to a network.

These new voice and video applications include things like Microsoft's Net-Meeting, CUseeMe Networks' CUseeMe, as well as *voice-over-IP* (VoIP) applications. Some of these applications are part of a class of applications that use the International Telecommunications Union's (ITU) H.323 protocol, which was designed as an industry standard for transporting voice and video across IP networks like the Internet. H.323 is an umbrella standard that describes the architecture of the system, but it refers to other standards, such as H.245 and H.225.0, to describe its actual protocols. A second competing protocol, the Session Initiation Protocol (SIP), has been standardized by the IETF. SIP can be used for the same types of voice and video applications as H.323, but it hasn't yet been as widely deployed as H.323. SIP may prove to be a major player in voice-over-IP applications.

The voice applications, as well as the audio support provided in videoconferencing applications, are frequently referred to generically as IP telephony applications. IP telephony is a broad category that encompasses most any application for carrying voice over IP networks. The most obvious application is transporting regular voice telephone conversations across the Internet. These Internet "phone calls" may be live audio chat sessions or a regular, full duplex phone call carried over the Internet. They may originate and terminate exclusively on computers connected over the Internet, or either side may be connected through a gateway into a PBX or the regular *public switched telephone network* (PSTN).

The problem with IP voice and video applications is that neither the Internet nor, for that matter, the IP protocol was intended to be used for real-time, delay-sensitive applications. That minor obstacle hasn't stopped the self-appointed mechanics of the Internet, new companies in the Internet space, and software developers from developing new and innovative ways to use IP and the Internet for voice and video applications.

NAT device vendors, such as firewall and router vendors, have responded to this trend by developing ALGs on NAT devices and firewalls that understand how these new applications work and accommodate their traffic. Some ALGs on NAT devices will support some of these video and voice applications. For example, the ALG functions of the NAT capabilities in Cisco routers running the newest versions of the Cisco operating system (Cisco IOS version 12.x and higher) will support most H.323 voice applications.

Embedding VoIP Addresses

The simplest possible VoIP system might be composed of two routers with VoIP capabilities connected together across an IP network, with two analog telephones connected behind them, as shown in Figure 7.2. The IP network might be an Ethernet, an IP wide area network, or the Internet. This may sound too simple an arrangement to be practical, but we'll use it as an example to illustrate why NAT may have problems with H.323 applications. We'll also focus on the addressing issues of H.323, rather than the details of an entire H.323 session. We will also look at an H.323 session between two PCs running Microsoft's NetMeeting software.

The fundamental issue in VoIP is getting IP devices to act as telephones. This is, they have to recognize off-hook conditions, pass dialing digits, and set up a bidirectional end-to-end channel across the IP network. It's not unlike setting up a regular TCP session, but there's a lot more telephone call administration to arrange. That's what those other protocols, such as H.245 and H.225.0, are all about.

In the network shown in Figure 7.2, the analog phones think the routers are telephone switches. In VoIP terminology, they're gateways, which use the H.323 protocols to set up the voice call between them. One of the protocols, H.225, sets up the call signaling channel between the two gateways. There

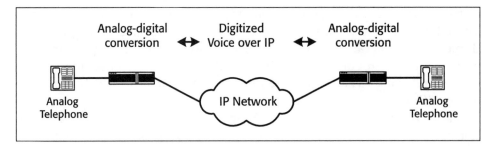

Figure 7.2   A simple voice over IP network, with two analog phones communicating through VoIP routers.

isn't "call signaling" in IP data traffic, but there is in telephone traffic. To set up the call between the two phones, one gateway sends the other an H.225 setup message. The setup message contains the source gateway's Call Signal Address (CSA), which is a combination of the IP address of the gateway router and a dynamically-assigned TCP port to be used for the call signaling channel.

Here's the rub between H.323 and NAT. If we impose a NAT box somewhere between these two routers, and the NAT box translates source or destination addresses in the IP headers, what happens to the CSA? It's in the data field of the IP datagram, and a normal NAT box won't see it. If only two gateways are involved in completing the call, it may work, but if a third or a fourth is involved, each forwarding traffic to the other, it's possible that the endstation's IP address and TCP port identity may become lost. The solution to this problem is a VoIP application-level gateway, which can see inside the H.225 messages and change them appropriately.

A more common voice-over-IP scenario is an H.323 session between two PCs running Microsoft's NetMeeting video- and audioconferencing application. NetMeeting also uses H.323, but it wasn't intended to emulate all of the administrative and control functions of regular phone calls. Consequently, a NetMeeting session eliminates problems with telephone issues like call forwarding, camp-on-busy, and call holding. Still, the NetMeeting client refers to a NetMeeting gateway to determine the address of the other NetMeeting client, and it uses H.323 to set up and control the session.

Some vendors are using SIP as an alternative to the more complicated H.323 protocol for voice-over-IP applications (see the sidebar titled *H.323 and SIP* for more information on SIP). H.323 is more widely implemented, but vendors like 3Com and Cisco have included support for SIP in their voice-over-IP products. Given the large installed base that H.323 enjoys, however, it may take a while before SIP becomes as widely used as H.323.

H.323 AND SIP

Some vendors of VoIP and multimedia systems have begun to support the newer *Session Initiation Protocol* (SIP) as an application-level protocol for voice and video services, in addition to H.323. SIP was established and standardized by the IETF in RFC 2543. SIP is similar to H.323, but it works in a slightly different way. SIP "invites" other SIP clients to VoIP or multimedia sessions, sending invitations across an IP network to another SIP user agent. A Redirect Server, which maps SIP connection requests to recipients' IP addresses, may be involved to locate the called party or to map a phone number back to an IP address. The SIP protocol also handles session management functions, such as call setup, call control, teardown, and session status.

Like H.323 protocol connections, NAT can interfere with those established by SIP. The problem is the usual one, in which the source address of the real SIP client may be embedded in the SIP connection request. As with other services, an ALG may be required to modify SIP connection request addresses.

Why use another protocol when the more established H.323 would seem to do? SIP is intended to be a simpler, faster, more flexible protocol than H.323, and it has a lot less protocol overhead. More important, H.323 was designed by the ITU to be used in a LAN environment, while SIP was designed under the auspices of the IETF, which intended it to work on the Internet. H.323 was designed from the ITU's telephone system perspective and adapted to IP, not the other way around. Most vendors that support IP telephony services and multimedia applications have long used H.323, but they are adding support for SIP as well.

Webcam Video Applications

The videoconferencing and live Webcam applications like CUseeMe (formerly from White Pine Software, since renamed CUseeMe Networks), Microsoft's NetMeeting, and Intel's Internet Video Phone also have the H.323 protocol. In many cases, the H.323 session is negotiated by each user's PC, although there are versions of each that go through a central server. In each case, the application doesn't work through a firewall or a proxy server, or through a regular NAT box.

For example, NetMeeting incorporates a number of capabilities, including data sharing, audio and video feeds, chat, file access, and whiteboarding, all of which are based on H.323. The data features use primary TCP connections, but the audio and video features use secondary TCP and UDP connections that are established after the primary TCP connection is established.

One of the specific limitations that NAT can place on NetMeeting is a restriction on the use of certain NetMeeting features on inbound connections. This may occur if the NAT device maps external addresses to a small number of internal addresses.

Games

A number of issues are involved in making multiuser games, such as Age of Empires, Battlenet, and Quake, work through NAT, particularly if NAT is part of a firewall. Games may use a number of TCP ports to establish gameplay sessions, then UDP ports to pass game moves across the network. All of these ports must be mapped back to the correct ports on the client machines, multiuser game servers, or other devices behind the NAT box. If a firewall shields the network, the firewall rulesets must be written to allow all of the ports. The NAT software must then be configured to translate the ports correctly. Because all of the traffic originates from the same host address, the NAT box may want to change the port numbers to its own port ranges, which may not be recognized by a server.

Many games use or are compatible with Microsoft's DirectPlay software, which establishes specific TCP and UDP port ranges for DirectPlay games. Games that conform to Microsoft's DirectPlay standard use TCP port 47624 to send and receive client connection requests and ports 2300 through 2400 for game playing communications. Newer versions of DirectPlay will simplify the NAT issue by sending all network traffic through a single port, rather than a range of ports.

DirectPlay also specifies the data format for DirectPlay server and client addresses. DirectPlay addresses include the IP addresses of clients, servers, service providers (who may host the games themselves), and the network address of a session, all of which NAT must translate successfully.

SNMP

The *Simple Network Management Protocol* (SNMP) is widely used by *network management systems* (NMS) to query the devices it manages. For example, a network management system that manages the routers in a network acts as an SNMP client, making periodic queries to the SNMP agent software in each router in the network. When each router responds to the query, it sends back to the network management system an SNMP data packet that identifies the router by its IP address and gives the network management system other indications about its status or operating condition. The data is formatted in fields, and each field has a unique *Object Identifier* (OID). The OIDs are numbers separated by periods, and they identify each data variable. The OIDs are like an index to the data, so that the network management system can identify the location and order of the data fields. The order and meaning of the SNMP fields vary with each implementation of a network management system.

The SNMP data frequently contains IP addresses, embedded in OID-tagged fields. Not all IP addresses in SNMP data are in OID fields, though, as some appear in dumps of routing tables and in other files. These addresses are the ones that each managed device uses, not necessarily the addresses that NAT uses to translate between inside and outside addresses. For example, take a network management system on the Internet that manages devices behind a firewall running NAT. The NMS will direct SNMP queries to an externally visible IP address on the external side of the firewall, using that address as the destination address in the IP header. The NAT software will translate the destination address to the internal address and forward the query to the managed device.

The NMS will identify each managed device by the data in the SNMP data fields, not necessarily by the address used in the IP header. The addresses of managed devices shouldn't change, so SNMP requires the real addresses of managed devices to be fixed, rather than dynamic.

When the SNMP agent in the managed device responds, it creates an SNMP data payload in an IP datagram. If the payload contains an IP address, it will be embedded in an SNMP response as data with a type of *IP address*. In this example, if the IP address were 192.168.20.5, it would be in the data field, not in the IP header. It's a private address, too, so the NMS can't use it as a destination address, and it can't be a source address on the Internet, either. In some cases, such as SNMP management of routers, the SNMP response may include the IP addresses of neighboring routers. Consequently, there may be multiple IP addresses embedded in the data field of an SNMP response.

The problem with SNMP through NAT is that if nothing is done to change the data fields, the addresses in the data fields will be different from the addresses known by the NMS. The datagrams, after their IP headers have been translated by NAT, will arrive at the NMS, but the addresses in the SNMP data payload won't match those known by the NMS.

In order for SNMP to work through NAT, the NAT device must be augmented with an ALG, as well as a standard address translator. That is, the NAT software must be able to read the SNMP data payload fields, locate the data fields that contain IP addresses, and change them. This task requires an ALG that can be programmed to do this and that can be configured to find and to translate the data payload addresses accurately.

For example, a NAT ALG uses rulesets that are similar to those used by a firewall to screen traffic. The NAT ALG ruleset indicates the identity and position of the OID, as well as the addresses to translate in the data payload. Like a firewall ruleset, the NAT ALG rulesets would identify the SNMP-managed device by the IP address in the IP header and translate those addresses.

The other issues in NAT ALGs for SNMP are performance, availability, and standards. An SNMP ALG adds a second set of rules and manipulations that the NAT device must perform. If the ALG function is part of the firewall software, the performance hit can be substantial. The second problem is availability. Only a few vendors make SNMP ALGs, and there are still a number of problems getting them to work reliably in all types of network environments. Last, there is no generally accepted agreement on standards for how SNMP ALGs operate. In fact, some SNMP people claim that it's doubtful that SNMP ALGs will ever work reliably enough to be practical.

Given the potential for problems with an SNMP ALG, assuming that a working SNMP ALG is available in the first place, it's probably best for network managers to deploy SNMP and NAT to avoid the whole issue. That is, the network should be arranged so that SNMP inquiries and responses won't traverse NAT at all. Network management has become too important an issue to sacrifice the benefits of network visibility and control for those of NAT. It's far more preferable and, in many cases, more effective to arrange NAT and SNMP so they don't get in each other's way.

RealAudio

The RealAudio software (RealPlayer, RealJukebox) is a streaming audio program for playing music, audio feeds, and other types of audio content across IP networks. The program uses a TCP-based protocol called the Real-Time Streaming Protocol (RTSP) to set up and control the audio feed. RealAudio clients use TCP ports 7070 and 554 to establish a session with a RealAudio server and to control the session. For example, the client can pause the session on port 7070.

Transmission of the audio content, however, uses UDP as the underlying transport protocol. The content streams from the server back to the client on UDP ports 6970 through 7170. It's UDP because once the audio or video content feed starts, timeliness matters far more than reliable data delivery. It wouldn't make much sense to retransmit lost or missing data in a streaming media feed. Data that arrives late or that has to be retransmitted is useless, so it's better to drop it and move along. RealAudio uses a number of UDP ports for the same reason that source ports are usually selected by the client. The client could be a user of a multiuser system, and using different ports allows a firewall or NAT device to distinguish where the UDP stream should be sent.

In many networks, clients access RealAudio servers through a firewall, which may also be doing NAT. A NAT device that supports RealAudio must remap the UDP ports back to the client ports and translate the datagrams' destination IP addresses back to the respective inside network addresses.

Resource Reservation Protocol (RSVP)

One of the problems of the TCP/IP protocols is that they were never intended to be used for applications that require fixed amounts of bandwidth or that could guarantee traffic flow. TCP and IP were always intended to be "best effort" delivery mechanisms. The traffic would most likely get there, but maybe it wouldn't. If it didn't get there, some protocol would try to send the traffic again, and it was hoped that that would get through. If that didn't work, then maybe the application would have to try again later. Neither the network nor the protocols gave any guarantees of Quality of Service.

The no-Quality-of-Service delivery model is markedly different from that of the switched telephone system. The circuit-switched phone network allocates fixed channels and fixed amounts of bandwidth for calls. A call can be used for voice or data, but the network guarantees delivery and, to a certain extent, the quality of that service. The only limitation on traffic delay is the normal propagation delay across the electrical, optical, or radio links of the network.

Remember those voice and video applications? And how about streaming video, Webcasting, Internet radio, and videoconferencing, not to mention online games and multipoint conferencing? They all rely on a reliable, continuous stream of audio or video, or both, as well as a fixed amount of bandwidth to accommodate the applications. In the case of high-definition, full-motion video applications, the amount of bandwidth can be as much as several hundred kilobytes per second.

Obviously, "best effort" delivery won't work for applications that require a regular stream of data, particularly over a network like the Internet. Some days the Internet seems to work fine, and some days it's slow. The regular, switched telephone system, by contrast, has busy days, but it's rare that it has the kind of bad day that's not uncommon on the Internet.

Several solutions have been proposed for this problem, one of which is the *Resource Reservation Protocol* (RSVP). The RSVP protocol has been defined in RFC 2205, but its actual implementation is up to network transmission vendors and application developers. The idea of the RSVP protocol is to create a mechanism for network routers to set aside, or "reserve," network bandwidth for specific application data streams, so that applications can have a constant, reliable, and continuous stream of voice, video, or multimedia content. As we will see, this is easier specified in an RFC than done. Furthermore, things like NAT at the entrance points to networks may have the same undesirable effects on RSVP as they might on the underlying voice or video data streams.

Network managers charged with enabling RSVP frequently perceive it as a transport-level protocol, like TCP. Unfortunately—or fortunately, depending on your viewpoint—it's not. Instead, RSVP is an Internet control protocol, like the Internet Message Control Protocol (IMCP), or more to the point, like a routing protocol, such as the *Routing Information Protocol* (RIP), the *Interior Gateway Routing Protocol* (IGRP), and the *Border Gateway Protocol* (BGP). Routers use routing protocols like RIP, IGRP, and BGP to pass routing table updates among themselves.

RSVP is an end-to-end protocol, but it's different from other types of end-to-end protocols because routers in the path must be aware of it and accommodate it. Its purpose is for RSVP-capable routers to set up an end-to-end path across a network, as illustrated in Figure 7.3, for the exclusive use of a client and a server that will run a *reserved bandwidth* application. Reserving that path or bandwidth is the "resource reservation" that the name of the protocol implies. Today, many vendors' routers are RSVP-capable, but the trick is getting a string of them together to arrange a reserved bandwidth path across a network. Then there's that problem of NAT, which introduces a further complication, as it may confuse the identity of those end-systems running the application.

As a practical matter, establishing an RSVP session across the Internet may be possible, but it's not likely. There are just too many different carriers that are

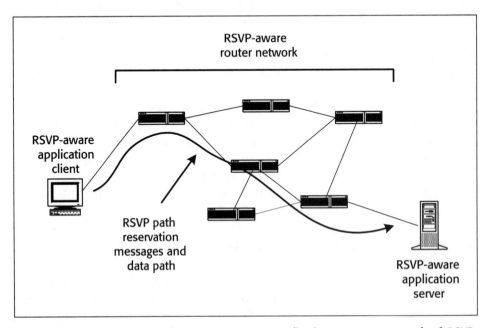

Figure 7.3 Path reservation by an RSVP-aware application across a network of RSVP-capable routers.

likely to be involved in the path across the Internet, many of which may have no interest in, nor see any advantage in, configuring an RSVP channel for users who aren't even their customers. What is more likely is to set up an end-to-end RSVP channel on a private IP network, such as an intranet, or between customer sites served by the same ISP. In those cases, there are likely to be fewer routers between the client and the server. More important, they will all be under the control of one organization, which may be more willing to configure its routers to use RSVP.

RSVP Sessions

The fundamental building block of RSVP is the RSVP session. It's similar to a TCP session, in that it implies prior arrangements to set aside, or reserve, enough bandwidth to carry the RSVP traffic. Unlike a TCP session, which is negotiated between the client and the server, an RSVP session is negotiated by the client, or sending system, with the network routers. The session setup designates, among other things, the IP addresses of the client and server, so that the RSVP-aware routers can identify the datagrams that get to use the reserved bandwidth channel. That's where NAT can complicate matters because a NAT device at the entrance or exit to a network may change one or both IP addresses.

An RSVP session is a flow of data between two IP addresses (the client and the server, which we'll refer to as the sender and the receiver), directed to a specific TCP port. In that sense, it's like any other type of TCP communications. It's also defined, though, by the path set up beforehand by the routers along the way. The sender creates a path message, addressed to the receiver, which is delivered by normal IP routing. The RSVP-aware routers along the way have to notice the path messages and record them, however, because it's their job to "reserve" this path for subsequent communications between the sender and receiver. Then the receiver sends a reservation message back to the sender, acknowledging it. The routers use the information they stored previously to make sure the reservation message takes the same path back that the sender's original path message took.

Transmission along that path is controlled by RSVP messages, which contain the IP addresses of the client or the server. A NAT box on either the client side of the connection or the server side will have to be able to replace the IP addresses in the RSVP messages, based on the direction and type of message. Obviously, this will have to be done correctly and quickly, so as not to interrupt the delay-sensitive flow between client and server.

NAT may introduce a second complication. RSVP can use a value, called *the RSVP Integrity Object*, which is similar to an IP or TCP checksum. It guarantees the integrity of an RSVP message. RSVP clients and servers may use it to determine if the RSVP messages have been corrupted en route. If a NAT box changes the IP address of the source or destination of RSVP messages, the Integrity Object may no longer be correct. Not only may a NAT device have to change the TCP and IP header checksums, but it may also have to monitor and change RSVP Integrity Objects as well. Note that NAT could make this change only if it also had the secret key that the client and server used to create the Integrity Object. Secret keys are usually available only to communications end-points, not to waypoints like NAT.

The net of this is that RSVP and NAT may not be the best of combinations. For that matter, using NAT in the path for most applications that are sensitive to delay may not be the best idea in any case. RSVP, or any arrangement that is designed to "pipeline" traffic of bandwidth between two points on an IP network, must be configured carefully to minimize any delays that NAT may induce.

Domain Name Service

The *Domain Name Service* (DNS) is a distributed network service that maps the text names of hosts or host names that are in Web site URLs back to their IP addresses. Its operation is covered more comprehensively in Chapter 8, "NAT and DNS," but it is one of those applications that by its very nature embeds IP addresses in its data payloads. Its data payloads are IP addresses, in that they are responses to DNS queries to map a host name, such as ftp.xyz.com, back to the IP address that corresponds to that host name. The DNS acts like a directory service for the Internet. It gives network administrators the flexibility to change the IP addressing plans of networks and to move hosts to other networks. Even if their IP addresses change, those hosts will still be accessible as long as their DNS records are updated.

NAT changes the addresses by which hosts are known. More accurately, NAT changes the apparent IP address of a host because its real address doesn't change. DNS, though, doesn't know that NAT exists, so the IP addresses in DNS records usually don't reflect any address changes that NAT makes. To make DNS work properly through NAT, the NAT software must be teamed with a DNS *application-level gateway* (ALG) that translates IP addresses in DNS payloads. As with ALGs for other applications, the ALG must be aware of the NAT process because the ALG must use the same addresses the NAT box uses when it translates host addresses.

One of the assumptions of a DNS ALG configuration is that a network DNS has been split into inside and outside DNS services. The inside DNS knows about hosts on the inside network, and therefore it knows their inside network addresses. It may also know about outside hosts, but the IP addresses it lists will be those from the point of view of a host inside the network. The outside

DNS lists the IP addresses of the hosts that are reachable from outside networks, such as a public Web server, a mail relay, an anonymous FTP host, and the DNS, as they are known from the point of view of a host outside the network. Inside network hosts may be advertised to the outside network, but their advertised addresses must be changed by the DNS ALG.

Handling Inquiries

DNS inquiries are usually UDP transactions, embedded in IP datagrams. When a DNS inquiry goes through a NAT device, NAT translates the IP addresses in the IP header, and if necessary, the ALG translates addresses in the data payload. For this example, we will assume that the network has only one DNS, located on the inside network. A DNS inquiry from a host on an outside network for the address of an inside network host will be answered by the DNS server on the inside network. If an inquiry from an inside host couldn't be answered by the inside DNS, it would go to an outside DNS. In both cases, the inquiries and responses will go through NAT and the ALG.

When an inside host makes a DNS inquiry to an outside DNS, NAT may change both the source and destination addresses in the IP header for both outbound inquiries and inbound responses. When the response returns from an Internet DNS, the DNS ALG may have to change the IP address in the response. Let's say that an inside host, called a.xyz.com, has an address of 10.0.0.1. That address can't be used by an Internet host because it's an unroutable address. An outside network inquiry for the IP address of a.xyz.com would be answered by the inside DNS, which would respond with the address of 10.0.0.1.

The response would go to NAT and to the ALG. The ALG would change the 10.0.0.1 address to whatever NAT uses for the external representation of that address. It might be a static address mapping that had been previously configured for externally reachable inside hosts or a dynamic mapping, created by NAT when the ALG requested a mapping. If NAT represents all inside addresses with a single outside address, that address would be used by the ALG as the host's address.

DNS zone transfers are more problematic for the ALG because each record in the zone file may have to be translated to its external address. For example, the inside DNS may maintain a zone file for the entire xyz.com domain, listing the host names and IP addresses for each inside host. If the zone file were transferred to an outside DNS, each of the IP addresses in the records in the zone file would have to be translated to its outside address representation, as determined by NAT. Because of the complexity of this task, and because name-to-translated-address mappings may not be established for all inside hosts, zone transfers usually aren't done through DNS ALGs.

NAT address mapping may change over time, particularly if NAT uses dynamic address mapping. A DNS ALG may also set a limit for the time that an inquiry response is valid, to keep it from being used beyond its "freshness date." The timer, expressed as a time-to-live value, may be only a few minutes, so that the DNS that received the response might cache the response for only a short time. This would force the external DNS to make a new inquiry each time it needed to resolve the address.

One other limitation on mixing DNS and NAT is Secure DNS (DNS Sec), a standard for securing DNS updates by encryption. Just as with several other types of encryption, which we will examine more thoroughly in Chapter 13, "NAT and Security," DNS Sec and NAT don't mix well. The purpose of DNS Sec is to give DNS servers a means to authenticate DNS updates, to prevent hackers from hijacking hosts by changing DNS records. The problem is that DNS Sec, like other forms of encryption, uses a cryptographic key that is shared by the sender and receiver. Intermediaries like NAT usually aren't part of the sender-receiver security relationship; they don't have the key, so they can't re-sign the encrypted data to preserve its validity.

Making Applications Safe for NAT

Some applications don't work quite right with NAT in the network path, but in the greater scheme of things, that's just so much water over the dam. FTP was designed more than 20 years ago, and it's too late to teach that dog a new trick. It's not about to change, but fortunately, its mode of operation and its use of embedded IP addresses and TCP ports are well enough understood that making FTP work through a NAT box isn't rocket science.

If we were to look into the future, it would seem reasonable to believe that NAT is neither going to go away nor change substantially. If anything, the pressure on IP address space will grow, not abate, which may well force more and more organizations to use NAT to hide overlapping address space or private address space. NAT, or something closely akin to it, will also play a key role in the transition to the next version of the IP protocol, IP Version 6, which we will examine in Chapter 19, "The Future of NAT."

Because it is unlikely that NAT will be going away, it would be wise for application developers to design new applications with NAT in mind. If application developers could make their applications "NAT-proof," then NAT could truly be transparent to new applications. Obviously, some of the problems that FTP, SNMP, RSVP, and other applications and protocols have with NAT are that they weren't designed with NAT in mind. Furthermore, it's too late to fix them. Some protocols and applications have special requirements that may make it difficult to make them NAT-friendly.

A further complication is that it may not be possible to make all applications NAT-resistant, just by the nature of what they do. Practically any application that separates setup, signaling, and control from data transmission, like SIP or H.323, can't necessarily be made NAT-safe. There's no known way to perform all of those functions without data and control functions being separate. The same thing goes for applications that carry configuration information, such as SNMP. By definition, those applications must carry IP addresses, and they can't be made NAT-safe either. ALGs may be able to solve the embedded data issues, but by itself, NAT can't necessarily do that.

Application developers who want their applications to work more smoothly should adhere to some relatively simple application guidelines. These guidelines are intended to make applications work properly with NAT, but they can also simplify the operation of the application, whether or not NAT is part of the network path.

Use a Single TCP Session

Although it isn't necessarily a NAT issue, FTP uses two linked sessions, the control connection and the data connection, on ports 20 and 21. There may have been a valid reason to do this 20 years ago, but common sense dictates that two TCP connections, each of which depends on the other, are twice as complicated as one, particularly because one goes from the client to the server and the other from the server to the client. Version 1.0 of HTTP, for instance, set up a separate TCP session to transfer each object on a Web page. Fortunately, subsequent versions of HTTP control most everything through the single TCP port 80 HTTP session.

Managing all application data exchange through a single session makes life easier for a NAT box that has to do address and port translation. It also simplifies the operation of the application, and it eliminates the problem of a "hanging" process that is dependent on a second (or third) process to terminate.

Originate Sessions from One End

Not to use FTP as a whipping boy, but it's a good example of an application that violates a second good design principle. If there must be more than one session, originate all of them from either the client side or the server side, but not both. The FTP client initiates the control connection, but the FTP server initiates the data connection. Sessions that originate from either end of the connection complicate matters for anything that is monitoring the sessions, such as a NAT device or a firewall. As with other applications, though, it may not be possible to restrict session origination to one side of the connection.

Both the sender and receiver of an RSVP session, for example, originate connections.

Use a Single Session

A NAT box has more than twice as much work to do when it has to translate TCP ports as well as IP addresses. Not only does it have to do the port and address translation work, but it also must keep track of each TCP session. An alternative to TCP is the User Datagram Protocol, UDP, which is a simpler version of TCP. Unlike TCP, UDP doesn't use sessions. It's intended to be a simpler, lightweight transport-level protocol for applications that don't require the overhead of TCP. Applications like ping and traceroute use UDP because they don't require the data delivery assurance of TCP.

Applications may use UDP or TCP through a NAT device. Either will work equally well, but if an application uses TCP, NAT will be much happier if there's only a single TCP session involved. To refine this single-session admonition a little further, we might say that applications should use in-band signaling. That is, if it is possible to do so, any signaling and control information should be sent between client and server over the same session as the data, instead of creating separate sessions for control and signaling. Most of the common Internet applications work this way, like HTTP and SMTP. Some of the newer applications do not. Some of the control functions that SIP and H.323 need must be done with separate, out-of-band TCP sessions because they won't work reliably with in-band signaling within the UDP data channel.

Detecting the end of a session can be a problem for NAT with either TCP or UDP. TCP sessions use a specific sequence to end a session, but UDP, which doesn't create sessions in the first place, does not. A NAT device may not know when to drop a TCP session that terminates abnormally or prematurely. If it's a UDP session, which has no end-of-session sequence (because there's no UDP session), the NAT box may be configured with a timer to indicate when it should drop the UDP connection.

Confine Addressing to Headers

Applications that embed IP addresses or TCP port numbers in data fields are clearly more difficult to support through NAT. Applications that confine addresses and ports to their respective headers are going to be easier to support through NAT. Of course, it's easy to prescribe this solution, but it does not allow for applications that may need to pass additional port and address information between clients and servers. There's no extra room in an IP or a TCP header for any other addresses. NAT boxes, however, will work better and more efficiently if they don't have to root through data payload fields to support applications.

Use DNS Names, Not IP Addresses

If it's impossible to build an application that doesn't incorporate embedded IP addresses, using host names instead of IP addresses may make it easier to create a reliable ALG for the application. Using DNS names implies that the ALG must resolve a host name to get an IP address, but it improves the chances of the ALG working properly. IP addresses are absolute references, but DNS host names are relative to whatever IP address a DNS service has for that host. IP addresses change, as do host names, but properly maintained DNS records are intended to be a reliable reference for current IP addresses.

Surely your mother told you, "Always wash your hands before eating." It is excellent advice, and perfectly sound from a hygiene perspective, but it isn't always possible. These guidelines are the same type of advice. They're good ideas, but it may not always be possible to apply them equally to every application. It might it be a good idea to use DNS names in embedded data instead of IP addresses, and to use a single TCP session and in-band signaling, but it might not be possible to do so for all applications. Some applications won't conform to these guidelines because they need to support certain types of functions to make the applications work properly. Instead of strict rules, application developers should keep these guidelines in mind, particularly when evaluating the different functions of applications. It may be possible to modify or eliminate functions that are less important than others, leaving important functions intact, even if the latter bend or break these NAT-friendly application guidelines.

That Management View

Given that NAT can cause a number of application problems, maybe the appropriate view for IT management to take is that NAT isn't a suitable technology for today's rapidly changing multimedia world. If NAT can cause so many problems and introduce so much uncertainty in network connectivity, maybe IT organizations should look elsewhere for less intrusive solutions.

The other side of this coin is that some of these problems aren't unsolvable. There are situations where NAT can't be used because it may interfere with applications or encryption, but they are well-known problems. For the most part, the NAT device vendors, who are the ones who make routers and firewalls, recognize that their products are both part of the problem and part of the solution. If a firewall is going to protect a network and use NAT to shield the identity and existence of the systems behind it, then it will also have to be able to handle most of the application protocol issues and problems that NAT may introduce.

IT organizations usually don't want to be in the business of creating custom solutions to application problems. They'd rather have the *magic box* solution, which handles problems transparently and which packages solutions inside hardware and software that the box vendor will support.

This is precisely what the firewall and router vendors have tried to do. NAT is a function built into their devices, so their manufacturers have also built into them the functionality of basic NAT, as well as functions to handle standard NAT-induced protocol problems. For example, Cisco has built NAT functions to accommodate widely used applications, such as FTP, NetMeeting, and CUseeMe, as has Nortel and other router vendors.

Besides, if the IT organization has made the commitment to use private addressing or overlapping address space in its networks, it has also made a commitment to NAT and to ALGs, even if they break some applications. An IT organization that has decided that NAT is justified because of other tactical or strategic reasons, such as security or better address management, probably won't want to forgo those advantages because of application-related issues. Unless there is a single killer app that NAT prohibits, it's really not worth giving up the advantages of NAT without researching alternatives to making the applications work in a NAT environment. Before deciding to deploy NAT, an IT organization should make a survey of the applications in use to determine how or if they would be affected by NAT.

Given that there will continue to be greater pressure to use IP address space more efficiently, and that the need for NAT may increase, not decrease, it is important that new applications take NAT into account. If new applications can't handle NAT, application designers must make that clear when specifying how an application works. The basic nature of some applications will preclude their being used with NAT. It's not always evident where NAT might be in use in a network, so application designers and network managers can't necessarily control where and when they will encounter NAT.

Summary

Nobody ever said that NAT was going to be free, and its effect on applications shows that it isn't without its problems. In previous chapters, we have seen that NAT can introduce delays in communications, and in this chapter, we have seen how applications can be affected by NAT, too.

Fortunately, the most commonly used applications aren't affected by NAT. The most widely used applications, such as HTTP and SMTP, usually don't embed IP addresses in data streams, so NAT handles them transparently. NAT is a technology that has been retrofitted on top of the existing TCP/IP architecture, so NAT must be made to adapt to TCP/IP and its applications, not the other way around. Application-level gateways are one of the primary ways in which NAT can accommodate most, but not all, of those NAT-unfriendly applications.

In the next chapter, we will take a broader view of how NAT affects other parts of the TCP/IP protocol architecture, specifically the operation of the Domain Name Service (DNS). The DNS is another one of those services that can be affected by NAT because IP addresses are part of the data referenced by a host in a DNS address lookup.

NAT and DNS

The *Domain Name Service* (DNS) is one of the collection of near-miracles that keeps the Internet running. It's practically a miracle because it works seemingly by magic, although DNS administrators know that it's hard work and attention to detail that make it work. DNS conceals a great many of the gory details of how the Internet operates from end users, giving them a highly simplified and extremely handy way to use a complex and convoluted system.

DNS services maintain tables that map the text names of network and Internet host computers, Web servers, PCs, and other objects back to their corresponding IP addresses. Everything needs an IP address, and the IP protocol uses IP addresses to route traffic to its destination. It's essential that a DNS service maintain accurate and correct lists of IP addresses and host names. Otherwise, the DNS information would be incorrect, and IP routing wouldn't be able to deliver traffic to the correct destinations.

As we have seen, NAT changes the IP addresses in IP datagrams. The problem is that a DNS service doesn't know about NAT, so the addresses given out by DNS may not reflect whatever changes NAT will make. Worse, NAT addresses changes may occur dynamically, which means that from time to time the addresses that NAT might use could change. In this chapter, we'll look at how the DNS operates and some of the complications NAT may introduce into the normal operation of DNS services.

What's a DNS?

The simplest way to view DNS is as a network service that provides a highly convenient utility: translating the text in *Uniform Resource Locators* (URLs) into IP addresses. Neither URLs nor host names, such as ftp.bigco.com, are useful to IP routers. Routers and the IP protocol work on IP addresses, not text names. If you type the URL http://www.microsoft.com into the Location:

URLS AND DOMAIN NAMES

URLs, host names, and domain names are often referred to as if they were the same thing, but they aren't. Web browsers work with URLs, but Internet Web surfers have become so accustomed to typing what is really either a fully qualified host name or a domain name in a Web browser that the distinction between domain names and URLs has become blurred.

The parts of a URL are these:

- The application type, such as http://

- A domain name, such as xyz.com

- A host name within that domain, such as www.xyz.com

- Any optional additional information after the host name that indicates the name of a file or subdirectory on the server, such as /documents/index.html

User-friendly browser features have made the distinction between URLs and domain names less clear. Browsers like Microsoft's Internet Explorer and Netscape Navigator will allow a user to type only a domain name, such as xyz.com, and the browser will convert it to a complete URL, such as http://www.xyz.com. In this example, the name of the host, which is a Web server, is "www," and the domain in which it is located is the xyz.com domain. The fully qualified name of the host is www.xyz.com. If the user does not specify a host name, the Web browser makes the assumption that it is "www," although the server we really want might have a different name, such as webserver1.xyz.com.

A domain name, by contrast, is a unique part of the DNS domain-naming structure, such as xyz.com, amazon.com, or domperignon.fr. Whoever holds the rights to a second-level domain name, such as these examples, may add third-, fourth-, and other lower-level subdomains under it. For example, if the XYZ Corporation has the rights to the xyz.com domain name, it may elect to create the sales.xyz.com subdomain, as well as the admin.sales.xyz.com subdomain under that, and name hosts within those subdomains.

box on your Web browser, the host name in that URL must be translated into the IP address that corresponds to the text host name. DNS provides that translation.

From a user's perspective, DNS simplifies using the Internet enormously by shielding users from the intricacies of IP addresses. Most Internet users don't have a clue what the IP addresses are of their favorite Web sites. In fact, most don't even know that Web sites have IP addresses. A big part of that miracle of the Internet is that users don't have to worry about the details of IP communications. As long as they can type a URL or a host name correctly, the DNS will translate it to an IP address, assuming that a DNS has a record for that host name.

From a network manager's or IT executive's perspective, DNS simplifies network administration and maintenance. DNS is a network directory service, which can be centralized, distributed, replicated, backed up, or restricted in a number of ways. Administering a DNS service, however, can demand a great deal of skill and experience because what may seem to be trivial errors and inconsistencies can leave networks incommunicado with the outside world. On the other hand, some of those same mistakes can leave enormous security holes, potentially exposing a network to intruders.

DNS Structure and Organization

DNS is a hierarchical, distributed directory service that runs on computers that are running the DNS program. The DNS servers are on local networks and on the Internet. DNS is a directory application that responds to client requests for directory information. On a Unix system, the DNS application is a Unix program called BIND, which is an acronym for the *Berkeley Internet Names Distribution* program. On Windows systems, the program is the Windows DNS Service, which is a Windows version of BIND. Most DNS services are various implementations of the original BIND program.

Network clients that need IP addresses for text host names or URLs request them from the nearest DNS service. In most cases, network clients know the IP address of at least one DNS, so that they know where to go to find a DNS service. On a PC running Windows, the IP address of a DNS service is usually configured in the Network icon of the Windows Control Panel. The IP address of the DNS may be entered manually in the Network icon's DNS tab. The IP address of the DNS server might change from time to time, which might leave a PC with a manually entered DNS address unable to find the DNS again. Many network administrators therefore use the *Dynamic Host Configuration Protocol* service (DHCP) to download a fresh copy of the IP address of the nearest DNS server to user workstations and PCs at the same time that DHCP gives the PC an IP address.

At the simplest level, a client request for directory information is a request, originated by a Web browser, to translate a host name in a URL into an IP address. As we will see, one DNS service may refer the request to several other DNS services to determine the answer. In this example, the answer is the IP address that corresponds to the host name in the URL.

Let's say a user who works at one of the offices of Small Co. types the URL of www.bigco.com into the Location: bar on his Web browser. It's possible that there is no host named www.bigco.com or that it doesn't have a DNS entry, but the Web browser, and certainly the user, doesn't know that. The Web browser takes the host name in the URL and passes it to the DNS client module in the PC. The DNS client formulates a request for DNS name resolution, locates the IP address of the DNS in the Windows configuration files, and sends the DNS inquiry to the DNS. In some cases, the DNS will be on the same local area network or on another LAN reachable through a router.

Before it sends the request to the network DNS, the DNS client may also check the PC's local hard disk for a file that maps text host names to IP

DOMAIN NAMES

Most everyone is familiar with Web URLs, which contain the names of Internet hosts. Internet naming is organized into a hierarchical structure called domains. The popular .com domain and the familiar .org, .net, .gov, .edu, and .mil domains are a hierarchical naming structure that organizes Web servers, hosts, and organizational networks.

At the top level of the hierarchy are the "top-level" domains of .com, .org, .net, and so forth, as well as domains for each country, such as .us, .nz, and .jp. Companies, people, and organizations may stake a claim to a second-level domain name, such as xyz.com or ietf.org, under one of the top-level domains. Host names usually fall under that lower or second-level domain, although other subdomains may be created under it. Whoever has the rights to a second-level domain may set up any number of subdomains under it or name hosts directly under the second-level domain.

So, in the host name www.bigco.com, .com is the top-level domain, bigco is the second-level domain, and www is the name of a host in the bigco.com domain. Because it has the rights to the bigco.com domain, Big Co. may create lower-level subdomains for network devices, such as servers.bigco.com and printers.bigco.com, as well as for company divisions, such as sales.bigco.com and legal.bigco.com. Then Big Co. could name hosts within those subdomains, such as fs1.servers.bigco.com or color.printers.bigco.com. Those hosts would also be listed in the Big Co. DNS, so that users could specify them by name, rather than by IP address.

addresses. This file, sometimes called the hosts.txt file or lmhosts.txt, is a small text table that maps a limited number of commonly-used host names to IP addresses.

When the DNS server receives the DNS client's request, it examines the host name www.bigco.com and looks for a file that contains host names in the bigco.com domain. The "www" part of the Web site name is the name of a host in the bigco.com domain. DNS services organize their host name-IP address records into separate files called *zone files*. The DNS will have a separate zone file for each domain it knows about. It may not know about very many domains, though, because each DNS service may know about only a small number of domains.

For example, the DNS for Big Co. might know only about hosts whose names end with bigco.com, such as www.bigco.com, mailgate.bigco.com, and ftp.bigco.com, as well as itself, ns.bigco.com. The user who typed www.bigco .com in the Web browser probably doesn't know where the Big Co. DNS is located or, for that matter, if it even exists. In fact, he probably doesn't even understand the problem, but fortunately, whatever DNS the client contacts first will solve the problem for him.

Finding the Right DNS

The first DNS that receives the request from a client to resolve a host name to an IP address assumes responsibility for resolving the name. That is, it will make requests of other DNSs until it finds the DNS that can answer the "What's the IP address for www.bigco.com?" question.

Most DNSs know about only a few other DNSs. The Small Co. DNS, to which the DNS client request was sent, may have only a zone file for other hosts in the smallco.com domain. What the smallco.com DNS needs to find the DNS for the bigco.com domain is a master index of all the DNSs for the .com domains. Each domain has a DNS for it, or at least it should have one, although there isn't necessarily a requirement for one. For that matter, it would be nice to have a master index for all of the DNSs for all of the domains in the other top-level domains, such as the .org, .net, .edu, .gov, and .mil domains. And, oh yes, all of those country code domains, such as .us (United States), .ca (Canada), .jp (Japan), and so forth.

By a huge stroke of luck, such a master index exists, and the smallco.com DNS, as well as every other DNS, knows how to find it. The master index of DNSs is a set of files on a group of 13 DNS servers, referred to as the *Top Level Domain* (TLD) servers. The master files on this set of servers are maintained by *Network Solutions, Inc.* (NSI, at www.networksolutions.com), as part of its role in registering domain names in the .com, .org, and .net domains. A company, organization, or individual who registers a domain name in one of the TLDs with NSI or with any of the 40 other domain name registrars must also specify the IP addresses of at least two DNS servers (a primary and a backup, or secondary, DNS) that will be able to answer requests to resolve host names in that domain.

So, when Big Co. registered the bigco.com domain name, part of the registration process required Big Co. to register a primary and a backup DNS for the bigco.com domain. Even if the domain name will only be registered and will have no real hosts in the domain (an "empty domain"), the assumption is that domain names are supposed to be real, and therefore they require DNS servers that know about hosts in them. Today, large numbers of domain names are registered just to reserve the domain names. Still, the registration process requires real DNS server IP addresses because domain names are supposed to stand for real, active domains, even if they don't really do that.

Part of a basic DNS server configuration is a small file, the root-servers.txt file, which lists the IP addresses and names of those 13 top-level servers. They're called the root-zone servers, and their host names are a.root-servers.net, b.root-servers.net, and so on, through m.root-servers.net. The servers are located around the world, although most of them are in the United States. Presumably, a DNS server will refer an inquiry to the closest DNS server, although it has no way of knowing which one is closest. It shouldn't matter which server it contacts because they all should have the same data.

One of the servers, the A-root server, is the master server, which maintains the master zone files for the top-level domains. That server, which is named a.root-servers.net (198.41.0.4), is located in Herndon, Virginia, at Network Solutions' headquarters. NSI maintains the master DNS files as part of its agreement with ICANN to register domain names and to maintain the TLD DNS files. The master server downloads changes to the TLD zone files twice a day, to update changes, adds, and deletions to domain name files and changes to DNS server addresses. By the summer of 2000, there were more than 10 million domains registered in the .com domain alone, an indication that the .com domain was the place to be on the Internet.

Asking the Right Question

Meanwhile, back at the ranch, the Small Co. DNS has received the request to get the IP address of www.bigco.com from the user's Web browser. The Small Co. DNS doesn't know anything about the bigco DNS, but it can find out by asking one of the TLD servers. Retrieving the IP address of one of the TLD servers from its servers file, the Small Co. DNS executes its DNS client program, called named, and creates a DNS request for the IP address of the DNS for bigco.com. It sends the request to the TLD server, which lists all of the domains in the top-level domains as well as their DNSs.

The TLD server receives the request and responds with the IP addresses of the DNS servers for bigco.com. Note that it doesn't answer the real question, which is "What's the IP address for www.bigco.com?", because the TLD server doesn't know. The name-to-IP address mappings for hosts in each of the second- and lower-level domains isn't of any concern to the TLD server. It's only a master index that can point another DNS to one of the DNSs for a secondary domain.

With the IP address for the DNS for the bigco.com domain, the Small Co. DNS can now ask the Big Co. DNS to answer its question because now it has its IP address. Furthermore, the bigco.com DNS should have the IP address because Big Co. is responsible for its own DNS. Big Co. may farm out DNS administration to its ISP or to a third party, but either way it should be able to resolve the address. If one of the Big Co. DNSs isn't available, the Small Co. DNS also has the IP address of at least one backup, or secondary DNS for BigCo, so it will have an alternative if the primary DNS doesn't respond.

The Small Co. DNS formulates a second DNS request, this time for the IP address for www.bigco.com. The request is enclosed in an IP datagram addressed to the bigco.com DNS. The bigco.com DNS server has a host name too, such as ns1.bigco.com, which the root server also sends back to the Small Co. DNS, but its IP address is what really matters.

When the Big Co. DNS responds with the IP address of www.bigco.com, the Small Co. DNS, which started all of this process, will be able to answer the original request from the Web browser. Finally—and only then—will the Web browser be able to initiate its request for the home page of www.bigco.com.

Fortunately, as experience using URLs in Web browsers attests, this involved process may take only a second or two. It's another one of the miracles of the Internet that such a communications-dependent process can be accomplished in so short a time. A request to resolve a text name to an IP addresses can literally go all over the world. Of course, if it does, the time to resolve a name may be affected by the speed of long-haul and local access communications circuits, congestion on the Internet, DNS server loading, and other factors.

Find the NAT in This Picture

So, you might ask, where's the address translation in this picture? For starters, it might not be there at all because there's no requirement that NAT be anywhere in any network. The initial request from the PC running the Web browser out to the network DNS might have gone through a NAT box, but the NAT box would have kept track of the source and destination addresses and the DNS TCP port (port 43) and made the appropriate address and port number manipulations along the way.

The most significant implication of NAT would have been on the addresses in the zone files maintained by the DNS services. As an example of one of a number of possible scenarios, the DNS for the bigco.com domain could have been located outside a firewall running NAT, as illustrated in Figure 8.1.

In this case, the request from the inside client passes through the NAT box. In itself, that's not a problem. The DNS, however, in public address space outside the firewall, might have records in its zone files for hosts, PCs, and servers behind the firewall. If those devices have addresses in private network space, they may be listed in the DNS's zone files, but they won't do anyone any good. Because they're private addresses, Internet routers won't recognize them as routable addresses, and they'll discard datagrams addressed to those addresses. Private and public addressing concepts will be dealt with more fully in Chapter 9, "Public and Private Addressing."

The DNS itself could be behind the firewall, with its own interfaces numbered from private address space. If that were the case, the IP address listed for the Big Co. DNS (ns1.bigco.com) in the TLD servers couldn't be the Big Co. DNS's real IP address. As in the previous example, Internet routers would discard traffic addressed to the DNS's private address, which would make it unreachable from anything outside the firewall.

In this case, the IP address in the TLD server records would have to be the external interface for the firewall or the NAT box, not the DNS's real address. Either the firewall address or the NAT box address would have to be in public address space in order for it to be reachable from the Internet or from else-

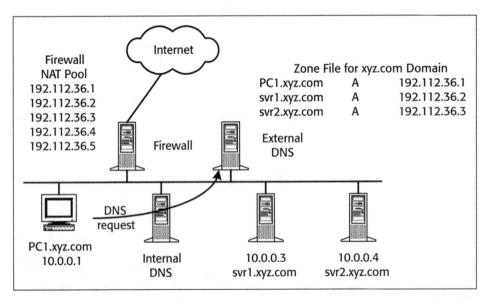

Figure 8.1 A host in private address space sends a DNS request to an external DNS in public address space.

where in public address space. The NAT box would have to maintain a static address translation table entry for the DNS to know how to readdress traffic destined for the DNS.

As we have indicated before, the firewall or NAT box external interface might be used for all kinds of traffic destined for hosts inside the network. And how would the firewall or NAT box know which requests were addressed to the DNS and not to other services inside the network? For inbound traffic looking for the DNS, the Destination TCP port number in the TCP header would be the port number for DNS, which is port 43. The NAT box would know that any traffic it received on its outside interface that was pointed to port 43 would have to be readdressed to the DNS's internal address.

Splitsville

A third DNS scenario is the *split DNS*, in which a network has not one, but two separate DNS services. One DNS service is located outside the firewall or NAT box, and the second DNS service is behind the firewall or NAT box, on the inside network. As with the previous two examples, NAT is again an issue because there are two separate sets of DNS files, and neither DNS necessarily knows—or cares—that there is NAT between them.

The split DNSs handle requests from, and have knowledge about, different addressing realms. The DNS inside the firewall or NAT box handles DNS inquiries from the inside network, and the second handles DNS requests from outside the network. This split of responsibilities works because PCs and workstations behind the firewall or NAT box are configured with the inside DNS as their default DNS. The outside DNS is listed as the primary DNS in the TLD servers, so it is accessible to outside inquiries.

The purpose in dividing the DNS into two separate and, as we will see, unequal parts is twofold. First, the inside DNS may know about the IP addresses of hosts, PCs, and servers in a private addressing realm behind a firewall. Those private addresses will be valid only within that realm or within other private addressing realms, not outside them. That is, the routers on the inside network must be configured not to discard traffic for private addresses, but instead to route it normally. After all, the routers on the inside network would have private addresses themselves on many or all of their own interfaces, so they couldn't summarily discard traffic with private destination addresses.

The second reason for the division between inside and outside DNSs is security. The inside DNS knows about inside network hosts, and the outside DNS does not. As we have discussed in previous chapters, hiding addresses with NAT isn't a security measure as much as an ancillary tool in a more comprehensive security strategy. It's far more useful for hosts with public addresses than those with private addresses. After all, listing hosts and their private addresses in an outside DNS is pointless. They can't be reached from outside the firewall or NAT box with those unroutable addresses. They might be attacked by an intruder who managed to penetrate the firewall and who could then use those addresses within the private addressing realm.

In a spilt DNS environment, inside network devices can still get to the outside world (the Internet), and they can still resolve Internet addresses. Any DNS address resolution request by a Web browser or other client on a PC on the inside network would go to the inside DNS. The inside DNS probably wouldn't be able to resolve the name to its IP address, unless it were for a host or Web site behind the firewall or NAT box. Instead, the inside DNS would forward the request to the outside DNS. The outside DNS would then resolve the address by requesting resolution from the TLD server and second-level DNSs, until it received the answer. The outside DNS would then forward the answer back to the inside DNS, which would answer the PC's original request.

For security reasons, the converse of this situation would not be true. That is, a request from an Internet host for the IP address of a host on the inside network could reach the outside DNS, but it wouldn't be forwarded to the DNS on the inside network. Both the inside and the outside DNS might know about hosts in the same domain, such as hosts in the bigco.com domain, but the outside DNS would return answers only to DNS queries about hosts listed in its zone files.

Internet security concerns have made the split inside and outside DNS combination an increasingly common scenario. The split DNS configuration has both security and performance implications. First, the outside DNS knows about only the relatively small number of hosts that can be reached from outside the network. These "outside accessible" hosts might include a public Web server, an anonymous FTP server, and an e-mail relay, as well as any other host whose name and IP address must be resolvable from the outside world. All other hosts on the inside network would be unknown to the outside DNS because there may be no reason for any outside host to know about them.

The performance issue is that DNS traffic, for the most part, is separated into inside and outside inquiries, few of which have to pass through the firewall or NAT box. If there were a single DNS service behind the NAT box, all DNS inquiries would have to pass through the firewall or NAT box, raising security and performance concerns on the NAT choke point. With a separate DNS outside the NAT device, DNS inquiries from the outside world don't pass through NAT and don't affect the performance of the firewall or NAT box.

Dem Zones, Dem Zones, Dem Crazy Zones

The reason that NAT can have a substantial effect on DNS inquiries is that DNS services don't know that NAT exists. DNS servers respond to inquiries for text-name-to-IP-address mappings. They're not supposed to do much else, although periodically they may go to another DNS to get an updated version of their zone files. There's really nothing in the DNS service to indicate to it whether NAT exists anywhere in a network, not to mention what, if anything, the DNS is supposed to do about it. In fact, a DNS doesn't do anything about it. The problem is that translating addresses through NAT means that the data in the DNS may not be correct anywhere but within the part of the network where the DNS is located, not necessarily on the Internet.

The data in the DNS is kept in a set of files called zone files. The zone files are relatively simple text files that match the name of a host, such as www.bigco.com, with its IP address. A zone file may have just a few or even hundreds of host-name-to-IP address matches in it. Each host name and its corresponding IP address is a single line of one of the zone files, in a *resource record* (RR).

The resource records in the zone file for the bigco.com zone in the Big Co. DNS might look something like the file depicted in Figure 8.2.

We'll ignore the text in the header of the zone file for now and just look at the resource records. Note that this zone file, which is for the bigco.com domain, has five hosts in it. Each line of the body of the zone file lists the host name on the left and its IP address on the right. The "IN" between the two indicates these are Internet resource records. At one time, this was significant, but it is no longer so. For purposes of backward compatibility among different versions of BIND, the "IN" remains in many DNS resource records, even though it no longer has any significance. Eventually, they may disappear entirely, but for now, it's like the coccyx. We don't need it, but it's there, and we hope that we'll evolve out of it.

Are all of the hosts in the bigco.com domain listed in the DNS's zone file? Maybe they are, and maybe they aren't. The DNS is created by the DNS administrator or the network administrator, who may elect not to put some hosts in the zone file. For example, let's suppose there's an FTP server outside

```
                     Zone File for bigco.com Domain

www.bigco.com            IN      A       192.112.36.5
mailgate.bigco.com       IN      MX      192.112.36.10
ftp.bigco.com            IN      A       192.112.36.3
bigco.com                IN      NS      ns1.bigco.com
ns1.bigco.com            IN      A       192.112.36.15
fwex.bigco.com           IN      A       192.112.36.50
watchdog                 IN      CNAME   fwex.bigco.com
```

Figure 8.2   Part of the zone file for the bigco.com domain.

the network that only a few people are supposed to use. It's not intended to be for general use, like the anonymous FTP server. It's on the outside network, though, so it's exposed to attack from the Internet, but we'll ignore the security issue for the sake of this example.

That FTP server is named ftpspecial.bigco.com, but it isn't in the zone file. It has an IP address, which is 192.112.36.76, and it's on the same network as the anonymous FTP host, the Web server, the mail gateway, and the DNS, but it's not listed in the DNS. All that means is that if you want to reach ftpspecial. bigco.com, you'll have to know its IP address. Pointing an FTP client to ftpspecial.bigco.com won't do any good. The inquiry will reach the Big Co. DNS (ns1.bigco.com), and the DNS will look in its zone file for ftpspecial.bigco.com, but it won't be there.

The point is that the DNS may not know about all hosts on a given network or in a specific domain. It's up to the DNS administrator or the network administrator to determine which hosts will be resolvable through the DNS. In most cases, all, or nearly all, of the hosts will be listed in the DNS. But some may not be because there's no reason for their names to be resolved by outside hosts or because they're just not contacted by other hosts.

The last host in the list of resource records depicted is fwex.bigco.com. That's the name of the external interface of the firewall. It might be the port through which internal services are reached, so it's possible it might be given a host name and listed in the firewall, too.

Note that the hosts listed in the sample zone file happen to be on the same IP network, 192.112.36.0. The hosts don't have to be on the same network. For that matter, the zone file for the bigco.com domain may list hosts on a number of IP networks. Remember that the primary purpose of the zone file is to map host names back to IP addresses. Inquiries are made for a host name in a specific domain. It doesn't matter what IP network the host is located on because the key to resolving the inquiry is the domain name, not the network on which the host is located.

Types of Resource Records

Most DNS zone files map host names to IP addresses, but there are a number of different types of DNS resource records, some of which don't do that. For example, some resource records identify specific types of hosts, such as DNS servers and mail exchange gateways. Others specify aliases for hosts, and another type of resource record maps IP addresses back to host names. There are movements afoot to create new types of resource records to map IP addresses to URLs, e-mail addresses, phone numbers, and other identifiers. In this section, we'll only examine the most common types of DNS resource records, particularly those that are relevant to NAT.

A Records

The *A* before the IP address in the resource records in the zone file means that this is the general-purpose resource record type (an *A record*), used for mapping host names to IP addresses. Most DNS resource records are A records. The general format of an A record is this:

    ftp.bigco.com   IN   A   192.112.36.3

Most DNS records are A records because they map hosts directly to IP addresses. If the Big Co. DNS received an inquiry for the IP address of ftp.bigco.com, it would use the A record shown here to resolve that inquiry. Obviously, the IP address in the record would have to be correct, but that's where the DNS administrator's typing skills come into play. Sometimes the DNS can create A records from information given to it by a DHCP server, which assigns IP addresses to hosts, which update A records automatically.

MX Records

An MX record is a special type of A record, in that it points to a Mail Exchange host or a mail gateway. That is, a system that is sending e-mail to a network through a general address must be able to identify an e-mail gateway. The MX record identifies which host is the mail gateway, even though the exact name of the mail gateway host is not identified in the e-mail.

For example, all users at Big Co. may have e-mail addresses like jonesj@ bigco.com, helpdesk@bigco.com, or webmaster@bigco.com. The Big Co. external DNS, the zone file and resource records of which are depicted above, doesn't have a record for a host named bigco.com. It does have an MX record for a host named mailgate.bigco.com, with an IP address of 192.112.36.10. The host named mailgate is the mail gateway for the bigco.com domain, and the MX record identifies it as such.

When a mail system on the Internet has e-mail for any address at bigco.com, the SMTP client asks its local DNS for the mail exchanger for the bigco.com domain. The DNS resolver request traverses the DNS hierarchy and finds the DNS for the bigco.com domain. The DNS request isn't just for any host that is named bigco.com—for which there is no resource record at all—but for the mail exchanger for the bigco.com domain. After all, it's e-mail because it originates from an SMTP client, so the DNS request includes a link to the higher-level application protocol that originated the request. For that type of request, the bigco.com DNS has an MX record for the host named mailgate.bigco.com. The bigco.com DNS returns that address to the DNS that originated the request, so the mail can be directed to the correct host.

The big advantage of MX records is that they help simplify e-mail addressing by offering a single point through which all e-mail for an entire organization can be accepted. The downside of the MX record is that a single mail gateway for an entire organization can be a single point of failure. Organizations with large mail systems can set up a DNS with multiple MX records, each of which points to a different e-mail gateway, and distribute mail among them. Other organizations use a single MX record and set up a load distribution system behind that host to distribute e-mail-handling chores.

CNAME Records

Sometimes hosts are known by one or more alternate names or aliases. The CNAME record lets the DNS administrator set up aliases for the same host. CNAME stands for *canonical name*, which means that it is an official, approved alternate name for the host. CNAME records don't have IP addresses in them. Instead, they list the alias and then the "real" host name. This also means that there must be an original A record for the host. If there weren't, the DNS would not be able to refer back to another record to get the IP address of the host.

Another way to identify aliases for a host is to use more than one A record for the same host. CNAME records are preferable, if only because they clearly identify aliases or alternate names for hosts, with the A record establishing a single master record in the zone file for the host's real identity.

NS Records

The *Name Service* (NS) records point to DNS services for a domain, typically another domain. The purpose of this is usually to identify another authoritative DNS for that domain. In the preceding example, the NS record identifies the host ns1.bigco.com as the DNS for the bigco.com domain. That's not how NS records are usually used, but it's listed as such in the sample zone file as an example.

More typically, there may be other name servers that provide DNS services for the domain. The other DNSs don't have to be located in the same domain that they serve. They can be anywhere as long as there are NS records that point to them.

PTR Records

A server that receives a request for a file transfer or for a Web page may want to determine the name of the host that originated the request. IP datagrams usually don't carry host names, only IP addresses. There is another DNS record type that matches IP addresses back to host names, the *Pointer Record*, or PTR record.

All of the other records we've mentioned map names to IP addresses, called *forward lookups*. Pointer records reverse this process, so they do *reverse lookups*. The format of a PTR record for the ftp.bigco.com host would be as follows:

    192.112.36.3   IN   PTR   ftp.bigco.com

There's a lot more to PTR records than we have indicated here, but we won't go into extensive detail about reverse address lookup. PTR records go in their own special zone file, called an in-addr.arpa zone file, that uses its own special way of indicating IP addresses. Suffice it to say that if a server receives a request from an IP address and wants to know something about the identity of that host, it must do a reverse address lookup on the IP address to be able to tell something about it. The reverse lookup zone file must be on a DNS for those addresses to be resolved to host names.

The traceroute program, for example, does reverse lookups on the IP addresses of ports it hits as it traverses the route from source to destination. Some of these IP addresses map back to host addresses, and some do not. Those that do, and that can be reverse-resolved, may show up as a host name on a traceroute result.

SOA Records

The first record in a zone file is the *Start of Authority* (SOA) record. It's considered a DNS resource record, but the SOA indicates administrative information about the zone file. For example, the SOA includes a timestamp, or *freshness date* for the zone file, a unique identifying number of the version of the file, an expiration date, and other administrative information. Backup, or secondary, DNSs read the SOA to determine if they have the most current version of the zone file. The SOA may also include the e-mail address of the DNS administrator to identify a real person who is responsible for the DNS zone.

Other Zone Files in the DNS

The DNS may have a number of zone files, each of which belongs to a different second-level domain or a different subdomain of each second-level domain. For example, the Big Co. DNS may have one zone file for hosts in the bigco.com domain and another for the hosts in the sales.bigco.com domain. The Big Co. DNS could also serve as the DNS for the Big Co. subsidiary, Medium Co., or for other organizations that aren't even related to Big Co. at all.

For example, let's say that Big Co. has a wholly owned subsidiary, Medium Co., which operates the mediumco.com domain. Medium Co. doesn't have its own DNS because Big Co.'s IT department controls the networks of all Big Co. subsidiaries. Big Co. has established a zone file for the mediumco.com domain in the Big Co. primary DNS, ns1.bigco.com. In the Internet's TLD DNS servers, the primary name server listed for the mediumco.com domain is the bigco.com DNS (ns1.bigco.com) because it answers for requests to resolve mediumco.com inquiries. An ISP's DNS servers typically host the DNS zone files for a number of their customers who don't have the resources or the desire to support their own DNS services.

Zone File Transfers

Each primary DNS should have at least one secondary, or backup, DNS for each zone it hosts. Periodically, a secondary DNS contacts the primary DNS and copies the zone files for the zones for which it is a secondary. The secondary checks the version number of the zone file in the SOA to determine if the information in the zone file has changed since it last copied the file. It also checks the freshness date to see if it is time for it to take a new copy. The secondary uses a DNS version of a file transfer protocol to copy the zone file. Copying a zone file is called a *zone transfer*.

As you might have surmised, a secondary isn't necessarily a backup DNS for all of the zones in a primary DNS. A secondary DNS might take copies of only the zone files for which it is a secondary and ignore the other zone files. It's quite all right to do that because DNSs are organized in any way that is convenient for the DNS administrator. There may be a number of secondary DNSs, which might act as secondaries for a number of other DNSs.

NAT Implications for DNS Zone Files

What does all of this mean for NAT? Remember that DNS services don't know about NAT. The addresses in the zone files may be correct only if traffic doesn't go through a NAT box. For example, a DNS behind a NAT box may give out an IP address that is valid for a host on a private addressing realm but not anywhere else. One of the challenges of running NAT is to get DNS services to work correctly because DNS information may be correct as long as you're behind the NAT box, but not anywhere else.

Some of the problems that NAT may introduce to DNS services are the following:

Inconsistent DNS results. Let's say the bigco.com DNS services were split because the company used private addressing on its internal networks and translated those addresses to public addresses on a firewall running NAT. The inside DNS zone files would map host names to private network addresses, which would be correct, routable addresses, but only on the inside networks. Those addresses wouldn't be routable anywhere else but on the private network. If the outside DNS were to resolve an address on the inside DNS, say for ftpinside.bigco.com, the inside, private address would not do an outside client any good.

Routing between overlapping networks. As we have already noted, one of the reasons for using NAT is that some networks use overlapping public addresses, which are public addresses that are in use on other networks. The problem is that an address resolved on a network that uses overlapping addresses will be a routable, public address. Traffic sent to that address might find its way to another network that uses that address range, and not the intended network. This is another case of the addresses on a DNS on an inside network not being reachable from another network. The reason is not because they're private, unroutable addresses, but because they're routable addresses for which there isn't a valid route from anywhere else on the Internet.

Embedded addresses in DNS replies. As we have already noted, DNS services don't know about NAT, so DNS services assume that the addresses in their resource records are correct IP addresses. We live in such a troubled world, so it's reassuring that DNS has such confidence in the accuracy of its resource records. The resource records for hosts behind a firewall might specify the IP address of the external interface of the firewall or NAT device, however, not the real address of the host behind it. That might be fine for most applications, but there may be some that need the real, translated IP address, which depends on the address NAT uses. It's possible to configure NAT with an application-level gateway (ALG) that knows this and that can modify the answer returned by the DNS on the fly. As we noted in the previous chapter on applications and NAT, ALGs aren't widely available, and those that exist can have an unacceptable effect on performance.

Zone file transfers through firewalls. Secondary DNS services that back up primary DNS zones copy files through the DNS zone transfer mechanism. In many cases, though, NAT runs on firewalls. If the primary DNS and its secondary are separated by a firewall—even if it isn't running NAT—the firewall may not permit DNS zone transfers through it. The reason is that a DNS zone transfer is an easy way for an intruder to determine what systems are on a network. Consequently, many firewalls, by default, do not allow DNS zone transfers unless they are specifically permitted by the firewall rulesets or configuration.

Summary

DNS is one of those "background services" that makes the Internet seem to run by itself. IT executives and managers in general, and DNS administrators in particular, know that little of the magic of the Internet, or any other network, for that matter, occurs automatically. If anything, NAT is one of those things that can affect the illusion of automatic networking most severely. The problem that the combination of NAT and DNS introduces is that NAT can cause DNS to give out addressing information that is correct only from within a specific network and nowhere else.

There's no easy solution to the problem. One solution is to partition DNS services so they give out DNS answers only to specific addressing realms where their answers will be correct. A second solution is to have NAT change the answer to a DNS inquiry because only NAT has the address manipulations it does. One of the solutions is to run a DNS *application-level gateway* (ALG), which will change the addresses in DNS records to reflect the address translation done by NAT. As with any kind of manipulation, there is a performance cost to a DNS ALG, so the simplest solution might be not to do address translation at all.

In the next chapter, we will examine public and private addressing, which is one of the issues that affects DNS. It's also one of the reasons why NAT exists. Private addressing is one of the solutions to the IP address exhaustion problem, and it gives network administrators a great deal of flexibility in configuring networks. It is also the source of a number of complications in networking that affect DNS and Internet routing in general.

CHAPTER

9

Public and Private Addressing

One of the primary justifications for using NAT is that the networks behind it use private addressing. That is, the addresses those networks use are valid only on that network and not on any other network. They are valid, dotted-decimal IP addresses, but they're not necessarily unique. They may be repeated on other networks, either within the same organization or company or anywhere else on the Internet. In fact, most of the private network addresses are repeated elsewhere on the Internet.

The original idea for private addressing was to allow for networks that were truly private, or not connected to any other network. Many of those networks were established with private network addresses, then later connected to public networks. The original network addressing was left intact, even though the private addresses were not routable on other public networks.

NAT makes it possible for networks to use private addressing, yet still connect to the Internet. Without NAT, or something equivalent to it, private networks would be left talking only to other devices on those networks, not to any other. Given the necessity and importance of Internet connectivity today, isolating networks that use private addressing is no longer a feasible course for many IT organizations to sustain.

An Interface, Not a Host

Every device in the Internet needs an IP address, one of those four-part, dotted-decimal numbers that identifies it uniquely from any other device. Computers that have IP addresses are referred to generically as "hosts," although a host computer could be a PC, a Unix workstation, a Windows NT server, or an IBM mainframe. In the future, it could be a Nintendo game console, a specialized e-mail and Internet access appliance, or anything else connected to any network or to the Internet.

IP addresses are assigned to things that are referred to as "hosts," but the one-computer-to-one-IP-address concept isn't really correct. Instead, IP addresses are assigned to network interfaces, which are usually synonymous with physical network connections. Most computers, such as users' PCs, have only one physical network connection, such as to a *local area network* (LAN). That connection is assigned an IP address, which is the address of the computer, or the host, on that network.

Some computers have more than one network interface, each of which is assigned a different IP address. Servers or multiuser computers may be connected to more than one network. If so, each network interface may be assigned a different IP address to identify it as a host on that network. Traffic addressed to the host addresses maintained by a single physical computer must be delivered to the appropriate network interface.

Specialized computers, such as routers or firewalls, may have several network interfaces, each of which is assigned a different host IP address on each of the respective networks. A router with eight active serial or Ethernet ports will have at least eight different IP addresses, one for each network interface. Devices that serve different types of functions, such as a firewall that acts as a *virtual private network* (VPN) gateway, may have a single host (interface) address and one or more additional virtual addresses that it uses to complete VPNs.

Consequently, even though we might refer to an IP addresses as a "host address," it's really an "interface address," and there may be more than one IP address on a specific interface. Even PCs actually have two IP addresses assigned to each physical interface. The first will be its address on the LAN, and the second will be a special host address for testing the interface, 127.0.0.1, called the *loopback address*. Routers may have a number of addresses assigned to each physical interface.

Much of the confusion over hosts, IP addresses, and interfaces is rooted in the historical definition of a host computer. Traditionally, referring to just any old computer as a host computer wasn't as common as it is today. Originally, a host computer was a multiuser system, such as an IBM mainframe, which served tens, hundreds, or thousands of users connected to it through dumb terminals. It could also have been a smaller version of the mainframe, a minicomputer, which supported a smaller group of users, still on dumb terminals. The big computer *hosted* the terminals, so it was referred to as the *host*. The host was the only device connected to the network, so it was the only system with an IP address.

As computers became less expensive and more powerful, those dumb terminals were swapped out for PCs that could run their own applications, and the PCs were connected to the network, too. When each PC was attached to the network, it got an IP address, which was different from that of the host and from that of every other computer. Even though the PC or workstation no longer "hosted" anything but itself, the convention of referring to it as a host stuck because it was connected to the network and because it had an IP address.

As other devices were added to the network, they too needed IP addresses. And, following the established convention, they were referred to as hosts, even though they may not have been host computers either. Routers, which are the special-purpose computers that switch traffic around a network and the Internet, are assigned IP addresses, too. Router ports, which are network interfaces, are assigned host addresses, too. They're referred to as interface addresses because a router is really a collection of network interfaces.

Part of the tradition of referring to IP addresses as host addresses is due to the structure of IP addresses themselves. As we discussed in Chapter 1, "What's NAT?," there are two parts to an IP address—the network part and the host part. Hosts are either host computers—however you define a host— or network interfaces, but hosts are located on networks, which are also identified by the IP address. The host or network interface addresses belong to the address designations of IP addressing.

Classful and Classless Addresses

At one time, IP addresses were separated into different *classes* of addresses, each of which was to be deployed on networks of different sizes. That relatively rigid system of IP address classification has since been abandoned and replaced by a more flexible system of address designation, called *classless* addressing. Today, ISPs use classless addressing, and most Internet routing protocols understand classless addressing and refer to address *blocks* instead of addresses classes. If asked what type of addressing they use, many network administrators would say they have a Class B assigned to their networks or so many Class Cs, and so forth. Many network administrators think of their addresses as being classful, even if their ISPs and routers don't think in those terms any longer.

Classful Addressing

When the IP addressing structure was first defined in the later 1970s, there was only one type of IP address. At the time there weren't that many networks, and there weren't that many computers, either. The one-size-fits-all approach was shortly abandoned in favor of a system of address types, or classes, to fit different network structures. The idea was that it was likely that computing and networking were in a state of flux, and the IP addressing scheme had to accommodate whatever was to happen in the future.

There were many chefs in the kitchen when the system of IP addressing was devised, but if we were to name its inventors, we might specify the people whose names are on the relevant RFCs that describes the IP addressing system. The root RFC for the IP addressing system is RFC 791, authored by Jonathan Postel. Through his long involvement with Internet standardization and his editorship of the RFCs, Postel is considered one of the founding fathers of the Internet. Other people, such as Vint Cerf and Robert Kahn, also played important roles in defining TCP, IP, and other protocols, Internet addressing and routing, and other key parts of the Internet infrastructure.

The IP addressing system they devised had several types of IP addresses, referred to as address classes, to accommodate different types of computing and networking environments. The first networking environment was the one that existed in the late 1970s and early 1980s. At the time, there were, compared to today, just a few networks and relatively few computers. They devised the first class of addresses, the Class A addresses, which allowed for a relatively small number of networks, but a lot of computers on each of those networks.

For Class A addresses, Postel and Co. decided to use the first byte of a four-byte IP address to designate the network and the last three numbers to identify hosts on that network, as depicted in Figure 9.1.

To make the numbers fall into specific numeric ranges, they decided that the first bit of the first byte of all Class A addresses would be a 1. The first byte of any Class A address fell in the range from 1 through 127 and designated the IP networks 1.0.0.0 through 127.0.0.0. On each of the Class A network addresses,

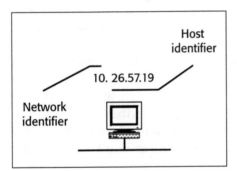

Figure 9.1   Class A address, indicating the network and host identifiers.

the second, third, and fourth bytes were used to number hosts within those networks. It's up to the network administrator to decide how to number hosts within any network address range. They may be numbered in any way the network administrator sees fit. It doesn't really matter how the host address ranges are used because Internet routers are concerned only with network identifiers to locate networks.

Postel and Co. devised a second class of addresses, the Class B address, to accommodate a different type of network environment. Class B addresses used the first two bytes of the IP address for the network number and the last two bytes for host numbers, as shown in Figure 9.2.

By convention, the first two bits of the first byte were always set at 10, so the first number of a Class B address always fell in the range from 128 through 191. With this addressing scheme, there could be more than 16,000 Class B addresses, each of which could have more than 65,000 hosts.

The third general-purpose address class was the Class C address to accommodate networking environments that were just starting to appear when the IP addressing scheme was devised. Class C addresses uses the first three bytes for the IP address for the network number and only the last, remaining, fourth byte for host addresses, as shown in Figure 9.3.

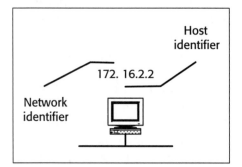

Figure 9.2   Class B address, indicating the network and host identifiers.

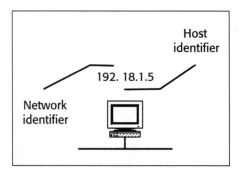

Figure 9.3   Class C address, indicating the network and host identifiers.

In order to force the first byte of Class C addresses into a specific range, the first three bits of the first byte of all Class C addresses was set at 110. The first number of any Class C address always fell in the range from 192 through 223. This addressing scheme allowed for more than 2 million Class C networks, but each of those networks could have no more than 254 hosts because hosts were numbered from a single eight-bit byte.

There were also two other classes of IP addresses, Class D and Class E, but neither was widely known, and only one of them was actually used. Class D addresses were designated for multicast networks, and Class D network addresses began with numbers from 224 through 247. Class E addresses were set aside as reserved addresses, to be used for research purposes.

Assigning Addresses

It's one thing to create address classes and another to put them into use. The original concept behind having different classes of addresses was to assign network addresses to organizations, companies, universities, the military, and to anyone else who needed IP addresses, according to their needs. Organizations that had big computer networks or that had established early computer networks were assigned Class A addresses. For example, the U.S. Department of Defense was assigned several Class A addresses for its communications networks. Stanford University, a pioneer in networks and computing, was assigned a Class A address, as were companies active in computing, such as IBM, AT&T, and Xerox.

Organizations that couldn't justify as large an address space as a Class A were assigned Class B network addresses. At first, it seemed that the Class C block, with room for no more than 255 hosts, wouldn't be that useful, but those were assigned to smaller networks. Over time, those small networks might grow into larger ones and need more Class Cs or even a Class B. As we will discuss in Chapter 12, "The Crisis in IP Addressing," those early address assignment policies were, in retrospect, profligate and led to today's real or imagined IP address crisis. NAT is one of the techniques that helps ameliorate this crisis, but it isn't a permanent solution to the problem.

Classless Addressing

The system of classful addresses worked fine, to a point. As long as the Internet was relatively small, composed of just a few thousand networks, the classful addressing system was suitable. Address were assigned whenever people, corporations, or organizations requested them. As the Internet grew, and as more and more of the classful addresses were used, several flaws in the classful addressing system became apparent. The problems were the following:

Inefficiency. Class A, B, and C addresses were easy to understand and use, but they were too large or too small to be used efficiently. A network that had more than 250 hosts was too big for a Class C network address, which allowed for 254 hosts, assuming it needed at least a little room to grow. The next larger size, a Class B, allowed for 65,536 hosts, which would be too much. The easiest thing to do was to assign the network a Class B network address. This worked, but it meant that, in this example, more than 65,250 host addresses would be wasted.

Request, not need. There seemed to be an almost limitless supply of addresses, so they were assigned to whoever requested them. Many address assignments were based on whatever the organization requested, which was not necessarily anything near what the organization needed. Many large corporations and organizations that were involved in the development of the early Internet were assigned Class A address spaces, whether they needed them or would ever use them.

Routing table expansion. As the Internet grew, so too did the number of separate networks that Internet routers had to list in their routing tables. If left to grow unchecked, these routing tables might grow to be too big for routers to handle.

The first solution to the address usage problem was subnetworking, which was first defined in RFC 950 in 1985. Subnetworking lets a local network administrator subdivide a network address into smaller parts, tailoring a larger address space into smaller parts. Since that time, it has been put to use extensively. At first, its objective was to give network administrators better control over their address space. Then, it was put to use to consolidate network references in IP routing tables.

One of the big advantages of subnetworks is that they aren't visible outside the organization's routing structure. For example, an organization that has the network address 140.49.0.0 may subnetwork it into a number of smaller networks, such as 140.49.1.0, 140.49.2.0, 140.49.3.0, and so forth. As far as the outside world is concerned, it's all network 140.49.0.0. Any subnetworking is invisible to Internet routers because it is only visible from within the organization's networks, not outside it. Even if the 140.49.0.0 network were to be subdivided into 255 subnetworks, Internet routers would have only one routing table entry instead of 255 separate entries.

Subnetworking introduces another level of hierarchy into the original division of an IP address into its network and host components. Subnetworking uses some of the bits that had originally been reserved for the host address for the network part of the address, making the number of bits reserved for the network part of the address longer than it's supposed to be. The customary way of indicating which bits belong to the network part of the address is the subnetwork *mask*. The mask is a dotted-decimal number that indicates the string of bits that are used for the subnetwork. It's actually just a string of bits, interpreted as a four-part dotted-decimal number. The network part of an IP address always comes first, so it's known as the *prefix*.

Another address conservation and routing simplification procedure, known as *Classless Inter-Domain Routing* (CIDR) described in RFCs 1518 and 1519, eliminated the distinction of *classful* addresses. Since the mid-1990s, the distinction of Class A, B, and C address classes has been eliminated. Instead, net-

---

SUBNETWORKS

The 10.0.0.0 address block is too large to be practical as a single network address space, so it is broken down into smaller blocks of address space called *subnetworks*. Each subnetwork is a part of the address block that is considered to be a network in its own right. As long as the routers in the network are configured to understand that the address space has been subdivided into subnetworks, network routing will work properly.

For example, the 10.0.0.0 address space is too large to be a single network, so a large organization may break it into a number of smaller subnetworks. The first three of the smaller subnetworks within the 10.0.0.0 address space might be these:

      10.1.0.0 – Host addresses 10.1.0.1 through 10.1.255.255
      10.2.0.0 – Host addresses 10.2.0.1 through 10.2.255.255
      10.3.0.0 – Host addresses 10.3.0.1 through 10.3.255.255

The network administrator may elect to carve a number of even smaller subnetworks from the same address space by using the first three bytes for a network identifier and only the last byte for host addresses. The first three of the smaller subnetworks in the 10.0.0.0 address space might be these:

      10.1.1.0 – Host addresses from 10.1.1.1 through 10.1.1.254
      10.1.2.0 – Host addresses from 10.1.2.1 through 10.1.2.254
      10.1.3.0 – Host addresses from 10.1.3.1 through 10.1.3.254

One of the reasons that subnetworking works is that routers at the entrance points to networks that have been subnetworked usually don't indicate that networks behind them have been divided into subnetworks. A router at the entrance point to a subnetworked network address will advertise to the outside world the whole address block. The router's internal configuration, however, will indicate to it through which interface the parts of the subnetworked address space are reachable.

work addresses are referred to with a slash prefix notation, indicating how the old classful address space is now subdivided.

For example, a Class C address, such as 192.168.1.0, had a 24-bit natural mask because the first three bytes (24 bits) were used for the network part of the address. The classless way of expressing this is to say that the network number is 192.168.1.0/24. A classful Class B address, such as 140.49.0.0, which uses a 16-bit natural mask, would be expressed as 140.49.0.0/16. If the 140.49.0.0 address space were to be subnetworked with a 24-bit mask, each of its subnetworks would be expressed as 140.49.1.0/24, 140.49.2.0/24, and so forth.

The "/24" at the end of the addresses is an expression of the length of the subnet mask. Today, the slash prefix notation is always included at the end of an address, whether it is a network or a host address. A network address would be expressed as 140.49.0.0/16, and the first host address in that network would be expressed as 140.49.0.1/16. It's also common practice to drop any trailing zeroes in a network address, shortening 140.49.0.0/16 to 140.49/16.

In modern routing protocol terminology, the slash prefix is called the *extended network prefix*. The prefix is simply a shorthand way to express the subnetwork mask, or the boundary on which a CIDR block has been defined. Modern routing protocols, such as *Open Shortest Path First* (OSPF) and the *Border Gateway protocol* (BGP) carry subnetwork masks, which actually indicate CIDR block ranges, as part of their routing announcements. Like expressing IP addresses as decimal numbers, the slash prefix notation is a human-readable accommodation. Modern routing protocols don't have an extra one-byte field in which they can carry the value of the prefix, so they carry the full 32-bit extended network prefix in routing information messages.

Public and Private Addresses

At first, all IP addresses were considered to be public addresses. This meant that networks that used them could be reached from any other network over a company or organization network, or over the ARPANET network. The ARPANET, a computer network established by the U.S. Defense Research Projects Agency, would eventually become what we know today as the Internet. The network didn't have dedicated routers. Instead, host computers, many of which ran the Unix operating system, functioned as routers, connecting smaller networks into the larger ARPANET.

At the same time, researchers also established a number of networks that were intended to be used for experimental purposes. These included networks that were used for testing new applications and developing new or improved communications protocols and new routing protocols. Some of these networks were isolated from other networks, including the ARPANET. A number of these "experimental" networks were also production networks, which were also connected to the ARPANET.

It's not such a good idea to mix experimental and production networks. Today, networking hardware and software are available for practically any type of system. In addition, networking hardware and software are relatively inexpensive to acquire and fairly simple to configure. In the early 1980s, networking was neither as easy or as inexpensive, nor were networking hardware and software so easy to acquire.

Many experimental networks weren't separate networks, but simply systems on other networks. The reason this isn't such a good idea is that sometimes traffic for experimental purposes, which may be harmful to other legitimate traffic, can become mixed with regular traffic. This can disrupt normal communications, corrupt data, or cause severe network errors. It's good operating practice to separate experimental traffic and operational traffic on different networks.

Unfortunately, creating a different network for that experimental traffic was sometimes easier said than done. A large number of those experimental, interconnected networks ran TCP/IP, so their hosts had IP addresses. One of the solutions that researchers on early networks developed to distinguish experimental traffic from operational traffic was to use specific IP addresses for experimental traffic.

Private Addressing Realms

The specific addresses that were adopted for use on isolated, experimental networks were referred to as private addresses. Private addresses are IP network addresses that have been set aside for use on isolated networks. Originally, private addresses were intended to be used only on those experimental networks. When NAT became a well-established networking technique, private network addresses could be used on any network, whether it was experimental or not. Then, when the Internet explosion occurred and demand for IP addresses began to threaten to exhaust the supply, private addresses started to be used for ordinary networks.

Both private and public addresses are IP addresses. They are all composed of four dotted-decimal octets, and they have extended network prefixes. When private addresses were defined in RFC 1918, they conformed to the normal rules of IP address classes, in that they fell into Class A, B, and C ranges. The only things that distinguishes private network addresses from public addresses are these:

Private address ranges. Private address space falls into specific address ranges that are set aside and recognized as private.

Routability on the Internet. Internet routers are usually configured to discard traffic to or from private addresses because traffic with private addresses isn't supposed to "escape" from an isolated network.

Just as Hester Prynne was forced to wear the mark of the scarlet "A," both of these characteristics serve as identifying marks on private addresses. They're intended to identify traffic that bears these addresses—either as source or destination IP addresses—as coming from or going to private address space. They're also the marks that make them unroutable by Internet routers, although there's nothing inherently wrong with them as IP addresses.

Private Address Ranges

So that private address space might be identified universally (or globally, we should say, until such time as the Internet reaches beyond our galaxy), specific network address ranges in the three classful IP address classes were set aside for use in private networks. Designating specific network addresses, instead of relying on filtering out experimental traffic, was a substantial improvement on the sometimes haphazard screening that was done before private address ranges were formalized.

The private address ranges are defined in RFC 1918, which sets aside the following address ranges for private networks:

- 10.0.0.0 through 10.255.255.255, also known as network 10.0.0.0/8; also expressed as 10/8.

- 172.16.0.0 through 172.31.255.255, also known as networks 172.16.0.0/16 through 172.31.0.0/16; also expressed as 172.16/12.

- 192.168.0.0 through 192.168.255.255, also known as networks 192.168.1.0/24 through 192.168.255.0/24; also expressed as 192.168/16.

10/8 Block Private Addresses

The 10/8 block encompasses the entire block of host addresses from 10.0.0.1 through 10.255.255.254. It's the biggest possible block of addresses, sufficient to number 16,777,216 hosts within the single address block.

As a practical matter, 16 million hosts is far more hosts than might ever appear on a single network. When the IP address system was designed in the late 1970s, Class A networks were created to accommodate networks that might grow to be very large, even by today's standards. In practice, public /8 network address blocks have been assigned to large corporations, universities, and military organizations, which have networks that are large enough to use this amount of space.

The 10/8 network address gives that same flexibility to any company or organization that wants a huge amount of address space but that can't justify 16 million hosts. Any organization can use any part of the 10/8 address space for any network, as long as it's isolated from other networks. That's where NAT comes in, to connect the private address space to the Internet's public address space. All addresses in the 10/8 space must be translated to public, routable addresses before they can be forwarded out of the network 10/8 space to the Internet, as illustrated in Figure 9.4.

The last host address in the 10.0.0.0 block, 10.255.255.255, is not a valid host address. The last address in the block, like the last host address in any address block, is a reserved address for broadcasting to all of the addresses in the block. It's a reserved address so that hosts will respond to broadcasts for the *Address Resolution Protocol* (ARP) and other networking utilities. Routers use ARP broadcasts to determine the host Ethernet address that corresponds to an IP address, so they need a broadcast utility to make this work. The standard "last host" broadcast address serves that purpose.

By common convention, another /8 address, 127.0.0.0/8, or 127/8, has been set aside, but it can't be used as private address space in the same sense as network 10/8. The host address 127.0.0.1/8 is a reserved address for local host loopback testing. It is a special address that hosts, PCs, servers, and other devices use to test whether their network interface cards can communicate with the IP protocol module. Even though it's the only address that is set aside within the 127/8 address block, the rest of the 127/8 address block is also a

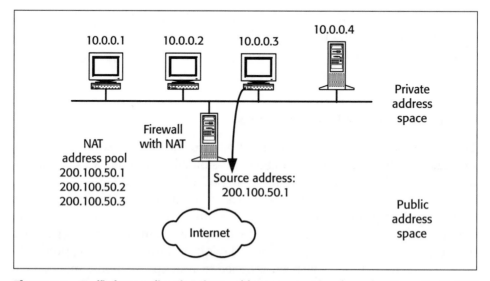

Figure 9.4 Traffic from a client in private address space going through a firewall with NAT to get to public address space.

reserved address block, and it can't be used as a regular, public network address.

172.16/12 Block Private Addresses

A set of sixteen /16 address blocks have been set aside by RFC 1918 as private address space. They are the networks from 172.1.16.0/16 through 172.31.0.0/16. Each of these networks may have 65,536 hosts on it, so there are more than a million possible host addresses (1,048,576, to be exact) within the reserved /16 address space. The block is expressed as a /12 block because the extended network prefix for the whole block of addresses is 12 bits long. Each individual network address has a network prefix 16 bits long, so each network has a /16 prefix.

As with the 10/8 address space, any network may be numbered from any part of the private 172.16/12 address space. Addresses from anywhere in that space are also deemed unroutable by Internet routers, so private 172.16/12 addresses must be translated by a NAT box at a network exit point to public, routable addresses in order to traverse the Internet or other public networks.

192.168/16 Block Private Addresses

In the last block of private address space, the 192.168/16 block, a total of 255 /24 networks numbered from 192.168.1.0/24 through 192.168.255.0/24 have been set aside as private address blocks. Each /24 network may have as many as 254 hosts, so 64,770 hosts may be numbered within this private address block. As with the other private address blocks, host address.255 is a broadcast address for each /24 network, so it can't be assigned as a host address. As with the other private address blocks, any network may be numbered from any of the /24 private address blocks, as long as those addresses are changed by a NAT box to routable, external addresses.

There's no reason either why a network can't use some combination of private addresses from all three private address ranges. Network administrators may find it easier to manage addresses from just one of the address blocks, but private address space is private address space, so it doesn't matter what private address blocks are used on an isolated network.

Aside from the complication of mixing public and private address space, there's also nothing wrong with an internal network using both public and private addresses, as shown in Figure 9.5.

Networks that mix public and private addresses may do so if the devices with private addresses talk only among themselves and not to anything outside the network. The addresses of hosts with public addresses, which communicate inside and outside the network, don't need NAT unless they're proxied or screened by a firewall for security or control purposes.

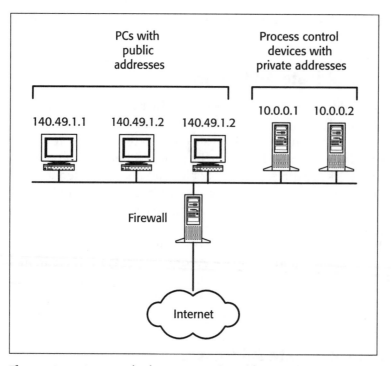

Figure 9.5 A network that uses 10/8 addresses for process control devices that communicate only among themselves and public addresses for PCs and servers that communicate with the Internet.

PRIVATE LINK-LEVEL NETWORK ADDRESSES

The *Internet Assigned Numbers Authority* (IANA) has set aside another private address block, the 169.254.0.0/16 block, which is reserved for use in isolated "link-level" networks. Microsoft Windows 98 and Windows 2000 servers use this special private address block to assign addresses on small networks that are isolated from other networks. Microsoft calls this *Automatic Private IP Addressing* (APIPA).

The assumption of APIPA is that a small network may have fewer than 100 hosts, although the address space allows for much larger networks. The idea of reserving this address block is to allow a network administrator to set up a small, isolated network, without having to get an address block from an ISP or from ARIN. The 169.254.0.0 block can be subnetworked into 255 /24 networks, each of which can have 254 hosts, so there's more than enough room for

Routers and Private Addresses

As a means to isolate networks that use private address blocks, Internet routers are usually configured to discard traffic that uses private addresses. This was the primary reason why NAT was invented, as a means to give hosts with private addresses access to outside networks.

The assumption that most routers make is that if they see traffic with private source or destination addresses, that traffic has unintentionally escaped from a private, experimental network. Private address traffic, therefore, may be harmful to other, legitimate traffic, so it should be discarded.

Routers may also be configured to route private network addresses. After all, the routers within a network that uses private addresses must be configured to route datagrams with private addresses. If private address routing were not allowed, all private networks would have to be flat, bridged networks, with no router links between networks.

The other complication of mixing private and public addresses on the same network is preventing the routers on the edges of the network from announcing the private address space to other networks. Unless they are restricted from doing so by the router configuration, routers will inform neighboring routers of the networks behind them. Private network address space shouldn't be advertised outside the private address space. The border routers on private networks must be configured to advertise only the public address space behind them (if there is any) and not the private space. Those same routers may be configured to accept inbound traffic for the private address space. That will work if there are hosts outside the private network that know about the hosts that use private addresses and if the external routers are configured to carry traffic addressed to those networks.

adding more subnetworks to the private network. Microsoft has embedded the 169.254.0.0/16 addresses in Windows 98 and Windows 2000 servers. Consequently, those servers can assign these addresses to network devices even if there isn't a DHCP server. It's just a way to provide network addresses automatically.

But isn't that what the reserved RFC 1918 private address blocks are for? Yes, the 169.254.0.0/16 addresses are reserved by IANA for private networks. They're not necessarily regarded as poisoned addresses by Internet routers, however, so traffic bearing those addresses won't necessarily be thrown away on the Internet. Many Windows 98 or Windows 2000 networks may be using these addresses. If these networks are ever connected to the Internet or to other networks, they need a NAT box to translate the 169.254.0.0/16 addresses into public, routable addresses.

Public Address Space

Private address space stands in isolation from public address space, which is anything in the rest of the IP address space. If private address space is for isolated networks, public address space is for everything else. That usually means networks that will be interconnected with other networks, such as the Internet, but it's also for any network, including private, experimental networks.

The only problem with public address space is that a network administrator must get it from an ISP or an organization that has it. Many networks may use the same private address space at the same time, but public address space must be unique. Consequently, it must be allocated and assigned by some organization that controls all of it, to prevent two networks from using the same public address space simultaneously. Internet routing may not work properly if the same addresses are advertised by networks in two different locations.

Public address space consists of any IP address that Internet routers will route. That is, it must fall within valid IP address limits, and it may not be any of the private addresses. Provided Internet routers know about networks in public address space, they will route traffic to those networks. How they know or learn about public address space in networks connected to the Internet is something that we will examine in the next chapter, "NAT and Routing."

ARIN and Address Assignment

RFC 1918 sets aside the private address space, but public address space is controlled by a not-for-profit corporation, the American Registry for Internet Numbers, or ARIN (www.arin.net). This organization, headquartered in the United States in Sterling, Virginia, assigns new (i.e., unique, not already used or assigned) IP address space to ISPs, corporations, universities, government agencies, and organizations that request it. It does so in order to assign unique, public addresses to new networks or to expand existing networks. ISPs get network addresses from ARIN to give to their customers, who use the addresses on their networks. ISP customers who run NAT use addresses they get from their ISPs as the external addresses to which they translate their internal network addresses.

Before ARIN was established, the cost of administering IP addresses was subsidized by the U.S. government, as part of its support of the InterNIC. ARIN is a self-supporting organization, so it charges fees for the address blocks it assigns to ISPs, corporations, and organizations. The cost for IP address space depends on the size of the address block. It's not so much that

IP addresses per se have value. Instead, the size of an address block corresponds to the amount of work that ARIN expects to have to do to register address subdelegations that ISPs assign to their customers. For example, in the spring of 2000, the cost of a new, unused /16 address block (65,536 hosts) was about $5,000 per year. ARIN must also maintain records on address space that was allocated before ARIN came into being, and the organization is contemplating charging maintenance fees for previously registered address space that was "grandfathered" into its database.

The Internet is a global network, so IP addresses must be unique everywhere. ARIN has responsibility for address assignment throughout the world. It has delegated that responsibility for some parts of the world, but ARIN has retained it for most of North America and South America, and for the Caribbean and sub-Sahara Africa. ARIN is also considering delegating address assignment authority to organizations in other countries and other parts of the world.

When it was created in 1997, ARIN maintained the delegation of address assignment authority to two other organizations, which had done this task before ARIN was established. It did so to maintain some regional control over address assignment and to make it easier for non-U.S. corporations, ISPs, and organizations to get public address space. For Europe, the Middle East, and northern Africa, responsibility for address assignment had been delegated to a European organization, Reseaux IP Europeean (RIPE), which is headquartered in Amsterdam. Responsibility for address assignment in much of the Pacific had been delegated to the Asia-Pacific NIC (APNIC), which is headquartered in Australia. APNIC's realm of responsibility includes most of the countries in Asia along the Pacific Rim, such as Japan, Korea, Taiwan, China, Hong Kong, and Singapore, as well as Australia and New Zealand.

Today, ARIN gets its authority over assigning IP address space from the *Internet Corporation for Assigned Names and Numbers* (ICANN). This organization was set up in 1998 by the U.S. government to assume responsibility for Internet governance from the U.S. Department of Commerce. The term *Internet governance* includes authority over IP address space, as well as Internet domain names, domain name trademark dispute resolution, the global, top-level DNS services, and other administrative powers over Internet infrastructure.

Transferring authority over Internet governance to ICANN was part of the U.S. government's exit from an active role in governing and running the Internet, to the extent to which the Internet could ever be governed or run. In the early 1990s, the *National Science Foundation* (NSF) had controlled many aspects of Internet governance. The NSF funded the operation of a number of organizations that supported the nascent Internet. These organizations included the *Internet Assigned Numbers Authority* (IANA), which controlled IP address space, and the InterNIC, then run by Network Solutions, Inc. (NSI), which assigned Internet domain names and ran the gTLD and TLD DNS servers.

As the Internet became more commercialized by the mid 1990s, NSF's management determined that a government agency like the NSF should not run what was to become a commercial entity. The NSF sought to transfer its authority over Internet governance to some other authority. To transition its authority to some other entity, the U.S. Department of Commerce assumed responsibility for managing the transition. The result was the formation of ICANN in 1998, although it took until late 1999 for ICANN to position itself to assume its new role.

Summary

In a perfect world, everyone would use public address space and be done with it. But perfect worlds exist only in the movies, and the movies haven't done a good job depicting the realities of the Internet, either. For reasons we've examined in this chapter, not every network needs or requires public address space. For one thing, experimental networks for which private address space was originally intended still exist. For another, private address space can give network managers or the IT organization a tremendous amount of flexibility in utilizing a vast expanse of addresses. Techniques like subnetworking allow network managers to tailor address space to their exact needs, and NAT devices on the network borders give as many devices as necessary connectivity to the Internet, or to whatever constitutes the outside world.

The issue for IT executives is whether the benefits of private addressing are worth some of the problems it may imply. For networks in flux, or for organizations that anticipate frequent changes in network connectivity, moving to different ISPs, or the turmoil of mergers and acquisitions, private addressing and NAT afford a measure of stability. A network with private addressing is a world unto itself, using NAT on firewalls or routers to screen itself from changes in external connectivity.

External connectivity is determined by the ranges of public addresses to which NAT translates private addresses, as well as how those addresses are advertised to other networks through routing advertisements. In the next chapter, we'll take a closer look at how NAT works with routing, to get a more complete picture of the role that NAT plays in the real networking world.

NAT and Routing

One of those things that always concerns the IT organization about NAT is whether it will affect the organization's connectivity to the Internet. Will it do some strange thing to routing, to cut off our networks' access to the Internet? Will NAT cause problems for us to get to our own, internal networks? Will NAT cause problems with our applications? What unknowns will NAT introduce to our networking environment?

These are legitimate questions and concerns. One of the roles of the IT organization is that of the organizational worry-wart, fretting constantly over all the strange things that may happen to the network. At the same time, the IT organization's job is to stay abreast and ahead of network technology, operations, and network management, so that it can operate the network reliably, efficiently, and effectively.

The short answer to the routing question is that NAT doesn't affect Internet routing, provided it has been configured correctly. One of the philosophical principles of NAT is that it breaks the normal end-to-end significance of IP addressing. When NAT is inserted in a network configuration, the source and destination IP addresses in the IP header no longer identify end-points in the network. Instead, those addresses may belong to intermediate NAT devices, not the end devices at all. And if NAT adds an element of deception about IP addresses, the thinking goes, might it not add an element of uncertainty about routing?

Just to make sure we've set the stage for the issue of NAT and routing, we should examine some common NAT configurations and look at how they affect routing. It may be more accurate to say that we will see if NAT affects routing and determine what to do about it.

To simplify a complex subject considerably, the basic principle of routing is that routers make routing decisions on IP datagrams, forwarding them to other routers for eventual delivery to their destinations. Routers usually don't have a complete picture of the exact location of a specific network. For most routers, there are too many networks to remember all of them, particularly in a huge network like the Internet.

Consequently, routers usually know about only a relatively small number of routers, forwarding datagrams for networks they don't know about to other routers. Presumably, these other routers, which are considered default routers by lesser-informed routers, know more about where a network is located. The assumption is that eventually the traffic will reach a router that definitely knows where the network is located and will deliver the datagrams to the destination.

Note that individual routers really don't know or care if the datagrams ever reach their destination. IP is a *connectionless* protocol, which means the IP protocol module in hosts or routers does not try to establish, or even determine if there is, a path or linkage to be established before sending the traffic. TCP, which is a *connection-oriented* protocol, establishes an end-to-end session before it ever sends any data. As for IP, each router just sends the data along to other routers, forwarding the IP datagrams in what it thinks is the right direction.

Routers and Routing Tables

The key to understanding how routers make these decisions is the routing table and how it works with route announcements. As we will see, NAT can affect routing because sometimes routes in front of or behind a NAT box have to be hidden, so as not to confuse routing. As for those routers, they determine the right direction by consulting their routing tables, which map networks to ports on the router.

Technically, a router uses the routing table to determine a *destination/next hop* association. This means that the routing table indicates to a router what is the best way to get traffic to a particular destination. The routing table specifies which neighboring router represents the best choice of a "next hop" to deliver traffic to a destination network.

A highly simplified version of a routing table, along with the networks reachable with that table, is depicted in Figure 10.1. This routing table, which

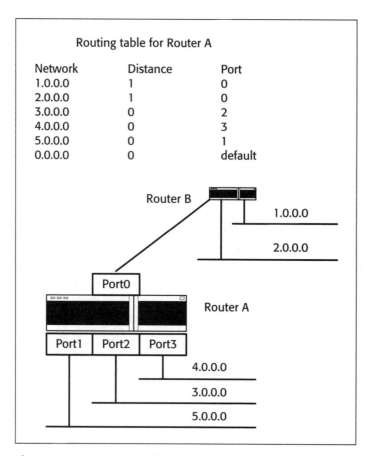

Routing table for Router A

Network	Distance	Port
1.0.0.0	1	0
2.0.0.0	1	0
3.0.0.0	0	2
4.0.0.0	0	3
5.0.0.0	0	1
0.0.0.0	0	default

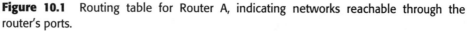

Figure 10.1 Routing table for Router A, indicating networks reachable through the router's ports.

has been pared down to illustrate the bare necessities of routing, shows only some of the information that might be in a real routing table.

Routers use the information in their routing tables to make routing decisions. For example, if the router received a datagram addressed to a host with an address on network 4.0.0.0/8, such as 4.0.0.1, the router would send the datagram out its port 3. The router doesn't keep any record of the traffic it handles unless it also screens traffic based on router administrator-specified screening criteria or on an *access control list* (ACL). The screening list and the ACL may specify IP host or network addresses on which the router must screen traffic, to block datagrams to or from those addresses.

Generally speaking, the entries in the routing table are created from two sources. First, the router administrator may create some of them. Second, they may come from other, neighboring routers, with which the router exchanges routing update messages. The reason there are two sources of routing table updates is that the router administrator may want to control how traffic is routed, by restricting how much a router learns about other networks from other routers.

Routing update messages from one router to another may consist of copies of entire routing tables or just updates of routing information. These updates may be based on changes in the connectivity the router sees to neighboring routers or on changes programmed into the router by the router administrator.

NAT and Routing

Routing tables reflect the connectivity that routers see to other networks. NAT changes the end-to-end significance of IP addresses, however, and it also changes the routability of networks and addresses behind the NAT box. For example, the networks on the inside network behind the NAT box may be numbered from private address space. If the NAT box is a router, the NAT box must not advertise the existence of those networks to outside routers. Traffic to those networks isn't routable on the Internet, so the router can't advertise the inside networks to other networks.

Instead, the router needs some group of public addresses, and a corresponding network address, that it can advertise to other routers. Figure 10.2 illustrates a simplified configuration of a network using private addresses, with a NAT box on its connection to the ISP. The NAT box advertises to the

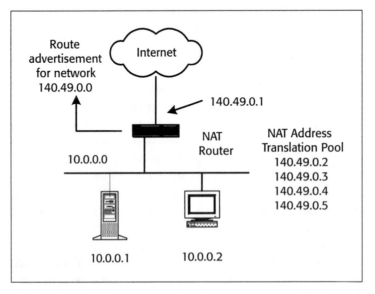

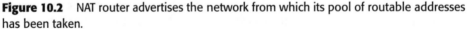

Figure 10.2 NAT router advertises the network from which its pool of routable addresses has been taken.

ISP's router that the 140.49.0.0/16 network is reachable through the NAT router. That network is only a pool of addresses that the NAT router uses for address translation purposes. They must be reachable over the Internet, so they must be advertised by the NAT router.

Numerous other configurations for NAT and route advertisements are possible, but a simple principle still applies: The networks that the outside addresses that the NAT box uses for address translation must be advertised to other networks outside the NAT box. Conversely, as we will see in the next section on NAT and multihoming, the NAT box may have to advertise only a few networks to the inside network in order to maintain the NAT charade.

Multihoming and NAT

Most Internet connection scenarios, including most of the ones presented so far in this book, make a key assumption. This assumption may not be correct. In fact, many networks aren't connected to the Internet under this simple assumption. The real world is much too messy for that.

The assumption is that most networks have only a single connection to the Internet, or to other networks, through which all traffic flows. We've made that assumption primarily because it is simple, and complicated topics like NAT, network routing, and firewalls are far easier to explain, understand, and illustrate in relatively simple scenarios. This hasn't been misleading, though, because many companies and organizations have only one connection to the Internet. The simplicity of a single ISP connection is not its only attraction. A single connection is also less expensive than multiple connections, and it's easier to secure. Given the cost of firewalls, intrusion detection devices, and network security software, not to mention the expense of maintaining and operating them, a single connection makes a lot of economic and operational sense.

Large organizations, particularly ones with several networks in different locations, may have more than one Internet connection. Their Internet access needs may be so great or so varied that it makes sense to do so, and they may often have the money to afford multiple Internet connections and multiple firewalls and security systems. Networks that have more than one Internet connection are called *multihomed* networks. A network with a single connection to the Internet or to another network is referred to as a *single-homed* network.

One of the benefits of a single-homed connection is that it's also the simplest and most straightforward situation in which to do NAT. A single entry and exit point simplifies the task of a NAT box because the single NAT box controls all address translation. As we will see, adding other network connections and managing NAT, not to mention routing, among several connections can be a serious challenge.

Reasons for Multihoming

If one Internet connection is good, two Internet connections must be better, right? This is not necessarily true, but there are a number of reasons why an organization might want to be multihomed to the Internet or to another network.

Reliability

A second connection increases the reliability of network connectivity. If the first connection fails, or if it becomes overloaded or congested, traffic may be able to flow through the second connection. Multiple connections may also be configured to give networks spare Internet access capacity that can be used as a shock absorber at times of heavy Internet use.

Multihomed networks don't necessarily have the same amount of bandwidth on each Internet connection. If one of the Internet connections is a backup to a primary ISP connection, the bandwidth of the secondary connection may be substantially less than that of the primary connection. Still, a second backup connection, even one with less capacity than the primary connection, increases Internet access reliability more than a single connection.

Diversity

Even though a lot of companies don't do this, it's a good idea to get Internet access for a second or third Internet connection from different ISPs. This is another aspect of the reliability argument because an outage in one network usually doesn't affect service on another provider's network. Diversity also means diverse routing, so that an outage at one location doesn't affect all connections. A company or organization may have two Internet connections, even to different ISPs, that both terminate in the same building or data center. The local loops that feed both connections may run through the same local telephone company *Central Office* (CO). Both connections could be knocked out if anything happens to the CO or to any common facility that both connections share.

Load Balancing

While this may be easier said than done, many companies try to distribute Internet traffic across different Internet access circuits, in order to balance the load across several connections. For reasons we will discuss in this chapter, that can be difficult to control because it depends on router configurations to work properly. The network manager may be able to control internal network routing to distribute the load on outbound network traffic. The network manager usually has no control over how Internet routing works, so inbound Internet traffic can't necessarily be balanced effectively across multiple Internet access points. Furthermore, it's difficult to get even one ISP to listen to routing announcements in such a way that it can support incoming load balancing, even if it is the only ISP providing Internet connections. Getting two ISPs to do it, and to coordinate their efforts so that it actually works, may be asking for too much.

Geographical Access

If a company or organization network spans a large geographical area, it may make sense to have Internet access points that serve users in different parts of the country or the world. For example, a company with offices in New York and London would probably want Internet access in both locations. First, it makes sense to do so, and second, it reduces the load on the internal network. If there were only one Internet access point in New York, all Internet traffic to or from London would have to be backhauled across the internal network's London-to-New York link to get to the ISP connection in New York. That might require a more expensive, high-bandwidth international circuit for backhauled traffic.

In any case, distributing access across several Internet access points is another dimension of the load-balancing problem discussed in the previous section. Geographical or multihomed load distribution depends on the ISPs' willingness and abilities to support it. Furthermore, once traffic reaches the Internet, the ISPs are powerless to determine how responses come back to them. Traffic sent out one Internet connection may return via another. It's controlled by Internet routing, over which an individual ISP may have little or no control.

Restrictive versus Permissive Access

A company or organization may have multiple Internet connections because it allows local variations in access controls, restrictions, and permissions. For example, the company's security policy may allow users at the company's headquarters unrestricted access to the Internet. At local branch offices or at offices that house a call or customer service center, access may be more restricted. If a firewall or screening router controls Internet access, it's a lot easier to control access permissions separately at each Internet access point. There may also be local proxy servers that intercept outbound Internet connection requests. While there's no requirement for a proxy server to access a local Internet connection, it's more efficient if it does so, to avoid backhauling traffic to a distant Internet access point.

There are also a number of drawbacks to multihoming, but some of these may not be obvious at first.

Cost

Internet access, particularly on a high-speed T-1 or T-3 connection, can be costly enough by itself, let alone doubling or tripling the cost by adding more connections. One of the roles of the IT organization is to justify IT expenditures by validating the benefits. The cost of multiple Internet connections may not be a consideration for users, but it's definitely an issue that IT executives must face in managing IT budgets and justifying expenses.

Multiple ISPs and Routing

Internal and external routing can be much more complicated in multihomed networks. Not only must routing from within the enterprise be controlled more carefully, but the ISPs must also control routing from the Internet or other networks into the enterprise. If network and Internet routing aren't managed carefully, it may be that effort to balance the load of Internet connections across two or more different Internet access points really doesn't work. Routers may decide that one of the Internet access points is better than the other. Unless network routing and external and internal route advertisements are carefully controlled, it's possible that most Internet traffic will flow through one connection, instead of being balanced across several connections.

Unbalanced Access Bandwidth

If the bandwidth of each Internet access point is different, and if internal and external routing aren't controlled carefully, multiple connections may perform differently, depending on how Internet traffic flows through them. This can be a problem if, for routing reasons, most Internet traffic may go through a lower-bandwidth connection, rather than a high-bandwidth path.

Usually, the benefits of multihoming outweigh its disadvantages. Companies and organizations that depend heavily on Internet access, particularly those that run operations online, must have multiple Internet connections.

Implementing NAT and Multihoming

Multihoming by itself is a routing issue, but frequently other networking issues become intertwined with it. For example, multihoming often complicates the addressing scheme used in a network. In addition, multihoming can make routing on the Internet more complex, as it can make it more difficult for the routes in a network to be aggregated at a network border. As we have noted, one of the objectives of multihoming may be to balance the flow of traffic over two or more network connections. The routers in a multihomed network may be able to control how outbound traffic flows into the Internet, but it may be difficult for them to control how return traffic from the Internet is routed back into the network.

RFC 2260 describes a multihoming configuration that addresses these issues. One of the drawbacks of the RFC 2260 configuration is that it may require renumbering, or changing the IP address, of the network if the organization switches ISPs. Part of the network may have also to be renumbered when the network switches from single to multiple homing.

About a year later, researchers at Cisco published a proposed solution to these problems. Their solution used NAT at each of the multihomed network access points as a means to resolve both of these problems. In the Cisco solution, NAT on each of the multihomed access points shielded the inside network from having to be renumbered, either if the organization changed ISPs, or if it went to a multihoming configuration. It also gave the organization better control over internal network routing.

NAT Multihoming

This NAT multihoming solution uses four different address ranges to control routing within the network, and how addresses appear on the outside network, which is the Internet or some other public network. On each NAT box at each network access point, the network administrator builds an address translation table that specifies how the addresses are to be translated. With four address ranges in use, one of the conditions of this configuration is that the NAT box must translate both the source and the destination addresses of IP datagrams, so that the addresses that are known inside the network are translated to their corresponding outside addresses.

Another condition is that the NAT box be a router so that it can act as the network's border router, connecting the network to the ISP's network. Another assumption is that the NAT router is an External BGP (EBGP) peering session with one or more of the ISP's routers, as well as *Internal BGP* (IBGP) peering sessions with other NAT border routers. For the sake of simplicity, we'll refer to the NAT box, which is also a router, as the *NAT router*.

Let's assume that we have a relatively simple multihomed network, such as the one depicted in Figure 10.3. Note that there are two ISP connections, to two different ISPs, each of which is controlled by a NAT router.

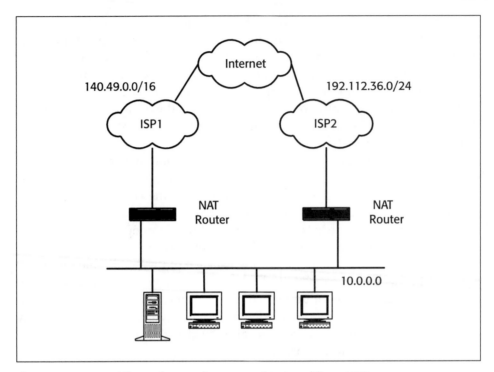

Figure 10.3 A multihomed network connected to two different ISPs.

Four types of addresses are used in this configuration, which are depicted in Figure 10.4. They are as follows:

Inside Local addresses (IL). Hosts on the inside network are given addresses from a public or a private address range. These addresses are the ones by which hosts inside the network are known to each other. In a typical NAT environment, the inside local addresses might be private addresses, such as those from the reserved 10.0.0.0 private address block.

Inside Global addresses (IG). So that they are reachable from the Internet, hosts inside the network are also assigned routable, public addresses. This address space typically comes from the ISP, which assigns routable network addresses to its customers. However, those addresses are known to the NAT router, not to the inside network hosts. The NAT router uses these addresses as a NAT pool to assign to inside addresses it translates to outside addresses.

Outside Local addresses (OL). The NAT router has a group of addresses that it advertises back into the inside network. Outside hosts on the Internet will appear to have these addresses because these will be the trans-

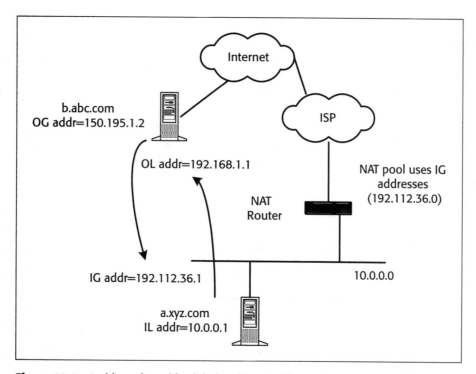

Figure 10.4   Inside and outside global and local address advertisements by a multihomed router.

lated addresses of hosts on the Internet, as they appear to hosts on the inside network. They are the addresses by which inside hosts address outside hosts, but the NAT router will translate them to their outside global equivalents.

Outside Global addresses (OG). Hosts on the Internet will really have their own unique addresses, called the outside global addresses. Internet hosts' real, outside global addresses will be translated to outside local addresses by the NAT router, in order to control routing within the inside network.

All of these address ranges are necessary in part because of NAT and in part because of the need to isolate the inside and outside address spaces from each other. By isolating the two from each other, the inside addresses don't have to change if the outside addresses change, should the ISP change.

These address ranges will control how inside hosts communicate with outside hosts because they will direct traffic to and from NAT routers on one ISP interface or the other. Because traffic will be directed to one NAT router or another, traffic flow to and from the Internet will be directed in and out one ISP connection or the other because each will have its own address translation table for the traffic it will handle.

To see how the address translation will work at the NAT routers in a multi-homed configuration, let's look at how one of them works. We will also note, where appropriate, any differences in how the second router would operate. We'll also focus on only the address translation part of the problem. There are a number of other issues that the network managers must also consider to make this multihoming configuration work, such as translating DNS response addresses and routing to and from the different ISPs, all of which are covered in extensive detail in the Cisco documentation. We will focus on the NAT issues, though, and touch only briefly on the DNS and routing issues.

The NAT Table

Each NAT router needs a special address translation table, which it will use to determine how to translate inside addresses to outside addresses, and vice-versa. If they use dynamic addressing, the address translation tables in each NAT router will have to be synchronized. Otherwise, they'll have to use static addressing. As a practical matter, static mapping may be the only workable option, so that each NAT router is responsible for only specific addresses.

There are two types of entries in the address translation table. The first is for inside address translation, and the second is for outside address translation. There are two components for each type of entry, a local address and a global address. In our example, the local addresses will be private addresses, which are unroutable on the Internet, and the global addresses will be public, routable addresses.

The first thing that the NAT router must do is build an address translation table entry for each inside and each outside host. It will need an address translation entry that matches the inside local address with the corresponding inside global address and the outside local address against the corresponding outside global address. Each NAT router will build its own translation table, using the NAT address ranges assigned to it.

Let's say that an inside host on the network behind the NAT box communicates with a host outside the NAT box, which is on the Internet. The datagrams will go through one ISP connection or the other. For inside-to-outside communications, which one the traffic goes through depends on which is identified as the inside host's default gateway. For outside-to-inside communications, it depends on whether the traffic is routed through the Internet to one ISP or the other.

Each NAT router must maintain static mapping between the inside and the outside addresses. Its address translation table will fix this mapping, but first, the entries for mapping inside hosts to outside addresses, or outside hosts to inside addresses, must be built by the NAT router. The NAT router may build an entry when it sees traffic from an inside host to an outside host, or vice-versa, or if it sees a DNS inquiry response.

The NAT router must also act as a DNS *application-level gateway* (ALG), translating external addresses to their internal or translated equivalents. By acting as a DNS ALG, the NAT router learns the real external addresses of Internet hosts. The DNS inquiry from an internal network host for the address of an external host address passes through the NAT router. The NAT router reads the response from the external DNS, which contains the external host's real IP address, and maps it back to one of the addresses in its internal address pool.

Translating Addresses

Let's say that the inside host sends datagrams for an application to an outside host. We'll call the former a.xyz.com and the latter b.abc.com. To focus on the address translation issue, we'll assume that A already knows B's IP address, through a previous DNS inquiry. The NAT router at one of the ISP connections has built an address translation table, to match the inside local and inside global addresses of A against the corresponding outside local and outside global addresses of B. The address translation table, depicted in Figure 10.5, illustrates the mapping of local and global addresses on one of the ISP connections.

There are two sets of entries in the translation table. The first, which is the top table in Figure 10.5, maps the inside local address of the inside host, a.xyz.com, which is 10.0.0.1, to its outside local address, which is 192.168.1.1 Like the inside local address, the outside local address is also a private address. It is assigned by the NAT router from a pool of private addresses that it uses to represent outside hosts.

The second entry in the address translation table maps a second NAT pool address, the inside global address, against the real outside address of b.abc.com, which is the outside global address. In this case, the inside global address is a real, routable address, 192.112.36.1, taken from a pool of routable addresses assigned to the NAT router. The inside global addresses have been assigned to the organization that runs the NAT router and the network behind it by the ISP. The outside global address is the real address of the Internet host. In this example, the outside global address is 150.195.1.2.

When the NAT router receives the datagrams that A addresses to B, it must translate both the source and destination IP addresses before passing them to the Internet. A's datagrams will use the inside local address (10.0.0.1) as the source address and the outside local address (192.168.1.1) as the destination address. The NAT router takes both addresses, translates each to its corresponding inside global address (192.112.36.1) and outside global address (150.195.1.2) addresses, and passes them to the ISP for delivery. Both the inside and outside global addresses are public addresses, so when they are on the Internet, the datagrams have valid, routable addresses.

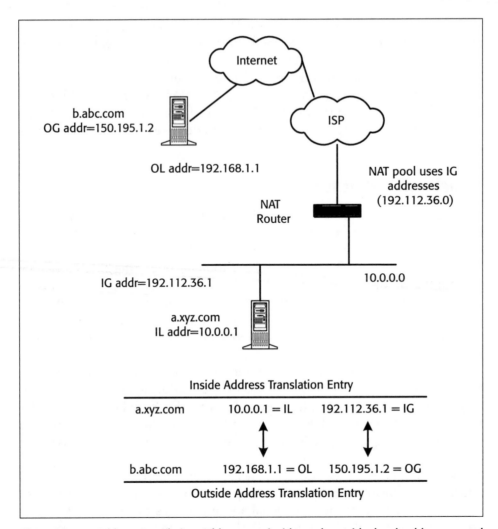

Figure 10.5 Address translation table maps inside and outside local addresses, and inside and outside global addresses, to each other.

When the NAT router receives the response from host B, it uses the same translation table entries to reverse the process. Host B will use the inside global address (192.112.36.1) as the destination address and its outside global address (150.195.1.2) as the source address. The NAT router will translate the inside global address to the original inside local address (10.0.0.1) and the outside global source address to the outside local address (192.168.1.1), then pass the data back into the inside network. Both of the translated addresses are private addresses, and they are routable on the inside network.

The NAT router translates addresses on traffic that originates on hosts on the outside network in exactly the same way. If B sends to A, B will use A's inside global address (192.112.36.1) as the destination address, and its outside global address (150.195.1.2) as the source address. Of course, host B won't have or need any knowledge of the inside global or outside global addresses because they're relevant only to the NAT router.

Is It Worth It?

Using NAT in the way described in this chapter is one way to insulate an organization's networks from changes in relationships with ISPs. In addition, it also avoids the thorny issue of renumbering the inside network, when or if the organization does decide to change ISPs. These are both worthwhile goals. The former gives the organization the flexibility to rearrange ISP relationships whenever necessary. The latter, renumbering, is the more problematic issue of the two. It's also the more expensive and time-consuming of the two problems, so it's also the one that network managers, not to mention IT executives who have to budget for these kinds of things, would like to avoid.

Multihoming with NAT doesn't happen without a price, and it can be a steep one, particularly when compared to regular NAT. First, it's much more complicated to manage any multipoint connections to multiple ISPs. Multiple connections to the same ISP are one thing, but multiple connections to more than one ISP are quite another. The routing and addressing issues can get to be quite complex, particularly when two or more ISPs have to make sure they announce each other's routes correctly to the Internet.

Second, the multihoming NAT router has a lot more to do. Except for internal route announcements to each other, different NAT routers in a multihomed network don't need to talk to each other. They can operate autonomously, which is good because they can each act as the internal gateway for a part of the internal network. That's bad, however, because they don't coordinate their efforts and learn from each other's translation tables. Furthermore, they can't necessarily serve as backup connections for each other because of their NAT-specific translation tables.

Then there are those translation tables, which must be created, with their static mappings between inside and outside local and global addresses. It's hard enough for the network administrator to understand what's happening, let alone the NAT router. At least the NAT router is a computer, which means it won't get sidetracked by all those other things the network administrator has to worry about.

Then there are the issues of how external and internal routing works in a multihomed environment and the magic of the DNS application-level gateway. Needless to say, there are plenty of complications to go around in a multihomed network—and plenty to go wrong. All of these are reasons why multihomed networks with NAT are relatively new, with configurations that are just being worked out.

Summary

Routing is the key to Internet and IP network communications. Even though all IP networks use routing, and routing is a widely practiced, well-understood technology, routing and addressing can be complicated and thorny issues, even in a single-homed network environment. Throw a second, independent ISP connection into the mix, and the routing and addressing complexities seem to escalate geometrically, rather than linearly.

This complexity is one of the reasons that network managers and IT executives should consider using NAT on multihomed network connections. As ever, NAT can complicate network configuration and routing issues, as well as inside and outside addressing. It can isolate the organization or company from depending on a single ISP or one that isn't performing properly. It is also an effective way to forestall problems with renumbering a network, either when going to a multihoming situation or when changing ISPs. In this chapter, we have ignored or given short shrift to several other complex issues that must be part of the solution, such as a DNS ALG and internal and external routing.

In the next chapter, we'll look at NAT as a solution to another networking problem, which is that of balancing traffic loads across several hosts or servers. As we will see, NAT is a handy and a workable solution that improves on previous efforts to control load sharing through passive means such as DNS. NAT isn't perfect as a load balancer, but it's a convenient and relatively efficient solution to another one of those network infrastructure problems.

Load Balancing and NAT

Many Internet sites that seem to be a single host, such as most of the heavily trafficked, popular Web sites, really aren't just a single computer. They are single sites in that they are identified by a single URL or identifier, such as www.xyz.com. They must handle so much traffic, or handle so many incoming and outgoing requests for mail exchange, FTP transactions, or Web page hits, that a single computer would be quickly overwhelmed.

Instead, many systems are actually a group of servers, which are known collectively by a single, external address. For example, www.xyz.com will be reachable through its single URL, and it may appear to be a single host. The reality might be that in order to handle the traffic to its online e-commerce widget-selling system, the XYZ Corporation needs three Web servers to handle the load. Instead of calling them www1.xyz.com, www2.xyz.com, and so forth, and forcing users to choose one server instead of another, the XYZ network administrator has created a load-sharing system. The system automatically spreads the load across the three servers while maintaining the appearance that there's just one host called www.xyz.com.

A number of techniques can be employed to create a load-balancing system. Several vendors produce load-balancing system hardware and software, while some networks rely on existing network utilities and infrastructure to do the load balancing. NAT is one of those network components that can be used to create a load-balancing system. Another is DNS, which can be configured to redirect traffic to the members of a pool of servers, to balance the load among them.

In this chapter, we'll look at load-balancing techniques and strategies, as well as the advantages and disadvantages of various load-balancing techniques. As you might expect, we'll also look at using NAT as a load-balancing technique. As we will see, NAT doesn't provide the same level of services as more comprehensive load-balancing systems, but it does work. Furthermore, NAT may already be part of the network infrastructure, and most load-balancing techniques involve some type of address translation or address substitution anyway.

Spreading the Wealth

Load sharing or load balancing isn't anything particularly new. The problem of spreading client requests for network services and applications across a number of servers has existed as long as there have been heavily used network services. For example, back in the mists of time, before the widespread use of the Web browser, FTP sites were among the most heavily used network servers. Instead of building a single, huge FTP system that could handle hundreds or thousands of simultaneous file download requests, many network administrators found it more practical to distribute the load across several systems.

In order to distribute applications or service request loads across several systems, network managers had to devise different methods to make it work. The first issue was making several systems appear to the outside world as one single system. That wasn't as much a load-sharing issue as it was an identity issue, which could be resolved through DNS. The problem is simple. If www.xyz.com, or ftp.xyz.com is really several host computers or several different servers, how do you let the world know that transparently?

Initially, the answer to the identity question lay in the Domain Name Service, DNS, which maps host names back to their corresponding IP addresses. Even if a Web site or an FTP server really isn't just one computer system but several, it's desirable that it appear as one site, referenced by a single name or URL. That makes it easy for clients to get to the site, as the actual number of hosts involved is irrelevant to clients. It also helps enforce the important site identity issue. There's only one www.xyz.com, not several, each known by a different URL.

The first DNS configurations that supported multiple hosts used multiple DNS A records, each of which used the same host name. Each host or system in the load-sharing pool has its own IP address. So, under this initial DNS approach, for a pool of three servers, there might be three A records in the

DNS, all listing the same host name, but each one would be mapped back to a different IP address.

This initial stab at load balancing worked, but how well it worked depended on how the client handled DNS responses. For example, the xyz.com DNS might have three separate A records for www.xyz.com and a different IP address in each record. A client inquiry for the IP address for www.xyz.com would return three different IP addresses, as illustrated in Figure 11.1.

Presumably, the content on each of the three servers would be the same, so it wouldn't matter too much which one the client decided to use as the destination IP address. In fact, in most cases, the client program wouldn't have made the decision or seen the variety of choices anyway because the selection would have been made by a local DNS resolver acting on behalf of the client. For the sake of simplicity, we'll refer to whatever makes a DNS request as the client, even though it might also be a DNS resolver. Technically, the DNS resolver is a client, but we'll ignore this fine point.

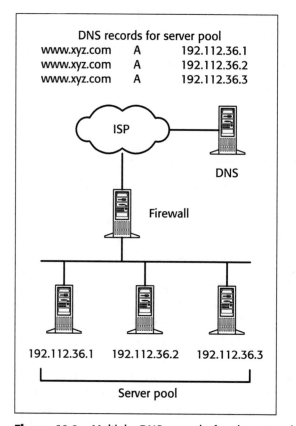

Figure 11.1 Multiple DNS records for the same host name pointing to different IP addresses.

This first load-sharing system worked, but only to a point. If there are multiple DNS records with the same host name in a specific DNS, it's common for that DNS to respond to an inquiry by sending all of the records that match the request. It's terrific that the DNS gives such a comprehensive response, but it makes certain assumptions about what the client that originated the inquiry will do with the answer.

The desired effect is that the client will choose one of the records and use the IP address in that record as the destination address for its application request. Each request from different clients will be filled with the same answers, and, at least theoretically, different clients will choose different records, spreading their responses more or less evenly across the group of three servers.

As is usually the case, the reality of this load-balancing scenario is not ideal. It depends on chance, and it depends on a distributed group of clients, who neither know nor care about what selections other clients make, to load balance by randomly selecting different DNS records. As a practical matter, most DNS resolvers that receive several different DNS A records in response to an inquiry will choose to use the first one and ignore the rest.

As a result, this first effort at load sharing or load balancing didn't really work too well. Even though there might be several DNS records for www.xyz.com, most all of the traffic might be directed at whichever A record was first. The rest of the servers might receive little or no traffic at all because their records were ignored by the clients.

Round-Robin DNS

Obviously, this first approach at load balancing through the DNS left too much to chance and depended on clients making load-balancing decisions, even if they didn't know they were supposed to do that. The second, more successful approach was still rooted in load balancing through DNS responses. This time, responsibility for making the selection of a specific server in the server or site pool was moved back to the DNS.

The new approach is called round-robin DNS, and it puts the responsibility for selecting different servers in a server pool back on the DNS. Round-robin DNS has been implemented in various ways, but the newer versions of the Unix DNS service (versions 8.x and above), Linux DNS services, and the Microsoft DNS Service all support round-robin DNS.

Round-robin DNS is simply a DNS capability that shuffles the order of the resource records returned to a DNS client. If the DNS service finds more than one resource record for a given host name in the zone file for the DNS zone, the DNS returns the responses in a different order each time it receives an inquiry. Presumably, the DNS inquiries originate at different DNS clients or resolvers, so successive inquiries get different lists of servers. They're all the same servers, but the order in which they appear in the DNS response is different each time. This technique redirects the traffic to a different server in the pool each time, as indicated in Figure 11.2.

For example, let's say there are three servers in the pool, and they are all identified by the host name www.xyz.com in the DNS zone file for the xyz.com. Each resource record lists a different IP address for each server, but that's OK because all three servers run copies of the same files. To the outside world, each one is www.xyz.com. In fact, each server could also have another name, a CNAME alias record, if it were a server for other services, such as FTP, Telnet, and so forth.

The DNS server for the xyz.com domain, which has been configured to run round-robin DNS, responds to each DNS inquiry for www.xyz.com by returning the three records in a different order. For example, in response to a first inquiry, the order might be 192.112.36.1, 192.112.36.2, and 192.112.36.3. In response to a second inquiry, the order might be 192.112.36.2, 192.112.36.3, and 192.112.36.1, and so forth. Even in a round-robin DNS, the order of the resource records in the DNS zone files doesn't change, only the order in which they are listed in the DNS server's response.

Note that DNS clients would still get all three records, so they would know about all three servers. The DNS server knows nothing about how the DNS client works, nor about how it would choose among several servers with the

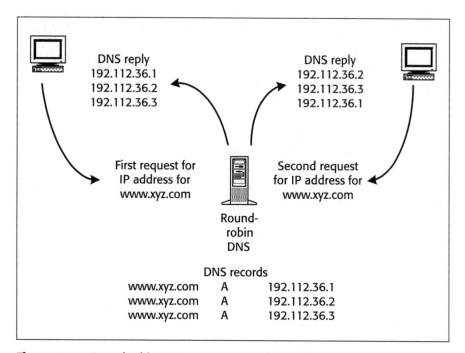

Figure 11.2   Round-robin DNS returns A records in a different order each time.

same host name. The DNS administrator's safest assumption is that even if a DNS client were given a choice of three servers, it would probably choose the first one returned anyway.

Round-robin DNS is a simple, low-overhead method of implementing a load-balancing scheme, but it does have its drawbacks. First, the DNS server has no positive control over what a DNS client will do with the responses, specifically if it will use the first record returned or select another one. The DNS server also doesn't know if a DNS resolver has cached a recent response for www.xyz.com and is reusing it repeatedly for subsequent inquiries for the Web site's IP address.

Taking It to the Border

As far as load balancing is concerned, round-robin DNS is a significant improvement over regular DNS name resolution. The round-robin DNS exerts at least some level of control over which server is the "preferred server," at least for that brief, shining moment when its record is at the top of the server list. What DNS clients or resolvers do with that list is another matter, as different DNS clients may be configured to use the DNS server's recommended order or any order the client has been configured to choose.

For load-balancing purposes, either round-robin or standard DNS will work with NAT, provided, of course, no IPsec encryption is being done on the data. Even if the network behind the NAT box uses private addressing, the NAT box can map whatever IP addresses appear in the DNS response back to their internal network equivalents. The NAT box must be configured to identify those addresses, and they must be externally-routable addresses in order for that traffic to get back to the external network interface.

For example, as shown in Figure 11.3, the NAT box may map an external address of 192.112.36.3 back to any internal address, such as 10.1.1.2. The assumption in this situation is that the network's external interface, be it a firewall, screening router, or NAT box, has been configured with those external addresses on it and that the network address space from which they have been taken is routable from the Internet.

The emphasis today is on network security and on hiding most or all internal network addresses behind one or a small number of IP addresses that are revealed to the outside world. Revealing the real internal addresses of servers in DNS inquiries may be contrary to company or organizational security policies and practices. Many companies have moved the task of selecting one server from a group of internal network servers away from the DNS server and back to the network entrance. The task can be done either by a NAT box or at a special traffic distributor or load-balancing system. The system may be

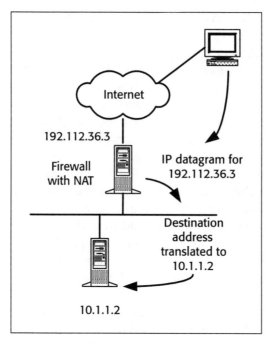

Figure 11.3   NAT device maps external addresses in DNS records back to internal network addresses.

considered an active or passive load-balancing system, depending on how much interaction it has with the servers in the pool.

On the Border

A NAT device falls into the category of a passive load balancer. It's considered a passive device because a NAT box that does load balancing usually doesn't have any contact with the systems over which it is balancing that load. In that sense, a NAT box or any passive load balancer isn't really a load balancer, but a traffic distributor. It distributes traffic to different devices, but it doesn't know anything about how much load is on any of them. Whether the load is balanced across several different servers is strictly a matter of chance, although there are techniques that can be used to make the selections less deterministic.

Like any NAT box, a NAT load balancer translates external addresses to internal addresses. The primary difference between the NAT load balancer and the DNS load balancer is that with the NAT load balancer, all of the IP addresses of the server in the server pool appear to be the same address. It's the external address of the NAT box. The NAT box knows the real, internal network addresses of the servers in the server pool and translates traffic to the external address sequentially to each server in the pool.

This means that no matter how many servers there are in the pool, they are all represented to the outside world as having the same IP address. The address is sometimes called a virtual server address because all of the servers are represented by the same address. It doesn't even have to be one of the real IP addresses of the servers in the pool. In fact, it usually isn't because it's the external address of the NAT box, through which all network traffic flows.

The NAT load balancer simplifies the DNS records for the zone on which the server pool is located. Instead of a different DNS resource record for each server, the DNS has only one resource record for the entire server pool. The host name in the record is that of the server, and the IP address is that of the external interface of the NAT box, not any one of the real pool servers. Remember that DNS doesn't really know or care where the real hosts are located, nor if their IP addresses are even remotely correct, as long as all of the records in a single zone file are actually in the same zone.

Internet clients direct traffic to any of the servers to the single virtual server address, as illustrated in Figure 11.4. The virtual server address is the only one

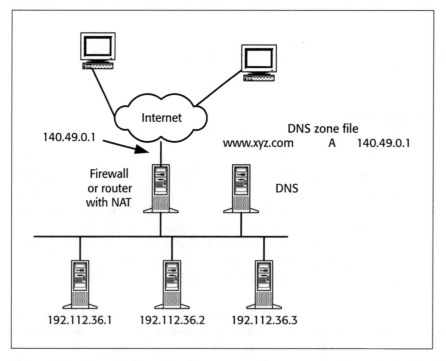

Figure 11.4 Many inside network servers may be represented by a single virtual server address.

visible to the outside world, which is usually the Internet. Unlike the situation with load balancing on a DNS server, hosts on the Internet have no idea how many hosts are really in the pool. DNS clients haven't a choice about which server in the pool to select, so the NAT load balancer improves the possibility that load balancing really will occur.

NAT as a Load Balancer

The operation of NAT as a load balancer is fairly simple and straightforward. The NAT box is configured with static mappings between the external interface address and the IP addresses of the servers in the server pool on the internal network. The NAT box translates traffic addressed to the single external interface to one of the internal pool server addresses, which remain hidden to external clients. Like the round-robin DNS, the NAT box rotates through the addresses of the pool servers, sending client requests sequentially to each server.

The NAT box must maintain the usual mapping of internal hosts to source and destination TCP ports. Responses from the internal pool servers will all be addressed back to the internal network interface of the NAT box. The source addresses of the responses will be the addresses of the pool servers, but the NAT box will have to translate each internal source address to the NAT box's external address, in order to maintain the fiction of the virtual server address. In addition, the NAT box will have to consult the address mapping table it created when it received the initial client requests, to translate each destination address back to the source address of the correct client. The address mapping table that the NAT box might build and use is depicted in Figure 11.5.

There is one additional complication to using the external interface of the NAT box as that of the virtual server address for the server pool. The external address of the NAT box may be the external address of a firewall that performs all NAT functions, including load balancing. Consequently, the NAT box must also be configured to check the TCP destination port of all inbound traffic, to separate traffic bound for the servers in the server pool from traffic bound for other servers. For example, if the server pool is a group of servers that act collectively as www.xyz.com, any inbound traffic to the NAT box addressed to TCP destination port 80, which is the HTTP service port, would be readdressed to one of the pool servers.

But what if there were a number of Web servers behind the NAT box or a number of different FTP sites, each represented by a different host name to the outside world? For that matter, there could be several different server pools behind the NAT box, each identified by a different virtual server name. If that were the case, the network would need multiple virtual server addresses, each listed in the external DNS and each mapped back to a different external

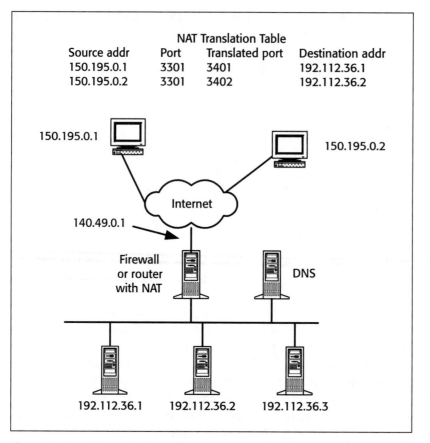

NAT Translation Table

Source addr	Port	Translated port	Destination addr
150.195.0.1	3301	3401	192.112.36.1
150.195.0.2	3301	3402	192.112.36.2

Figure 11.5 NAT translation table maps external addresses and port numbers to server pool addresses and port numbering.

address. The NAT box might still have only one physical external interface, but that one interface might have several IP addresses assigned to it, as illustrated in Figure 11.6.

In a sense, load sharing is a role reversal for NAT. In traditional NAT situations, the NAT box translates the addresses, and frequently the TCP ports, on outbound traffic, from the internal to the external network. Address translation occurs the other way, too, when the server responds to the client's request, but the initial translation is inbound. Load-sharing NAT does address translation in the other direction, initiating its translation table entries and performing address and port translation from the outside to the inside network realm.

Evaluating Load-Sharing NAT

Load-sharing NAT is a relatively simple improvement on basic NAT capabilities. If NAT already exists at the network border, the NAT box need only be

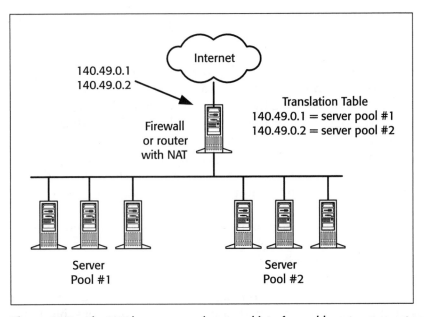

Figure 11.6 The NAT box maps each external interface address to a separate server pool on the inside network.

configured to do load sharing, assuming it's one of the NAT capabilities supported by the NAT software vendor. NAT load sharing may also be used even if there is no other requirement for NAT. That is, there's no requirement that NAT be done on all internal addresses in order to implement NAT load sharing. Instead, NAT load sharing may be configured by itself, and it may be the only address translation done on inbound traffic. Unlike other NAT capabilities, NAT load sharing may be installed as a point solution for load sharing, without requiring NAT for any other traffic.

Furthermore, NAT load sharing has other advantages. Typically, NAT translates between private and public address spaces. NAT load sharing, however, may be used for either public or private address spaces. The inside address space behind the NAT load-sharing box needn't be private space at all. In fact, the inside network can be numbered from routable, public address space.

NAT load sharing is also relatively simple. There are no changes or special accommodations required on either the client or the server side. Like most other forms of NAT, load sharing is transparent to clients and servers, minimizing the time for network reconfiguration for load-sharing NAT. From a DNS perspective, it's easier to administer than separate resource records for each host. All of the servers are represented by one DNS record for all of the hosts in the pool. As long as the NAT box knows the addresses of the servers in the pool, more servers can be added, or others taken out of service for maintenance, without changing any DNS records.

This is not to say that NAT load sharing is without its limitations. As we have already noted, even though it's called NAT *load sharing*, it doesn't have any knowledge of whether the load is distributed or shared equally over all of the servers in the pool. NAT load sharing doesn't make use of any inquiry mechanism to determine how heavily loaded or how busy any of the servers in the pool may be before sending traffic to the next server. Round-robin DNS works the same way, only it's even more removed than NAT load sharing from what's happening on the servers. At least the NAT box might be able to tell if a pool server is handling any traffic at all, based on whether traffic comes back from it, to be changed by NAT. The DNS server is completely removed from any pool server transactions, so the entire server pool could be out of commission, for all the DNS knows.

As with many load-sharing techniques, once a job is sent to a pool server, how that job is handled is completely up to the server. If the job or the server fails, there's no way to switch it to another one of the pool servers. The client may sense that the contact has been lost and reinitiate the task, but it would appear to the NAT box as a new transaction. The NAT load-sharing box must account for and manage those failed, dropped, or lost connections, but that's no different from the chore that any NAT box handles.

Load-sharing NAT also imposes some limitations on network configuration. For example, unless the NAT load-sharing software has been configured to translate the virtual server addresses, which we will discuss later, all of the pool servers must be on the same stub network behind the NAT box. The pool servers can't be distributed on other networks. In practice, the servers in a pool of servers are often in the same physical location, only because it's easier to manage and control them in one place. For reliability and redundancy, however, some organizations prefer to distribute server pools across several locations. In any case, a given pool of servers must be served by a single NAT box, which manages back-end access to the server pool.

Last, there are the usual restrictions on applications that have problems working with NAT. There's no point in going to the trouble of configuring NAT load balancing on servers that run applications that may not work with NAT. The same restriction applies to applications that use encryption. Even some types *of virtual private network* encryption (VPN) won't work properly through NAT, whether configured as a single NAT box or a load-sharing NAT device.

Modifying NAT Load Sharing

NAT load sharing is normally a passive activity, in that there's no coordination between the NAT box and the server pool. NAT load sharing has the potential to be more active, and less passive, if other capabilities can be configured into the NAT load-sharing software. Whether any of these capabilities can be configured on a NAT load-sharing box depends on whether it has been incorporated into the design of the vendor's NAT software.

Some of the potential improvements on basic NAT load sharing are the following:

Server weighting. The network administrator may be able to assign a server "weight" to each server in the pool, to direct how the NAT load-sharing software distributes loads. For example, if some of the servers in the pool have less processing capacity than others, they might be assigned a lower weight. The NAT software may then redirect more traffic to servers with higher weights and fewer sessions to those with lower weights.

Application weighting. Just as servers themselves may be assigned weights, so too might the applications on those servers. For example, if the servers in the pool run HTTP and FTP server processes, the NAT software may assign a higher weight to either process. The HTTP process might be higher if the site's Web pages have a lot of graphics or multimedia files, or the FTP servers may have higher weights if clients can download large files.

Response testing. A NAT box may be able to estimate how heavily loaded the servers in the pool are by sending periodic inquiries to each pool server. Without access to a performance monitor on each server, this test might be only a periodic ping from the NAT box to each server. The NAT box may be able to estimate the load on a server by comparing how quickly the ping responses come back from different servers. Other factors, such as network configuration and network bandwidth, would have to be part of these estimates, but they may give the NAT box an indication of server availability and loading.

Session tracking. The NAT box tracks sessions when it translates addresses back and forth for transactions between inside pool servers and outside clients. The NAT software could be configured to track the number of concurrent sessions to each of the pool servers and to send new sessions to whichever server has the least number of active sessions.

Any of these refinements to NAT load balancing is possible, but some may require more sophistication than might be found in a standard implementation of NAT. Some of these techniques demand more processing power, and therefore they may consume more CPU resources in the NAT box. If the NAT box is a router that doesn't do much else, that's one thing. If it's a firewall that is also running a DNS, a mail relay, and NAT, in addition to screening traffic, that's another matter.

Breaking the Stub Limit

One of the most common configuration limitations to NAT is that all of the servers in the server pool must be on the same stub network. That is, they must be on a network directly behind the NAT box, not somewhere else on the internal network. It's true that they must all be located behind the NAT box because NAT must change the virtual server address to that of a host behind it.

The stub network restriction can be broken if the NAT load-sharing software is configured to translate both the real client address and the virtual server address. The result is that responses back to clients from the pool servers will go back to the NAT box, wherever it's located on the network.

For example, in a standard NAT load-sharing configuration, the client, which is on the outside network, uses the virtual server address as the destination IP address and uses the client's own IP address as the source address. The client also uses the appropriate TCP service port as the server destination port and a port of its choosing as the source port. As illustrated in Figure 11.7, the NAT load-sharing software changes the virtual server address and port to that of the selected pool server address and port. It leaves the client address and port unchanged, as the server will use that address and port in its response.

Note that this implies that the external network on which the client is located is routable from within the internal network. If the external network address isn't advertised inside the internal network, at least there must be a default route to the outside network on which the client systems are located. It's usually the default route to the Internet because the clients could be anywhere on the Internet.

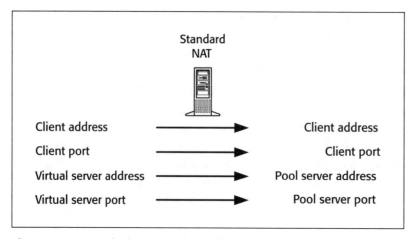

Figure 11.7 Standard NAT translation changes virtual server address and port to the pool server's address and port.

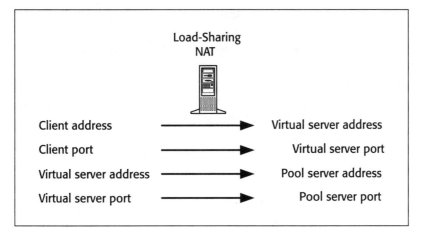

Figure 11.8   Load-sharing NAT changes client address and port to virtual server address and port.

The pool servers could be on any inside network behind the NAT box if the client address were translated to the inside address of whatever device has the virtual server address on its outside network interface. For example, if the virtual server address were on the outside interface of the NAT box, the client's source address and TCP port could be translated to the inside address and port of the NAT box. For outbound responses from the server, the NAT box would have to do a second translation, changing the inside interface address and port to the external, virtual server address and port, as shown in Figure 11.8.

The primary advantage of this configuration is that it removes the restriction of placing all of the pool servers on a single stub network. This configuration may also be used if there are multiple links into the stub domain, as each NAT load balancer can keep its traffic captive, directing responses back through the NAT box that originated the session back to the servers in the pool.

On the downside, this is a more complicated NAT configuration, one that may not be supported by certain NAT devices. It also doubles the amount of translation the NAT box must do, at least on outbound responses, as the destination addresses are translated from inside to outside virtual server addresses. If the NAT box handles a large number of sessions, this may affect the performance and throughput of the NAT box.

Active Load Sharing

Most people who are responsible for operating Internet Web or e-commerce sites that have to handle very heavy traffic loads find that DNS or NAT load balancing doesn't give them enough control over the server pool. Under heavy traffic loads, and for sites that must maintain close control of every session, it's important to give the load-balancing system more active control over network traffic.

Those requirements have created a market opportunity for active load-balancing systems. These systems, which are hardware or software solutions, impose themselves between the outside network and a pool of servers. They act like NAT devices, redirecting client requests addressed to a single virtual server address back to individual servers in a server pool. Unlike NAT load balancing, these devices take a more active role in managing traffic flow to and from the servers.

For example, the Cisco LocalDirector and F5 Networks' BigIP devices represent slightly different technical approaches to solving the load-balancing problem. Both are virtual servers, through which traffic to a server pool must pass to get to the server pool. The LocalDirector permits servers in the pool to be taken out of service and returned online. It may also be integrated with the routers and LAN switches on the inside network, to integrate LAN switching with routing, to pipeline traffic back to the servers. Both systems are intelligent load balancers, in that they query the servers in the pool to determine loading, availability, and system status. The F5 BigIP box is also designed to be a load balancer for other parts of the network infrastructure, such as firewalls and Web caching servers, expanding the utility of load balancing out to the network perimeter, instead of just to inside servers.

The IT Case for NAT Load Sharing

In principle, load sharing among the servers in a server pool is a practical solution to providing network services and Web site applications. As we have seen, NAT isn't the only choice for load sharing. Considering the whole range of load-sharing options and capabilities, ranging from DNS to NAT to active load-sharing systems, NAT falls in the middle ground. Provided the NAT software can be configured to fit specific network loading scenarios, it offers more flexibility than DNS, and it incorporates more direct control over load distribution. It's also a simple, relatively unobtrusive load-balancing solution that may already be in place in a firewall or a screening router.

IT executives and network managers must recognize the limitations of NAT as a load-balancing solution. High-traffic, high-availability e-commerce sites have very different operating thresholds than standard Web sites and other applications servers. In those situations, NAT load balancers will work, but they don't exercise enough positive, active control over network traffic. It's not that a NAT load-balancing solution won't work. It will work, but it has limitations. A NAT load balancer is usually blind to the performance of the individual members of the server pool and the throughput back to those servers. A high-availability, high-performance Web site, particularly one that accesses mission-critical or secure applications, must be managed and controlled carefully. Despite the simplicity of its approach, a NAT load balancer may not fit the bill for those applications.

For high-traffic sites that don't have tremendous requirements for control and manageability, a NAT load balancer, or even a DNS load balancer, may be an adequate solution. They're simple, and both may already be part of the network infrastructure, eliminating the cost and operational responsibilities of an additional part of the network infrastructure.

Summary

Most NAT systems weren't originally designed to do load balancing. The capability was added when it became apparent that load balancing or load distribution was becoming a requirement for many types of networks, many of which already had NAT in place. If they didn't, NAT could be added relatively simply, with little impact on network performance.

NAT load balancing represents a middle step in load-balancing systems. It takes the completely passive approach of DNS load balancing, including round-robin DNS, and incorporates at least some measure of active allocation to server traffic management. Traffic-intensive, heavy-duty load sharing for e-commerce or transaction applications, however, requires an active server monitoring and traffic management system. NAT load balancing wasn't meant to be used in those types of environments, even if they may be pressed into service to do the job.

In the next chapter, we'll switch gears and look at the crisis in IP addressing. It's one of those infrastructure issues that has been smoldering for several years, and NAT is one of the answers that's frequently cited as a solution to the problem. Are we running out of IP addresses for all of those networks in public address space, or are private addressing and NAT the only real hope for the future? Some people say there's no real crisis, but others say that until the next version of IP becomes widely used, NAT will be the only effective solution to the problem.

CHAPTER

12

The Crisis in
IP Addressing

Network managers tend to take a parochial view of routing and addressing issues. Their problems encompass the networks they manage and oversee—and not anything beyond them. What happens on the Internet is not their problem, they say, because that's the ISP's job?

One aspect of the magic of the Internet is that it seems to work without anyone doing anything to make it work properly. Traffic flows out to the ISP, and magically Web pages flow back. Type in a URL, and as if by magic, a DNS somewhere resolves the text to an IP address.

Except for advertising internal networks properly to an ISP, Internet routing has always been somebody else's problem. The same is true for IP addressing. As long as the network uses valid addresses or translates private, internal addresses to valid public addresses through NAT, the thinking goes, IP addressing really doesn't matter all that much.

Crisis? What Crisis?

This cavalier attitude has worked for quite some time, but the dramatic growth of the Internet has made what were originally someone else's problems all of our own problems. For a long time, we, the users of the Internet, haven't had to be too concerned about what made the Internet work. It was nice that somebody, somewhere was making it all work right, and, to a certain extent, that's still true. But just as we can no longer pollute the environment and consume natural resources at an uncaring pace, we can't consume IP address space at the present rate, and not care a whit about Internet routing.

Unfortunately, the ideas that IP addressing and Internet routing are someone else's problems are no longer entirely accurate. Contrary to popular belief, neither the Internet nor any other network works by magic. In fact, one of the magical things about networking that has been concealed to most users, and to many network managers, is the crisis in IP addressing. Depending on your viewpoint, it's either a real or an imagined crisis.

Growing Like a Weed

The Internet has grown far more dramatically in the past decade than any of its inventors ever imagined it would at any time. In early 2000, some estimates of the size of the Internet put the number of computers connected to it at more than 80 million hosts. By using the widest possible definition of an Internet "host," any user's PC or workstation is an Internet "host." Given the current use of the Internet as a vehicle for the World Wide Web, an estimate of the number of Web servers might be the most relevant count.

One of the consequences of the growth of the Internet has been the consumption of public IP address space. Everything on the Internet needs an IP address, and while the supply of IP addresses seems endless, it's not infinite. In fact, we, the users of the Internet, have been using up new IP address space at a tremendous and rapidly escalating rate.

Despite the fact that it adds a measure of complexity to network design and operation, one of the benefits of NAT is that it has reduced the pressure on the demand for even more public IP address space. Networks that use NAT could be using private address space, overlapping public address space, unallocated addresses, or illegal addresses, which are addresses that a network administrator simply chooses to use without being allocated those addresses by an ISP or by ARIN. In a number of cases, NAT boxes hide networks that use legitimate, allocated, public address space, either for security reasons or to make certain systems unreachable from the Internet.

In many of these situations, NAT has taken some of the pressure off the demand for public address space. Still, the crisis in IP addressing persists because given a choice between public and private IP addressing, most network administrators would choose to use public space.

HOW BIG IS THE INTERNET?

If the U.S. Census Bureau wanted to take on another challenge—as if the Year 2000 U.S. Census wasn't enough—it might try tackling a census of the Internet Just as the population of a country is changing all the time, so too is the "population" of the Internet. Because there's no one in charge of the Internet and no "registration fee" besides an IP address, estimating the size of the Internet is as much guesswork as it is science.

Most estimates of the size of the Internet are either educated or wild guesses, but some organizations have tried to approach the issue methodically. One method of sizing the Internet is to try to poll Internet hosts. The theory is that pinging all IP addresses in usable, public, and assigned IP address space may return a reasonable estimate of the number of Internet hosts. This method won't be entirely accurate because firewalls and screening routers hide large numbers of systems. Then there are networks that hide hosts that use private addresses behind NAT boxes, which also won't be counted accurately.

The Internet Domain Survey Project, conducted annually by the Internet Software Consortium (see www.isc.org) has made estimates of the number of Internet hosts since 1987. In January 2000, its estimate of the number of Internet hosts stood at more than 72 million. Until 1997, the survey queried DNS servers and counted "A" records in DNS zone files, which map text names of hosts back to IP addresses. Today, many DNS services are configured not to permit such detailed examination of DNS zone files, so the survey has resorted to making DNS inquiries for host names assigned to active IP addresses.

Even that method won't be accurate because a great deal of active IP space is behind firewalls, screening routers, and NAT devices, which hide the IP addresses that are in use in networks behind them. Even so, the survey makes reverse address lookups on all of the addresses that are in address ranges that are in use. Obviously, the error margin of such a technique can be great or small, but then again, the results are intended to be only an estimate. Even so, the survey takes about eight days to run, even running at 600 to 1200 reverse address lookup queries per second, as the ISC estimates that there are about 223 million addresses in use worldwide.

So How Bad Is It?

When the IP addressing plan was first devised in the late 1970s, it seemed that the possibility of an IP addressing crisis was impossibly remote. After all, with an IP address space that encompassed more than 2^{32} possible addresses, there could be more than 4 billion hosts on the Internet. From the perspective of the late 1970s, that seemed to be more than enough address space for all of the hosts that could ever be on the Internet, even if it grew beyond anyone's wildest guess.

The fact is that the IP address space does indeed allow for a huge number of IP addresses. The way the IP address has been devised and the ways that IP address space have been allocated over the years have led to huge inefficiencies in address usage. In RFC 1715, Christian Huitema, a widely recognized authority on Internet routing, argued that any scheme to allocate finite resources through a central authority usually leads to tremendous inefficiencies. By his calculations, only a quarter of all assigned IP addresses are actually in use, and less than half of the available ten-digit phone numbers are used.

Both of these factors have led to today's crisis in IP addressing, in which we are running out of this essential part of the Internet infrastructure. It might be worse, if it were not for several factors we'll examine in this chapter. NAT is one of those things that helps alleviate the crisis in IP addressing because it allows the same IP addresses to be reused on many different internal networks. There are other techniques that also help alleviate the IP address crunch, including address conservation, address reclamation, and new address consolidation techniques.

The long-term solution to the addressing crisis is an entirely new version of the IP protocol, IP Version 6, but it may be a long time before IPv6 ever hits a router in your neighborhood. In the meantime, of all of the IP address crisis-intervention techniques, NAT at the border to networks using private addressing is the most workable, immediate way to deal with the problem. It isn't a permanent solution to the problem.

The Problem of Classful Addressing

As the Internet keeps growing, we are using up IP addresses at an alarming clip. To most users, the pace of IP address usage isn't evident because addresses are available. At least they are for now, although network managers may have noticed that ISPs are far less generous these days than they used to be about handing out as many IP addresses as a customer wants. A less evident reason for the apparent shortage of IP addresses is the IP addressing system itself, which has some built-in inefficiencies that can lead to unnecessarily excessive waste of perfectly good address space.

Let's make the assumption that all network managers are wholesome, socially conscious individuals, who want to do *the right thing*. Given this assumption (which is true in most, but not necessarily all, cases), one of the problems network managers face in trying to make the most efficient use of their IP address space is to use as much of that space as possible. Unfortunately, the IP address class structure doesn't necessarily let them do that. Those network managers will try to use the address space as efficiently as they can with subnetworking and other tactics, but they can't escape the inefficiencies of the IP addressing class system.

The problem with the basic IP address classes of Class A, B, and C addresses is that they are intended to be for large, medium, and small networks. In practice, though, the size categories work out to be gargantuan, large, and tiny networks. Each Class A network can accommodate more than 16 million hosts. A Class B network can have more than 65,000 hosts, and a Class C network can have 254 hosts.

Unfortunately, these sizes don't effectively match the size networks that we have today. The large Class A and B networks, as we will see, were simply too large. In practice, most of the address space in Class A and B networks is wasted and not used at all. That so much of that address space is wasted isn't the fault of network administrators. It's a fundamental flaw in the way the IP addressing system has been designed.

There is a fix to this fundamental flaw in the addressing structure, which is *Classless Inter-Domain Routing* (CIDR), which will be discussed later in this chapter. CIDR removes the distinction of classful addressing, replacing it with the concept of *classless* addressing. From the perspective of ARIN and the ISPs, there are no more IP address classes per se, just IP addresses. ARIN assigns addresses to ISPs in CIDR blocks, and the ISPs assign address ranges in CIDR blocks to their customers.

Many network managers, however, regard CIDR address allocations as background noise because they think in terms of classful addressing. If they are using private addressing behind NAT, they'll still think in classful addressing terms because they'll use the Class A, B, or C private address blocks. The router administrators know better than to think about classful addressing, particularly if they deal with their ISPs and how their internal routes are advertised to the ISPs. The router people deal in CIDR blocks because their route advertisements to ISPs usually carry subnet mask notation, so they must be thoroughly familiar with CIDR.

As far as the ISPs are concerned, IP addressing is classless, and classful addressing is history. From their perspective, there hasn't been any classful addressing since CIDR was defined in an RFC and put into practice in 1995. To be completely accurate, we should note that network managers may use IP address space as if it were classful. The ISPs, whose opinions make Internet routing to those addresses work, no longer think of addressing as having any classful distinction. From ARIN's address assignment perspective, all addressing is classless CIDR addressing.

From today's perspective, we can see that Class A networks are too large to be practical. They were intended to be for very large networks run by corporations or research institutions and universities. Few networks run by a single corporate, research, or educational institution even approach that size. The problem is that large corporations, research organizations, universities, and agencies of the U.S. Department of Defense have been allocated Class A addresses. Most of those companies and organizations use the Class A address space they have been allocated, but they use only a small part of that space. Regardless of how much address space they use from a Class A block, whatever they don't use is wasted.

The same problem exists with Class B address space. Class B networks have room for more than 65,000 host addresses, but in practice, few networks have that many hosts. Whatever host addresses aren't used in the network to which the Class B address has been allocated are wasted, as they can't be used elsewhere. For that matter, a Class A address has the same problem, only it's magnified because there are more Class A addresses that are wasted, or marooned, if they're not used.

For example, the U.S. Department of Defense has a number of Class A addresses assigned to it. The early ARPANET was designed for the Department of Defense (DoD), so it's not surprising that some large DoD networks use Class A addresses. There is a large DoD common-user data network, the NIPRNET, that uses the network 33.0.0.0/8 address space. The NIPRNET connects more than a million military users to exchange unclassified e-mail, transfer files, access client/server applications, and access the Internet.

The only network interfaces that are numbered from the 33.0.0.0/8 address space are the routers that connect thousands of U.S. military installations to the DoD backbone network. There are only a few hundred of these routers, but most of them have multiple interfaces on the backbone network. Of the 16 million addresses in the 33.0.0.0/8 network, approximately a thousand are in use. The others can't be used by other networks because they belong to the NIPRNET.

Even though the old Class B-size /16 addresses can accommodate only 65,000 hosts, marooned addresses appear widely in Class B network address spaces. Many large corporations, research centers, military bases, and universities have been assigned /16 addresses. Many also have only a few thousand hosts in use, which can strand a high percentage of addresses. It's not uncommon to find that only a few thousand of those 65,000 addresses are in use. It leaves the rest either available for future network growth or, more likely, stranded high and dry, unable to be used anywhere else.

The former Class C /24 space, the tiny size, at 254 hosts per network is actually a lot more flexible than either Class A or B space. Large networks of several thousand hosts can be built from a group of /24 addresses, which can be tailored to just the right size, with very little waste. The most commonly used building block of CIDR addressing is the /24 address block, which contains 254 host addresses, which is the same size a classful Class C address block contained. With CIDR notation, a network that needs about a hundred host addresses might be assigned a /25 block, which contains 128 host addresses.

NAT makes it possible for any network manager who wants to use private address space in whatever way is suitable for the network. It doesn't matter how much or how little of any private address space is either used or stranded by a network manager because it all comes out in the wash, so to speak, when those addresses go through NAT at the network border. The only point at which a network that uses private address space internally puts any pressure on the public address space is in the small CIDR block the ISP assigns for address translation. Even in a big network, the public address translation block may be a relatively small CIDR block of 16, 32, or 64 public addresses.

Conserving What We Have

One of the most effective ways to ameliorate any supply shortage is to make better and more efficient use of whatever resources you have, instead of consuming them willy-nilly until they run out. Today, IP addresses aren't as easy to get as they once were because address allocation organizations have tried to conserve new address space carefully. It's not exactly to the point where it could be called rationing, but it's not like an all-you-can-eat salad bar either. RFC 2050 specifies the address allocation guidelines for address registries and the conservative address use guidelines they must follow.

The people who allocate IP address space, such as the American Registry for Internet Numbers (ARIN, which we introduced in Chapter 9, "Public and Private Addressing") and its delegates in Europe (RIPE) and the Far East (APNIC), have become downright stingy with IP address space in recent years. ARIN and the other registries allocate new, unused address space to those who request it. The requesters might be corporations or organizations that want their own, provider-independent public address space. More often, the requesters are ISPs who need address space that they can assign to their customers. The U.S. military also requests address space from ARIN for use on its unclassified and classified data networks. ARIN is also responsible for the IP address space that has already been allocated, including addresses that were allocated before ARIN came into existence in 1997.

The problem that ISPs and other organizations face today is that ARIN won't give them all the address space they want just because they ask for it. In an effort to conserve the use of new address space, ARIN requires ISPs, companies, and other organizations that want public space to justify all of the space they request. ISPs allocate address space to their customers, so ISPs are held responsible for making sure that their customers' address space allocations are used efficiently, in accordance with RFC 2050. ICANN's Address Supporting Organization (ASO) holds the responsibility for changing the address allocation rules, if that should become necessary.

Specifically, ARIN tasks ISPs with several responsibilities in order to qualify for any additional address space allocation beyond whatever they have already been assigned. The responsibilities are for an ISP to do the following:

- Use up at least 80 percent of the previously assigned address space before being eligible to apply for more address space.

- Demonstrate how the ISP has assigned large address blocks to customers, if possible, in order to minimize the impact on the top-level Internet routing tables.

- Forecast demand on the new address space in the first three months of its allocation, to prevent ISPs from stockpiling address space.

- Return any previously assigned address space that the ISP and ARIN have agreed should be returned.

ARIN imposes much the same types of responsibilities on corporations and other organizations that request their own address space. The assumption is that corporations and other organizations will act like ISPs for other parts of their organizations, so they must follow the same requirements as "regular" ISPs for assigning and using address space efficiently.

Are We Really Running Out of Address Space?

In 1999, ARIN assigned the equivalent of 84,839 Class C network-sized CIDR address blocks to ISPs and to corporations and organizations. If there are about 2 million CIDR-equivalent Class C blocks available (in the address space from 192.1.1.0/24 through 223.255.255.0/24), that's about 4 percent of the former Class C address space. The problem is that more than two-thirds of the Class C address space has already been allocated. At the current rates of address consumption, even with address conservation measures, the rest of the old Class C address space might be gone in another 10 years.

If we take this at face value, we could conclude that techniques like NAT are definitely part of the solution to the address exhaustion problem. NAT makes it possible for networks to reuse addresses that are also used elsewhere, whether they are public addresses or private addresses. NAT might be a permanent solution if most networks used it, but it's highly unlikely that would happen.

In reality, the Doomsday scenario, in which the world runs out of IP addresses and the Internet fragments and drifts off into space, has been overdrawn. It is true that the growth of the Internet is consuming an increasing number of unassigned IP addresses year after year and that the pace of usage is likely to increase for the foreseeable future, not decrease. There's still a good bit of IP address space left, even if the current pace of address usage continues for the next 20 years.

The Strategic Reserve

So, where's all this address space if it's being used up so quickly? A little more than half (more accurately, about 55 percent) of the IPv4 address space has never been allocated. Most of the old Class A address space was set aside in reserved address blocks that have never been used. In fact, the Class A address blocks from 62.0.0.0 through 126.0.0.0 (62/8 through 126/8, in CIDR notation) have never been used, and neither have the Class A blocks from 21.0.0.0 through 30.0.0.0 and 45.0.0.0 through 52.0.0.0. In those blocks of the old, classful Class A address space, there are more than 80 Class A networks, encompassing more than 3.5 billion host addresses. All of that space is in unassigned or reserved address blocks that essentially have not been used. Figure 12.1 illustrates the parts of the IPv4 address space that have and have not been used, as of 1999.

The old classful Class B and C address blocks also have unassigned space, although little of the old, classful Class C space is reserved. In the Class B address space, the address blocks from 173.1.0.0 through 191.255.0.0 have also not been assigned. ARIN is now working its way through the unassigned Class C address space, using it as the basic assignment block, although it has also started assigning addresses from the address ranges covered by the unused parts of the classful Class A address space. The reserved address blocks sitting out there represent about half of all of the IP address space. What

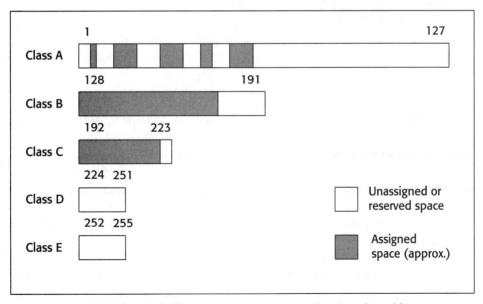

Figure 12.1 Shaded areas indicate approximate ranges of assigned IP address space.

is really needed is a way to break the available address space into blocks that can be tailored to the precise address block needs of a specific network or ISP.

The CIDR Rules

Fortunately, there is just such a method to break large address blocks into smaller, more convenient sizes. It's called Classless Inter-Domain Routing, or CIDR. As its name implies, CIDR removes the class distinctions of IP addresses. Under the rules of CIDR, there are no classful addresses, like Class A, B, and C addresses. In effect, any part of the IP network address spaces can be carved up into whatever size is required to fit the needs or size of a specific network or ISP customer set.

All of that Class A address space that is sitting out there is now being carved up into smaller blocks of address space and assigned as CIDR blocks to ISPs, corporations, and organizations. It makes available a lot of that address space that has been locked up because it's been reserved by the IETF, but also because it has been in address blocks that are too large to be of use by any one organization or ISP. This assumes, of course, that those big Class A address blocks haven't been used for some other purpose in the meantime.

CDIR has two major benefits, but it requires a methodical, organized approach to assigning address space. The major benefits of CIDR are these:

- CIDR allows larger address blocks to be broken into smaller, more appropriately-sized address blocks, which can be tailored to the addressing needs of specific networks or ISPs.
- Addresses that are in CIDR blocks can be listed more compactly, or "aggregated," in the routing tables of the routers at the Internet core, which helps them operate more efficiently.

CIDRized addresses assigned to network interfaces look the same as any other IP addresses because they're those familiar, four-part, dotted-decimal numbers that we all know and love. To network administrators, they're just like other IP network addresses, and they can be managed the same way, too, and subdivided into subnetworks. The only difference is that CIDR network addresses are represented a little differently in router address tables, which we'll discuss shortly, to indicate what part of a large address block they represent. They're also commonly referred to in slash prefix notation, so 10.0.0.0 is referred to as 10/8.

In practice, when a large network address space is broken into smaller address blocks by CIDR, it is commonly treated as if it were a number of smaller, Class C address blocks, although any size larger or smaller than a classful C block is possible. For example, the 100.0.0.0 Class A address space could be broken up into more than 65,000 smaller address blocks, each the same size as a

Class C address and assigned to ISPs, corporations, and to other network providers. As far as address space use is concerned, the benefit of this is that instead of assigning the whole Class A address block to one ISP, it might be broken into smaller address blocks and assigned to ISPs all over the Internet. ISPs aren't limited to Class C-sized CIDR blocks, as they may assign a /24 to one customer, a /26 (64 addresses) to another, and a /16 (65,536 addresses) to another.

But wait, you might say, what's the difference between breaking up a larger block of Class A space into Class C-sized units with CIDR and doing the same thing with subnetworking? The difference is that Internet routers would know that the larger address space had been broken into smaller address blocks because their routing tables can carry an extra notation to indicate that addresses belong to CIDR blocks. The slash prefix CIDR notation means the same thing as a network mask, in that it indicates the length of the part of the address (the prefix) that represents the identity of the subnet (if it's an interface) or what's in the routing table (if it's in a routing advertisement). All routing protocols except Version 1 of the Routing Information Protocol (RIP-1) support CIDR addressing.

The other side of the CIDR coin is that part about simplifying the routing tables of the routers at the core of the Internet. Their problem, as we noted in Chapter 10, "NAT and Routing," is containing the growth of their routing tables. As the Internet continues to grow, the number of routes that have to be carried in the routing tables of the routers at the core of the Internet has threatened to become almost too unwieldy for those routers. Network addresses that have been put into CIDR blocks can be represented more efficiently in the routing tables of those top-level routers. This helps preserve Internet routing and helps to keep the Internet from falling apart, which would happen if those top-level routers couldn't keep track of all Internet addresses.

CIDR Notation

The initial objective of CIDR was to reduce the size of the routing tables of the core Internet routers. CIDR did this by supernetting blocks of Class C network addresses. There are more than 2 million possible Class C networks, even though many still remain to be assigned. Adding all of the Class C addresses, or even a small percentage of them, as individual routing table entries would soon overwhelm the Internet's core routers. This was never perceived to be a possibility when the IP addressing class system was first devised. Today, with the Internet growing by leaps and bounds, it's a real threat.

The basic CIDR supernetting concept is to assign contiguously numbered blocks of Class C addresses to individual ISPs, instead of assigning Class C network addresses individually to many different ISPs. Let's say that a group of 64 Class C addresses is assigned to a single ISP, which we'll call ISPOne.

Let's say the Class C addresses are in a contiguous block of addresses that starts with 204.200.1 and runs through 204.200.64.

In a router's routing table, the network addresses would be listed individually, along with the corresponding Autonomous System Number (ASN) for ISPOne's network. The Autonomous System Number is a numeric designation that identifies different networks, such as those of different ISPs, major corporations, and government and military agencies. Like IP addresses, ASNs are another of those parts of the Internet infrastructure that are controlled by ARIN. A complete discussion of ASNs and Internet routing is beyond the scope of this book, so we'll simplify this by saying that Internet routing tables map network addresses to ISPs.

At the top level of the Internet routing hierarchy, each ISP's networks correspond to another routing entry that maps to a network through which that ISP is reachable. For example, if ISPOne and ISPTwo were smaller, regional ISPs that passed their Internet traffic to a larger ISP, BigISP, both ISPOne and ISPTwo's networks would be routable through BigISP's network.

The routing table wouldn't really look like the one depicted in Figure 12.2, but the concept is the same.

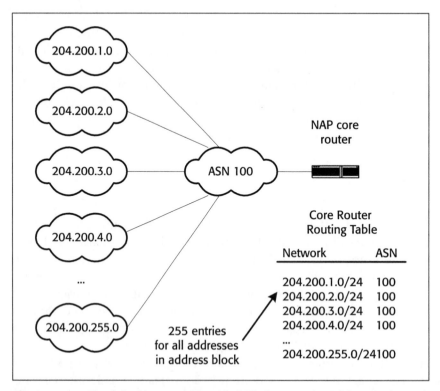

Figure 12.2 Classful address routing table includes a routing table entry for each routable network.

Note that to represent all 64 Class C addresses, there would have to be 64 separate routing table entries. With ARIN assigning more than 80,000 Class C equivalents each year, it wouldn't take long for those core router routing tables to become too unwieldy for ARIN to manage.

Because all 64 of those addresses are in a contiguously numbered block, we could represent all 64 of them with one routing table entry. The single routing table entry, which would be done with CIDR notation, might look like Figure 12.3.

Note that with the CIDRized address block, all 64 networks can be represented with a single routing table entry. The "/18" after the 204.200.0.0 is CIDR notation. It is interpreted by routers as meaning "the group of 64 consecutively numbered Class C networks, starting with 204.200.1.0." And why does "/18" mean that? It's similar to a subnetwork mask, which indicates bits of the 32-bit IP address space that will be used for the network portion of the address. In CIDR notation, it indicates the number of Class C network addresses in the CIDR block.

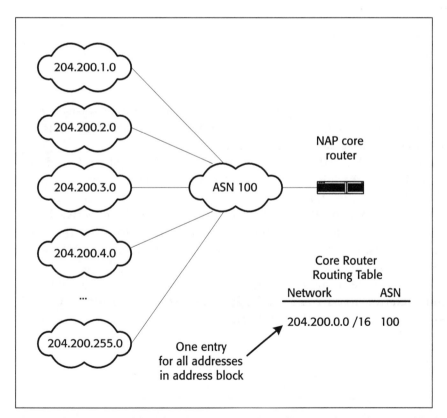

Figure 12.3   CIDR address notation summarizes all networks in the CIDR block in one routing table entry.

CIDR Prefix	Class C Equivalent Networks
/ 8	65,536
/ 9	32,768
/ 10	16,384
/ 11	8,192
/ 12	4,096
/ 13	2,048
/ 14	1,024
/ 15	512
/ 16	256
/ 17	128
/ 18	64
/ 19	32
/ 20	16
/ 21	8
/ 22	4
/ 23	2
/ 24	1

Figure 12.4   CIDR block sizes.

CIDR blocks aren't arbitrarily sized. They are sized in powers-of-two increments, so the number of Class C network addresses in CIDR blocks falls into specific ranges, as indicated in Figure 12.4.

For example, the 10.0.0.0 Class A private address is frequently referred to as 10.0.0.0 /8. That means "all of the 65,536 Class C equivalent addresses starting with 10.0.1.0." In practice, it means the whole Class A address space of 10.0.0.0, however it is subdivided. As we have noted earlier, if a private network uses 10.0.0.0, it may be used in any way the network administrator likes, provided, of course, that those addresses are translated to public addresses by NAT at the network exit.

In another example, a single Class C network address, such as 204.200.1.0, is frequently referred to as 204.200.1.0 /24. This means, "the whole Class C address space for network 204.200.1.0," running from host numbers 204.200.1.1 through 204.200.1.254.

Internet, CIDRize Thyself

At the core of the Internet, compacting the routing tables of the core routers at the NAPs and MAEs of the world has been elevated to the level of a crusade.

Top-level ISPs, such as Sprint, MCI, UUnet, and the like, which route millions of datagrams of Internet traffic every hour, have a vested interest in keeping the core routers working efficiently because they run a number of the core routers, as well as some of the NAPs and MAEs.

Several years ago, the top-level ISPs started to force the use of CIDR blocks in newly assigned Class C address space. Their goal was to force ISPs to CIDRize address space, to reduce the size of the address tables maintained by the core routers. In 1995, the routing tables of some of the top-level core routers held more than 60,000 routes. By 1998, that number had been reduced to about 45,000. The reduction was accomplished by their own rigorous enforcement of the use of CIDR blocks in newly assigned address space and by ARIN's assigning new address space only in CIDR blocks. There are graphs available on the Internet indicating the growth of the size of some routing tables (www .telstra.net/ops/bgptable.html) that show a drop in the mid-1990s when CIDR was turned on.

Some of the top-level ISPs unilaterally forced the use of CIDR blocks by ISPs as a means to protect the integrity of their core routers. For example, in 1996, Sprint decided that any IP addresses from newly assigned address space would have to be announced to its core routers in CIDR blocks of at least 32 Class C equivalents (a /19 CIDR block). Addresses in newly assigned space that weren't in CIDR blocks of at least /19 size, Sprint said, would not be carried by its core routers. In effect, Sprint forced the issue by requiring that ISPs use CIDR blocks. Since then, many of the other top-level ISPs followed Sprint's lead. The result has been that CIDR is now a commonly accepted practice for ISPs.

Summary

Is the world running out of IP addresses, or are there really enough to last us for a while? Frankly, there is plenty of IP address space out there. The problem is that the original IP addressing system wasn't designed for the current Internet environment, and as a result, the IP address space hasn't been used as efficiently as it might have been.

From our vantage point in history today, we have the benefit of perfect 20/20 hindsight. Might the inventors of the TCP/IP protocols and the IP addressing scheme have done it differently, had they foreseen this problem today? Probably, we would think, they might have made everything a Class C address and invented CIDR, to boot, as a means to allocate those IP addresses as efficiently and as economically as possible.

Fortunately, all of this business with CIDR and the real or imagined crisis in IP addressing is just so much distant thunder to NAT. If anything, NAT is part of the solution to the address consumption issue because NAT reduces the pressure on the IP address space. It is true that IP address space, at least in the Class C address space, is being used up at a rapid clip, and the pace doesn't seem to be slowing appreciably.

In the next chapter, we will shift gears and look at how NAT affects network security. The subject will be the effect of NAT on encryption and how network security can be enhanced—or possibly threatened—by NAT.

CHAPTER 13

NAT and Security

Network security has always been an issue for network managers and IT executives, but it has never been as high on the priority list as it is today. It wasn't too many years ago, just before the advent of the Internet Age, that security meant passwords on Telnet and FTP sessions.

Today, the security landscape has changed radically. No network manager or IT executive in his or her right mind would think of leaving an entire network exposed to every Tom, Dick, and Master of Deception on the Internet. Network security has become a booming industry. Security devices and capabilities, ranging from firewalls to screening routers to intrusion detection systems, are no longer nice-to-have network features. They're a necessity.

They have become a necessity not because network managers are paranoid. Actually, many are paranoid, but it's because they're under the impression that network users and IT executives are out to get them. That's only an illusion because users only want computers and networks to work right, and IT executives don't want any operational problems.

The justification for network security systems is an operational issue and less a privacy issue. Today, denial-of-service attacks, hijacked password files, and network intrusion attempts have become alarmingly commonplace. In fact, the ingenuity of hackers and intruders to probe, attack, and disable systems has become quite sophisticated. Network managers and IT executives are engaged in a costly and complex arms race against hackers and intruders.

As we have discussed in previous chapters, NAT isn't much of a security measure. Hiding the identities of systems behind a NAT box doesn't really secure them any more than trying to deceive anyone outside the network that most of the systems on the internal network really don't exist. It's obvious to a hacker or an intruder that there are more systems on the networks of corporations, organizations, or military agencies than are evident from the outside. A NAT box on a firewall may represent all the interior systems with a single outside address, but that bit of fiction is intended only as a first line of defense against outsiders.

Besides, many security problems originate from within the enterprise, not from outside. Internally originated security problems are usually of a different type than those of external origin. External threats tend to be more destructive in nature, deleting files, creating floods of extraneous e-mail messages, and exposing credit card and customer information to unauthorized uses. Inside threats usually involve compromising confidential information, such as personnel data and salary information. Hiding inside addresses is of little help when dealing with internal threats.

Hiding by Encryption

Encrypting data is another tool in the network manager's security toolbox. Encryption addresses a different element of security than firewalls, screening routers, and single network interface systems. Encryption addresses the issue of data interception, not system intrusion. In fact, one of the assumptions of encryption scenarios is that encrypted data is likely to be intercepted. The other aspect of the encryption scenario is that even if it is intercepted, encrypted data can't be read or seen.

Just as has happened in the network intrusion environment, hackers have been engaged in a rapidly escalating arms race over encryption. Even as computer scientists have developed more and more sophisticated and complex data encryption algorithms, hackers have developed more and more sophisticated methods of cracking those algorithms. Not all attempts to crack encryption algorithms are malicious. Some are experiments in massively parallel computing, harnessing tens or hundreds of smaller computers together to work on a complex, computational exercise like cracking an encryption algorithm. The objective of these experiments is not to crack encryption schemes, but to develop better encryption algorithms and to determine if existing encryption schemes are really as unbreakable as they are believed to be.

There are a number of widely used encryption techniques and algorithms, but only a few that are widely implemented and accepted in IP networks.

Some networking techniques, such as Virtual Private Networks (VPNs), use encrypted tunnels to pass encrypted data from the VPN client to the VPN server or gateway. In VPNs, the data is encrypted to secure the VPN "circuit" over the Internet.

As we will see in this chapter, encryption can be one of those networking techniques to which NAT is blind. Like embedded IP addresses in data payloads, encryption can be one of those things that requires special techniques or networking arrangements to make NAT work properly. In some cases, NAT won't work at all with encrypted data because its import and arrangement are completely hidden from the NAT functions on a firewall or router.

Some types of encryption are completely impenetrable to all kinds of networking gear. Military communications systems frequently employ link-level encryption, in order to protect transmissions on secure or sensitive systems. A link-level encoding device encrypts IP datagrams that arrive asynchronously on one of the encryption device's interfaces. The encryption box creates a continuous, encrypted data stream on its outbound port, embedding the IP datagrams in a continuous, encoded data stream. Anyone who intercepts the data stream has two data interpretation problems. An interloper must break the encryption algorithm to decipher the IP datagrams, but first, he or she must decipher the data stream to determine where the encrypted datagrams are located.

Most IP data encryption algorithms aren't so complex. Most network managers deploy only a few encryption techniques and protocols, so the varieties of IP encryption with which NAT must be configured to work are considerably reduced. In fact, only a few types of encryption are commonly employed in IP networks. We'll examine three of these, IP Secure, Point-to-Point Transmission Protocol (PPTP), and Level 2 Protocol Translation (L2PT), before seeing how or if NAT can—or can't—handle each at the network boundary.

IP Secure

The IP Secure protocol, commonly known as IPsec, is a security standard for encrypting, securing, and authenticating IP traffic. It has become one of the standard methods employed to protect data when it's transmitted on the Internet, both through encryption and authenticating senders and receivers. In addition, IPsec can also be employed in Virtual Private Networks, particularly to carry data across the Internet on a secure, encrypted VPN tunnel.

IPsec is an IETF security standard, as it has been specified in a number of RFC standards. The fundamental RFC defining the IPsec architecture is RFC 2401, but there are several other RFCs that have followed RFC 2401 to define more fully other technologies that implement the IPsec architecture. Although most network managers and IT executives don't think of it as such, it is correct to refer to IPsec as a protocol. Like other protocols, such as TCP and IP, IPsec defines rules and agreements between two devices exchanging data across an IP network.

IPsec isn't just an encryption algorithm, although the protocol does specify how data can be encrypted. Instead, it is a set of rules for secure data transmission, some of which cover encryption. And, like a lot of protocols, the specifications of IPsec don't necessarily map back to how it is actually implemented.

IPsec is more than just authentication. Instead, it defines a set of services for securing data transmitted over IP networks. The services provided by IPsec include the following:

- Encryption
- Authentication
- Ensuring data integrity
- Defense against unauthorized retransmission of data
- Security key management

There's another security standard that is associated with IPsec that covers another element of data encryption. The *Internet Key Exchange* protocol (IKE) is the IPsec security key management protocol. It is a series of steps that establish the keys for encrypting and decrypting information sent over IPsec. Together, IPsec and IKE standardize the way that data protection is performed.

The most significant benefit of this set of protocols is that it makes it possible for security systems that have been developed by different vendors, and that are intended to be used on different types of systems, to still be compatible with each other and still interoperate. In the same sense, different systems, such as those running Unix, IBM's MVS, and Microsoft Windows, can all run TCP/IP, even though their implementations of the protocol may be slightly different. And, if they run compatible client and server applications programs, all of those systems can interoperate.

IPsec Modes

IPsec works in one of two ways, each of which is referred to as a *mode*. The differences between the two modes, called the transport mode and the tunnel mode, lie in whether the client and server know anything about IPsec or whether IPsec data security responsibilities are handled for the client and the server by some other device.

The first mode, the transport mode, is the simpler and more direct mode, but it requires that the client and server understand IPsec and that it has been implemented on each system. In the transport mode, both the client and the server are running modified TCP/IP protocol stacks. The IPsec protocol has been configured in both systems to run on top of the IP protocol, as depicted in Figure 13.1.

In the transport mode, the client and server may encrypt the data, authenticate each other, and maintain the integrity of the data they transmit. They may take all or just some of these security measures. It all depends on the level of security each side wants or that the user or administrator has implemented.

The second IPsec security mode is called the tunnel mode. In this mode, neither the client nor the server need know anything about IPsec. They simply create IP datagrams, which are addressed to each other. The IPsec part is provided by other devices, which are usually called security gateways, which implement IPsec for the IPsec-challenged client and server. The gateways encrypt and decrypt the data for the client and server.

It's called tunnel mode because the gateways do more than just encrypt the data. The gateways encrypt the datagrams created by the client and the server, but they also hide the existence of the client and the server by wrapping their encrypted IP datagrams in another IP datagram that has the source and destination IP addresses of the security gateways. In other words, the original client and server's traffic is tunneled across the Internet within the datagrams created by the security gateways, as shown in Figure 13.2.

Note that to an observer on the Internet, the datagrams appear to be traffic between the two gateways, not the two hosts behind the gateways. By hiding the datagrams from the real hosts, and by encrypting the data in those datagrams, the gateways tunnel the traffic through the Internet.

Virtual private networks use IPsec tunnels, managed by VPN gateways that use IPsec tunneling. The chapter on VPNs and NAT (Chapter 14, "NAT and

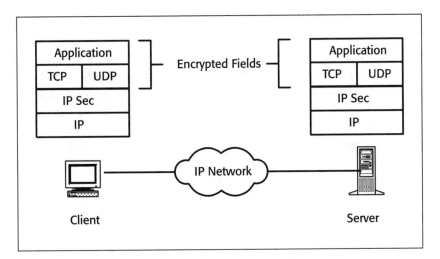

Figure 13.1   Encrypted fields in IPsec transport mode.

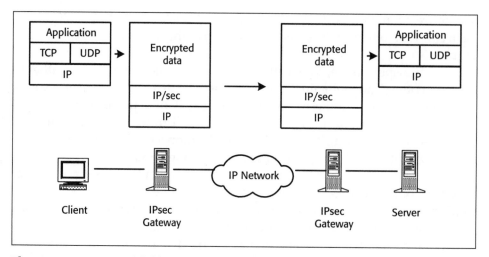

Figure 13.2 Encrypted fields in IPsec tunnel mode.

Virtual Private Networks") has more detail on the implementation of VPNs and VPN tunneling and how NAT works with VPN gateways.

Note that a protocol stack that includes IPsec positions it just above IP. In a standard VPN configuration, IPsec encrypts and authenticates the layers above it, which are usually TCP and the application-layer protocol header and the data payload data, such as FTP, HTTP, or another application. IPsec may also be used with any other protocol that sits above the IP layer. Consequently, the IPsec transport or tunnel modes are also suitable for other types of higher-layer protocols, such as UDP, BGP, or ICMP.

IPsec Encryption

As its name implies, one of the ways in which IPsec may secure data is by encrypting it. It's correct to say that IPsec may encrypt the data, not must encrypt it, because a specific implementation or application of IPsec may not include encryption. As we will see, one circumstance in which encrypted IPsec data may not be desirable is if IPsec-secured datagrams have to pass through a NAT box.

Whether or not IPsec uses encryption depends on how it has been implemented, as well as those other extenuating circumstances, such as the presence of NAT somewhere in the path between the client and the server or between two IPsec security gateways. The type of encryption used also depends on how encryption has been implemented. For example, many vendors use two of the most popular data encryption standards, the *Data Encryption Standard* (DES) and its close relative, Triple DES.

Both DES and Triple DES are secret key algorithms. That is, they are mathematical algorithms that specify the way in which the data in, say, the fields of an IP datagram, can be converted into what appears to be a random string of bits. In other words, it's encrypted. Running the same algorithm with the same secret key at the destination simply reverses the process and decrypts the data. The encrypting and decrypting algorithm is called a cipher, and it's usually a widely available piece of software.

But anyone can get the encryption algorithm, so what's to prevent anyone from decrypting the data? The encryption algorithms use a unique value each time they run the encryption and decryption algorithm. The unique value, called the key, determines the content of the encrypted data string. The same key, applied to the encrypted data string by the decryption algorithm, reverses the encryption and decrypts the data. The key to keeping the encrypted data secure is for the encrypting end and decrypting end of the exchange to keep the key secret. The sender and receiver must share the same key, so they can encrypt and decrypt the data using the same key value.

The DES cipher simply uses a single shared, secret key. The sender uses the key to encrypt the data, and the receiver uses the same key to decrypt the data. The key doesn't travel with the data, nor is it sent over the network. It stays with the sender and the receiver to keep it secure.

Triple DES works just like DES, in that it uses the same DES algorithm, only it compounds the encryption by doing it several times. Triple DES uses either two or three secret keys to generate the encrypted data, which is known as ciphertext. With the three-key version, the first pass encrypts the data with the first key, then the second pass encrypts the encrypted data with the second key. Finally, the double-encrypted data is encrypted a third time, using the third key. With the two-key version, the first key encrypts the data, the second key encrypts the encrypted data again, then the first key encrypts it again. The two-key version is slightly less secure than the three-key version, but it is simpler to administer than the three-key version as it has one less security key.

Triple DES is far more secure than single DES because it takes three different keys and three different decryption steps to encrypt and decrypt the data. An interloper who intercepted either Triple DES- or single DES-encrypted data couldn't tell which type of DES had been used, unless he or she had some knowledge of the number of keys held by the sender and receiver. For that matter, just by looking at the encrypted data, he or she wouldn't even know if DES or another algorithm had been used. In any case, the data would appear to be a random string of bits, so encryption also conceals the method used to encrypt the data.

Why use only single DES if Triple DES is three times better? The reason is that encryption, like any of those side trips data may take as it goes through the network, adds delay, affects throughput, and requires a hefty increase in processing power to work properly. All devices that examine, translate, screen, or encrypt data, such as NAT boxes, firewalls, screening routers, and encryption devices, add subtle amounts of delay that together can slow down network traffic significantly. Encryption, which involves real processing, can cause the most significant delays of all. In many cases, it's the performance hit that encryption adds that discourages many network managers and IT executives from using encryption more widely.

Encryption and IPsec Modes

There are differences in the way that the two modes of IPsec encrypt data. In the transport mode, only the data payload and the application- and transport-level protocol fields are encrypted. In tunnel mode, the entire datagram is encrypted, but a new, routable header wraps the encrypted data.

IPsec uses a type of encryption known as packet encryption. It is referred to as packet encryption because it takes place at the network layer, or Layer 3 in the ISO Model. If you recall, IPsec is implemented in the TCP/IP protocol stack just above the IP layer, but it's still considered to operate at the network level.

In IPsec packet encryption, the entire packet or, to use the correct IP term, the datagram isn't encrypted. The IP datagram header, which is the IP header and the source and destination IP addresses, isn't encrypted. Some parts of the IP header must remain unencrypted because some parts of the IP header contain information that the destination system needs to decrypt the data.

For example, a system that uses IPsec may be communicating with several different hosts, each of which is doing IPsec encryption, using a different cipher key. The destination system needs to know which system has sent a specific block of encrypted data, so that it can use the correct key to decipher the data. More important, if the source IP address has been decrypted, the destination system won't be able to tell which system sent the data and won't be able to make a correct routing decision.

The IP header must remain in the clear for the data to be routed properly, too. For that reason, both transport and tunnel mode IPsec encryption leave an unencrypted IP header on the higher-level encrypted fields. In the transport mode, the IP header isn't encrypted at all. In the tunnel mode, the entire original IP datagram is encrypted, but it's wrapped in a new IP datagram that has an unencrypted IP header. The source and destination addresses in that new IP header are those of the security or VPN gateways. If the data can be routed to the destination gateway, it will remove the IP "wrapper," decrypt the encrypted datagram within, and pass the unencrypted data on to the network behind it for final delivery.

IPsec and NAT

As long as the client and the server implement IPsec in the same way, IPsec works fine as a means to secure traffic sent between two hosts, or between VPN clients and servers, over the Internet. It won't work with NAT because the NAT box doesn't see the payload IP datagram buried inside the datagram that constitutes the VPN tunnel. NAT can't change encrypted addresses because it can't see them, and it can't change the contents of an encrypted datagram without invalidating the encryption integrity check.

Not even an *application-level gateway* (ALG) will help NAT do this. The ALG would have to decrypt the IP datagram payload in the tunnel, change the addresses and TCP ports inside, and then reencrypt the data before sending it on its way. Besides the substantial performance hit this would imply, it also means that the ALG would need to know the private cipher keys known by the client and server. They are supposed to be known only to the VPN client and server, so distributing them to an intermediary, such as the NAT box, would compromise the security that IPsec or any private key-based encryption system is supposed to provide.

Another VPN security protocol, the *Level Two Tunneling Protocol* (L2TP), which we will discuss later in this chapter, also uses IPsec and also presents problems for NAT. Instead of focusing on problems, let's look next at a VPN security protocol that does have a chance to work with NAT before going back to L2TP and more IPsec issues.

Point-to-Point Tunneling Protocol (PPTP)

For a number of reasons, many organizations elect not to use IPsec. It may be implemented differently by different vendors, managing the encryption keys can be a pain (although there are few things about security that aren't), and many organizations just don't think that much protection is worth the trouble. They may change their minds sometime in the future if their networks and communications are successfully hacked, but that's part of the security learning curve. Then there's the problem with NAT. As we've seen, NAT can't deal with IPsec-encrypted data because of those encrypted, hidden data fields and those problems with cryptographic checksums.

There must be a simpler solution, you might say, and yes, there is. It's the *Point-to-Point Tunneling Protocol*, also known by its acronym, PPTP. This is intended for simple, easy-to-use VPN security. It can use encrypted or compressed data payloads, all of which are tunneled through regular IP datagrams. PPTP eliminates the complexity and expense of *public key infrastructure*

(PKI), which IPsec may use. Better yet, as far as we are concerned, PPTP is compatible with NAT, as long as NAT is the end-point of the tunnel. In fact, it's the only one of the three tunneling and security protocols we'll address in this chapter that doesn't create problems for NAT.

PPTP was designed to encapsulate Point-to-Point frames in IP datagrams, for transmission over an IP network. One of the standard implementations is for dial-up users who connect to the Internet through an ISP, then execute a PPP session on their PCs. In the era before security paranoia, that kind of access was suitable for getting into an organization's internal network. It's still a common way for ISP subscribers to access the Internet through an ISP dial-up connection.

Using that dial-up connection to access an internal network over the Internet has become a capability that many organizations eye warily. Their response has been to allow PPP over dial-up ISP connections, but to require users to implement PPTP security, to encrypt the PPP data, and to tunnel it through the Internet over a VPN to a VPN gateway. PPTP is the protocol that "warps" the PPP data and delivers it to the VPN gateway.

PPTP uses a TCP connection, called the PPTP control connection, to set up, manage, and end the tunnel. Then it uses a UDP connection to pass the data across that tunnel. The PPP data sent across the tunnel may be sent in the clear, or it may be encrypted or compressed, or both. Typically, data sent over a PPP session through a dial-up ISP connection isn't encrypted. If that dial-up connection is the client side of a VPN connection, it might be encrypted with a lightweight encryption scheme. In dial-up Microsoft networks, for example, the encryption protocol might be Microsoft Point-to-Point Encryption (MPPE). Some implementations of VPN tunnels may also use IPsec, but it would be applied only to the PPP data payload, not the IP datagram.

The PPTP control connection, which is originated by the VPN client, uses TCP port 1723. The datagram contains no data, only PPTP control commands and responses, so it's not encrypted at all. Once the control connection has been established, it's followed by PPP data, encapsulated in IP datagrams. The PPTP data flow sequence is illustrated in Figure 13.3.

First, the client creates a PPP header, which is tacked onto the PPP data payload. Then, another header, the *Generic Routing Encapsulation* (GRE) header, is placed in front of the PPP frame, which may be encrypted. GRE, described in RFC 2784, is a simple, lightweight, general-purpose mechanism for encapsulating data sent over IP networks. As Figure 13.3 shows, the PPP packet and the GRE header are encapsulated in an IP datagram, addressed from the client to the VPN gateway. The source IP address is that of the client, and the destination is the VPN gateway.

At the destination side of the VPN, the VPN gateway simply reverses the encapsulation process to strip out the data. It removes the IP and GRE headers

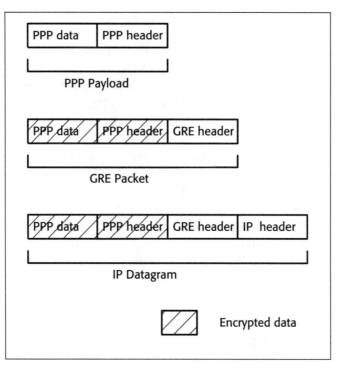

Figure 13.3   Encrypted fields in PPTP data flow.

and, if necessary decrypts or decompresses the PPP data and passes the traffic back to the destination server on the network.

PPTP and NAT

Fortunately, there's one security and encryption scheme for IP networks and VPNs that works with NAT. As we have already seen, it isn't IPsec, and as we will see next, it isn't the Layer Two Tunneling Protocol. The only one that usually works cleanly with NAT is PPTP. The only hitch to making PPTP and NAT work together transparently is that it may require one of those ALGs or a NAT editor to work properly.

When the PPP data is tunneled inside IP datagrams, the tunnel is identified to the VPN gateway by the source IP address in the IP datagram and an identifier in the GRE header, the Call ID field. If there are a number of PPTP clients on the inside network side of a NAT box that have set up VPN tunnels to the same VPN server, all of the tunneled traffic, as seen from the Internet, has the same source IP address. That's the way it's supposed to be because the

NAT box translates the source addresses to its single external interface address.

The Call ID values in the GRE headers can present problems. It's possible that some of the VPN clients might pick the same Call ID number when they establish the VPN tunnel. The Call ID is like a source TCP port number, which is established by the client. If some clients picked the same GRE Call ID, their VPN traffic would arrive at the destination VPN with the same IP source address and the same GRE Call ID.

To prevent this problem, an ALG or a NAT editor must monitor the PPTP connection establishment sessions, and the GRE header, to create separate mappings between real source IP addresses and the Call IDs. The ALG or the NAT editor may have to change the Call ID and map it back to the read source addresses, to keep track of which client originated the VPN session. Fortunately, some network operating system software includes just such an editor. For example, the Microsoft Windows *Routing and Remote Access Service* (RRAS) includes a NAT editor that monitors the GRE Call IDs, to change them, if necessary, and map them back to the original source addresses.

Level Two Tunneling Protocol

A third option for encrypting Internet and VPN traffic is the Level Two Tunneling Protocol, known by the acronym L2TP. This is another tunneling protocol, with encrypted data wrapped in IP datagrams. L2TP uses IPsec as its encryption protocol, but for several exotic reasons, like regular IPsec, L2TP is incompatible with NAT.

L2TP is a combination of two tunneling protocols, which have been combined into one protocol for the sake of industry standardization. L2TP is a compromise combination of the PPTP protocol and a Cisco-developed tunneling protocol, *Layer Two Forwarding* (L2F). Both do approximately the same thing, but one was a public standard and the other a standard supported by a major networking vendor. To avoid having two competing but incompatible security protocols duke it out in the market, the IETF proposed that the two be combined into one protocol that takes the best features of both protocols. The result is L2TP, which has been standardized in RFC 2661.

One of the common ways in which L2TP is implemented is in a VPN gateway. The gateway connects a client and a server over an encrypted, secure tunnel over a public network, which is usually the Internet. Like the PPTP protocol, L2TP encapsulates encrypted data in IP datagrams for transmission over a secure tunnel over the Internet. Unlike PPTP, the L2TP uses more complex encapsulation techniques. More important as far as NAT is concerned, L2TP also uses IPsec, whereas PPTP does not. Because L2TP uses IPsec, a VPN using L2TP won't work with NAT.

If we look at how L2TP works, we can see what causes problems for NAT. It's really quite simple, as it comes down to a matter of mapping port numbers and IP addresses through a NAT box. As with regular IPsec security, the IPsec encryption that L2TP uses foils attempts by NAT to read addresses and port numbers correctly.

On the surface, L2TP should be relatively simple. Its basic construct is that the data payload is framed in PPP data blocks, which are then placed inside UDP blocks. The PPP frame and the UDP block are encrypted and put inside an IP datagram wrapper, which tunnels them over the Internet.

That simple summary doesn't explain the port and address problem, though, because we have to look in more detail at how L2TP works to see that. L2TP uses several different levels of encapsulation, each of which encapsulates other, lower-level data, only part of which is encrypted. The encapsulation process is summarized in Figure 13.4.

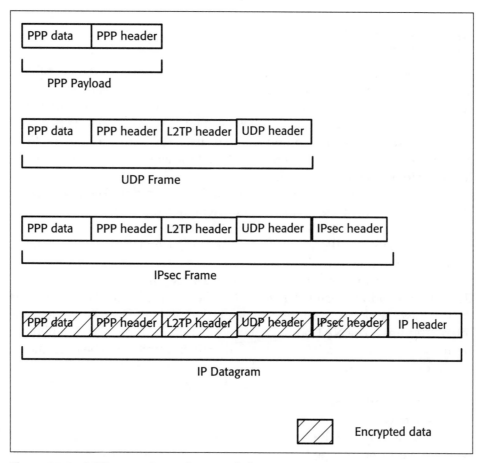

Figure 13.4   L2TP encryption and encapsulation.

The L2TP process starts with the data that is to be sent to the destination, formatted as a PPP payload. A PPP header is added to the PPP payload, as is a L2TP header. The receiving VPN gateway, which is the L2TP peer of the sender, will read the L2TP header to establish the L2TP connection and to manage the flow of data that is sent over the connection. Then, a UDP header is added onto the frame, using the L2TP standard source and destination UDP Port 1701.

Then the entire UDP message is encrypted with IPsec. An IPsec header and trailer are added to the encrypted UDP message. The IPsec header will be used by the destination gateway's IPsec process to manage the decryption process. Finally, the entire IPsec packet is encapsulated in an IP datagram, addressed to the destination VPN gateway.

At the destination gateway, the VPN gateway reverses the process, decapsulating the messages and payload and decrypting the payload. In the last step, the gateway passes the payload back to the destination system on the internal network behind the gateway.

L2TP and NAT

L2TP implies IPsec, so that alone means it's sure to be trouble for a NAT box. The reasons aren't clear until we see how the VPN gateway manages the data sent through it. The problem lies in that encrypted UDP port number in the UDP header. It's encrypted, so it can't be read by NAT, which means that NAT can't track traffic by mapping port numbers back to internal addresses. Even an ALG or, to use Microsoft's term, a NAT editor won't help because neither has a key to decipher the encryption.

There's another problem, too, that's related to encryption. The IPsec header contains a field called the Security Parameters Index, or SPI. The SPI value is used in conjunction with the destination IP address in the outer IP datagram wrapper to control an IPsec *security association* (SA), by which the two sides of the IPsec connection identify each other.

When L2TP traffic travels outbound from a VPN gateway to a NAT box, the destination IP address isn't changed. For inbound traffic, the NAT box must change the destination IP address, which is that of the VPN gateway, to some internal address. The NAT box uses a single external address for all outbound traffic, so the destination IP address for all inbound traffic will be the same.

In order to distinguish one IPsec data stream from another, the destination address and the SPI can be mapped back to an internal destination address and a corresponding SPI. The IPsec header contains a cryptographic checksum, generated as part of the encryption process, which verifies the IPsec header and its payload. If the destination address were to be changed, the SPI would have to be changed, but that would invalidate the checksum. As a result, the IPsec process on the destination VPN gateway would think the checksum was incorrect and discard the data because it failed the integrity check.

There's a second reason why L2TP with IPsec and NAT don't mix well. Both the UDP header and the TCP header of the outer IP datagram wrapper include checksums, calculated on the source and destination address of the outer IP header. If the source or destination address were changed, the checksum would be invalidated. While the TCP checksum is outside the encrypted packet, the UDP checksum is inside. Consequently, it can't be touched by a NAT box that can't decrypt the data.

Where Do We Go from Here?

What's an IT executive or network administrator to do? Unfortunately, IPsec, as terrific as it is at encryption, doesn't mix with NAT. The choice may be that VPN tunnels that must use IPsec should go through a special VPN gateway that doesn't use NAT. The other choice might be to set up VPN gateways on special networks that are outside the NAT boundaries and use proxies behind the VPN gateways. If the real clients and servers are in private network space, the proxies could then pass the traffic unencrypted back through a NAT box into the private network

Another alternative to IPsec is *Secure Sockets Layer* (SSL), from secure Web browsers. SSL works just fine through NAT, and it's simpler than IPsec. It's not as secure as IPsec, but for most purposes, it's sufficient for general-purpose use.

Most vendors take a stand on the VPN security issue and recommend specific types of tunneling for VPNs. Microsoft, for instance, recommends L2TP with IPsec, instead of pure IPsec. The company's reasoning is that IPsec has not been fully standardized by the IETF, and some vendors use their own proprietary implementations of the still-developing IPsec "standard."

Security concerns aren't going to go away, and the trend is for companies and organizations to use the Internet more, not less, for all kinds of traffic. That means that VPNs are here to stay, as are methods to secure VPN traffic. The only general-purpose security standard that's out there is IPsec, although other, proprietary PKI systems could be used as well to secure VPN traffic.

Summary

For people who manage networks that use NAT, there are only three easy answers to the question of how to run VPNs and secure Internet traffic through them. The first is PPTP, the second is SSL, and the third is not to secure it at all. PPTP doesn't provide the same level of security as IPsec, or an IPsec-based solution like L2TP, and neither does SSL. They're certainly simpler solutions than something that uses IPsec because they don't involve the administrative overhead of managing PKI security keys. Note that IPsec doesn't always imply the use of PKI, but it frequently does.

But are these the right answers? For networks that need secure channels and secure VPN traffic, probably not. It also means that until a better solution comes along, NAT and highly secure VPN traffic don't mix. That's cold comfort to networks that use private addressing or that use NAT as a means to represent all internal addresses as a single external address.

In the next chapter, we will move to another related NAT issue, which is using security systems like IPsec and PPTP for virtual private networks. Many organizations and companies are using VPNs to replace leased lines, substituting Internet connections for those dedicated circuits. In most cases, VPNs assume some type of encryption, in order to provide some level of security to VPN channels.

CHAPTER

14

NAT and Virtual Private Networks

Once the Internet became all the rage, all kinds of long-distance, worldwide communications became as effortless (although not necessarily as fast) as communications across the street. IT executives and network managers who paid telecommunications bills every month for the leased lines, dial-up ports, and special communications circuits that connected their far-flung global operations started thinking about that worldwide network.

It didn't take long for them to put two and two together, and to take Internet communications to the next logical step. If the Internet goes everywhere—at least the same places where all those leased lines and specialized facilities take us—why can't the Internet replace all of those specialized, costly communications facilities? If there are reasons why it can't replace all of them, are there at least some for which it can provide at least an equivalent level of service?

Thus was born the idea of the Virtual Private Network, a network that is virtual, not real. The distinction comes down to using a generalized network—the Internet—as if it were a more specialized one. A VPN is really an overlay network running over the Internet, a virtual network on top of a real one, acting like a direct point-to-point link. But communications is communications, right? All that matters is that it works, not what provides it.

In this chapter, we'll examine how NAT affects the ability of organizations to configure and use VPNs. They're all the rage now, but it's often not clear to

IT executives or to network managers how or if existing facilities and technologies, such as NAT, affect the creation and operation of VPNs. The short answer is that NAT isn't supposed to affect VPNs, but that it usually does. In this chapter, we will also examine the issue of VPNs as it affects Windows networking. Many of the VPNs that have been established are relatively new, and most have been done on Windows networks. Doing so does not restrict the coverage of VPNs to Windows networks, but it does help explain how VPNs and NAT are implemented in a commonly used networking environment.

It's Not Virtual Anything—It's Real

The term *virtual private network* is somewhat of a misnomer, particularly if it refers to something that goes over the Internet. The Internet isn't virtual because it's composed of real communications circuits, routers, and switches. The Internet isn't private, either, as most everyone has become aware of the open nature of the Internet and the security risks its openness implies. It is a network, though, so at least some part of the term describes something that really does exist.

As the term is used today, a VPN is a communications link that uses the Internet, instead of a dedicated circuit or network, to connect two devices or locations together. For instance, take an insurance company with its data center in Atlanta and a claims adjustment office in Los Angeles. In years past, the claims adjusters in Los Angeles sat at terminals that were connected to a cluster controller in the Los Angeles office. The cluster controller acted as a multiplexer, managing communications from all of the terminals to the mainframe in Atlanta. The insurance company rented a dedicated point-to-point line from a long-distance carrier to connect the two locations. Times have changed, and so have communications costs, but let's say that 10 years ago, a dedicated leased line between Los Angeles and Atlanta, running at 56 Kb (then a reasonably high-speed circuit) cost $1000 per month.

Fast forwarding to the present, the terminals in Los Angeles have been replaced by PCs running a special claims adjustment client program, and the mainframe in Atlanta has been replaced by a server running a claims adjustment server program. The application may not have changed, just the interface and the applications processor. Neither has the requirement for communications between the client and the server.

Now both the Los Angeles and the Atlanta offices have Internet connections. Each location has a T-1 link to a local ISP that provides Internet access. Let's say that each ISP connection costs $1000 per month. That's twice the cost of the dedicated 56 Kb connection, but about 60 times as much bandwidth. The purpose of the ISP connections is to provide each office with Internet access, but the insurance company's IT organization has taken a slightly different view of it. Instead of leasing a separate line to connect the users in Los Angeles with the server in Atlanta, they've decided to send that traffic over the Internet connections at each location, as illustrated in Figure 14.1.

In using its Internet connections in place of a leased line, the company has eliminated the cost of the leased line. Instead of a point-to-point network between Los Angeles and Atlanta, which was actually a leased private line, the company no longer has a "real" private network, but a virtual private network. It's not really a private network, but it acts like one. If the company wanted to do so, it could connect claims offices in other locations back to the Atlanta data center over the Internet. That would eliminate other leased-line costs and bring more traffic and more locations into the virtual private network.

The same company may want to use the Internet to give its telecommuters and road warriors a means to connect to e-mail, file servers, and applications in their field offices, or back to the main office in Atlanta. Instead of paying for many hours of long-distance toll charges, remote workers dial into a local ISP and connect to field offices through their ISP connections. In this case, the Internet acts as the equivalent of a virtual private network of dial-up phone lines.

To be fair, we should say that the intent is always that a VPN will perform just like a real private network, even if it isn't actually a dedicated private network. The cost of a real private network is usually higher than that of an Internet VPN. Cost is usually the motivating factor behind creating Internet VPNs, although a VPN may not duplicate a real private network in every other way.

The reality of a VPN may be somewhat different, for many reasons. IT executives and network managers have a number of factors to consider when choosing between a VPN and a "real" private network connection. These

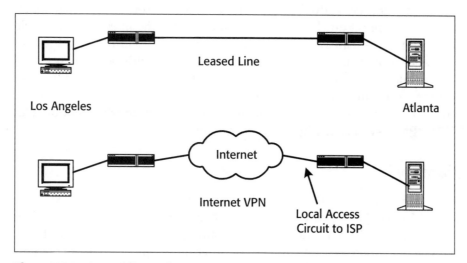

Figure 14.1   Leased line and Internet VPN connection between two locations.

factors include the following considerations: security, performance, reliability, routing, and NAT.

Security

One of the distinct advantages of a private network is that it is, by nature, a relatively secure network. No one else is using it, even though the local telephone companies and long-haul carriers usually multiplex traffic over circuits that are shared by other traffic. Anyone who can access the wires of a leased line can monitor the traffic going across them, but that's basically wiretapping. You'd need access to the physical wires themselves, either in a wiring closet, a point of presence, or in a telco central office or switching center. Tapping into wires is not impossible, but it happens more frequently on TV and in the movies than it does in real life.

The network paths, however, are usually dedicated, not shared. We might contrast this with the Internet, in which virtually everything goes across a number of shared circuits. On the Internet, there is no security, but on the surface, at least, Internet transmission is no less secure than leased-line transmission. Most of the Internet is composed of leased lines, and if they weren't being used for the Internet, they might be used for point-to-point leased-line traffic. Most anyone in the world may be "on" the Internet, so it's not as safe a bet to assume that the Internet is secure. We must assume that VPN security means adding encryption, and the complications that entails, to retrofit the Internet VPN with security.

Performance

As most Internet users know, performance is all relative on the Internet. Sometimes we can connect quickly to Internet sites, and sometimes it's impossible to get through. There are no guarantees to Internet bandwidth, nor to Internet performance. Private lines, on the other hand, do guarantee performance, and most guarantee bandwidth, too. Consequently, the performance of an Internet VPN may be erratic compared to that of a regular private line network. Because it relies on the Internet for transmission capacity, the throughput of an Internet VPN may vary wildly from day to day.

Reliability

As any Internet user can attest, reliability is a relative term in the context of the Internet. Most of the time it works, but there are those days when something, such as the local ISP connection, Internet routing, local network connectivity, the firewall, DNS services, or a number of other things, just isn't feeling like its old self. As a result, there are times when Internet connectivity just doesn't seem to perform well or just doesn't work at all. Private lines have their bad days, too, but their problems are frequently (but not always) easier to assess, and fixes tend to be permanent. The world of private lines is relatively stable, while the stability of Internet connectivity is a transient thing. If you want reliability, maybe a private line is a better choice than a VPN.

Routing

Many private networks are point-to-point networks because that's the way that private lines are usually configured. Some types of private line networks, such as frame-relay networks, aren't really point-to-point networks, although they act like they are. In either case, routing across a private network is straightforward and direct. By contrast, routing across the Internet, or across a VPN that uses the Internet, may be anything but direct. NAT adds complexity, and so does using private addressing, where routing must be kept separate from the Internet. In addition, VPN gateways may have to assign different IP addresses to the clients coming through a VPN connection. Those addresses must be routed, and the networks to which they belong must be announced, both to the internal network and to the Internet at large.

NAT

As with other network configurations, NAT at the VPN gateway, or NAT on the client side of the VPN connection, may add a number of complications. The foremost of these complications is encryption, which is frequently added to VPN traffic to deal with the security issue, or lack of it, in normal Internet communications.

Despite these complications, VPNs are here to stay. If we make the assumption that practically every company and organization has Internet connectivity, the economics of a VPN are hard to beat. VPN performance and reliability may not necessarily be the same as that of a private network. Security is an even more problematic issue for VPNs, and NAT and addressing and routing issues add their own complexities to the issue. The logic of using the ubiquitous Internet connection for all it's worth may overstress that connection, but it won't stop it from being used for more and more networking solutions.

VPN Elements

There are several different types of VPNs, but most share some common elements that are found in the majority of VPN configurations. The elements of a VPN, which are depicted in Figure 14.2, include a "local" side and a "remote" side, as a means of distinguishing the side of the VPN connection where server processes are running (the "local" side) and the side where client processes are running (the "remote" side). Many VPNs are circuits that connect equals, such as two routers that use the Internet to route traffic between networks located behind them.

Generally speaking, we could classify VPNs into two categories. There are a number of variations on these themes, but most VPNs fall into one category or another. The two types are as follows:

Client-based VPNs. A VPN client running on a PC at a remote location connects to a local ISP and establishes a connection across the Internet to a VPN gateway. The VPN gateway may be running on a firewall, and the transmission from the client or the gateway may be encrypted. The VPN gateway authenticates the client and gives the client access to resources on the network behind the gateway or firewall.

Network-based VPNs. Two routers connect networks behind them together by a VPN link the routers establish between them. The link between them is a VPN running over the Internet, instead of a dedicated leased line. The VPN link may be encrypted. Neither clients nor servers on either network are aware of the existence of the VPN.

In either case, the VPN is composed of a number of discrete components or elements. The elements of most VPNs are these: VPN gateway, VPN client, VPN local access, VPN transit network, encryption, authentication, and tunnel.

VPN Gateway

If we make the generalization that a VPN connects systems on one part of the Internet to a network on the other side of the Internet, there should be a system

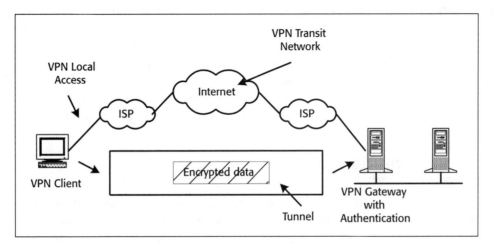

Figure 14.2 Elements of a VPN.

on the destination network that accepts VPN connections from clients. This system is called the VPN gateway, as it is the entrance point from the Internet into the network. The VPN gateway could be a firewall, a screening router, or a special-purpose security system. It's the same device that might perform NAT functions, by translating inside addresses to outside addresses, maintaining connection state, and doing other NAT tasks. In most cases, VPNs incorporate a strong authentication security capability to prevent unauthorized users from using the VPN as a channel into the internal network.

VPN Client

The VPN client is the software running on the client systems, on the remote side of the VPN. Just as in regular client/server communications, the client usually initiates the VPN session. The exception is a peer-to-peer VPN session, such as one between two routers that use the Internet VPN as if it were a leased line. If the VPN gateway incorporates encryption or authentication for VPN clients, the VPN client will have the appropriate encryption keys and encryption algorithms to match those on the VPN gateway.

VPN Local Access

VPN clients use the Internet to connect to the VPN gateway, but the VPN client connection must be made through an ISP. This means that remote clients must have Internet access, either through a dedicated or a dial-up connection. Users who are in a remote location usually have a dial-up ISP connection, either through a local ISP or toll-free number access.

VPN Transit Network

An IP network substitutes for the long-haul portion of a private line network. The IP network is usually the Internet, but it could also be any private or shared IP network. If the Internet forms the transit network for the VPN, it does not imply any of the usual benefits of leased-line connectivity, such as performance, bandwidth, response time, or security.

Encryption

While traffic sent over a VPN does not have to be encrypted, VPNs almost always incorporate some sort of encryption. One of the assumptions made in a VPN environment is that the transit network is a public network, like the Internet, or a private network that is run by a single organization or shared by several. In either case, the data is usually encrypted because there is some assumption of privacy in the communications.

Authentication

Remote VPN clients gain admission into the local network by authenticating themselves. The authentication mechanisms are usually built into the client software, although they may be managed externally by a separate password generator. VPC clients may be authenticated by the VPN gateway or by a destination system, or both.

Tunnel

A tunnel is the encrypted channel over which the data is sent through the VPN. The tunnel is usually a wrapper around the data or the data stream, in order to protect and secure its transmission through the transit network.

Encrypted or secured data may be tunneled across the VPN through another protocol, such as the Point-to-Point Tunneling Protocol (PPTP) or the Layer Two Tunneling Protocol (L2TP) with IPsec. These protocols manage the tunnels, and they encapsulate the data for transmission across the VPN channel.

Other elements may be incorporated in a VPN, but many are variations on these basic elements. For example, different VPN configurations may use different types of encryption and authentication techniques, but the principles of authentication, encryption, and tunneling remain the same. As we will see, some types of encryption won't always work if NAT capabilities have been configured on the VPN gateway.

VPN Addressing and Routing

Network addressing and routing are both affected by the creation of VPNs, whether they are created to replace leased-line-type connections with Internet VPNs or to allow remote users to access a network over the Internet. In order to establish a VPN connection to a VPN gateway, the gateway establishes a new, virtual interface to the gateway. The new virtual interface must be assigned a new IP address. Furthermore, new routes must be established, or old ones changed, so that this new IP address and interface can be reached by Internet routing. If NAT is involved in the operation of the VPN gateway, the IP address assigned to the gateway's virtual interface must be compatible with the address translation performed by NAT, in order to pass traffic back into the network successfully.

The virtual interface on the VPN gateway is necessary so that the VPN traffic can be separated from the regular traffic that comes to the VPN gateway's external interface. The VPN gateway may be a firewall or a router that is serving double duty as a VPN gateway. It already has an external interface IP address, on which it sends and receives all non-VPN traffic. The VPN gate-

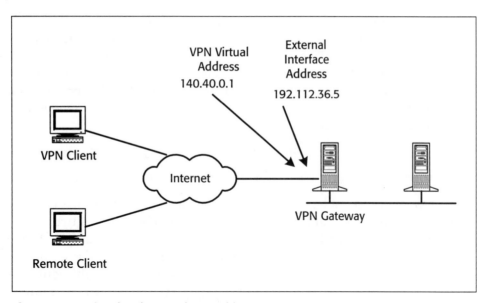

Figure 14.3   Virtual and external VPN addresses.

way's virtual IP address is simply another IP address for its external interface. The second address, illustrated in Figure 14.3, identifies the "receiving end" of the VPN tunnel, so that VPN traffic is clearly separated and distinguished from normal Internet traffic.

To make matters more confusing, the client side may be assigned either one or two new addresses, depending on the type of VPN connection the client side requests. The client may need a second IP address to be its VPN virtual address, so that it too can distinguish VPN traffic from other, standard Internet traffic.

To simplify the coverage of VPNs, addressing, routing, and NAT, we'll limit this discussion to two different types of VPNs. The first will be the fixed, or permanent VPN, which is often deployed as a replacement for a leased line between two routers. The second is the transient, or dial-up, VPN. In this situation, a dial-up user connects to an internal network over a VPN channel established over the Internet, instead of over a long-distance or toll-free 800 number.

The Router-to-Router VPN

A VPN between two routers connects two portions of a private network together. The VPN substitutes an Internet connection for a dedicated line between the two routers. As far as the routers are concerned, they still route data to each other over the connection. As far as the IT director is concerned, the organization's monthly telecommunications costs have been reduced, although the load on its ISP connection probably will have been increased.

The router-to-router VPN connection is relatively straightforward. Unlike a dial-up VPN connection, which will be discussed next, there may not be any temporary IP addresses to be assigned to clients or servers. Router-to-router VPNs fall into two types, one of which resembles the dial-up VPN model. The two types of router-to-router VPNs are these:

Transient VPNs. Router-to-router VPNs over dial-up connections.

Permanent. Router-to-router VPNs that are left in place permanently.

The two types of router-to-router VPNs fit into different usage circumstances. The former is suitable if there is only sporadic traffic between two LANs or if ISP access and connection costs are an issue. For example, if two Exchange e-mail connectors on two different LANs are configured to exchange e-mail once every two hours on weekdays, and once every eight hours on weekends, there may not be a need to keep the VPN operational, consuming system resources on both routers, all the time. It can be reestablished only when it is needed, then taken down when the e-mail exchange is done. A timer and dialing instructions are usually programmed into the client end of the transient VPN, so that the dial-up connection can be established automatically.

The latter, the permanent router-to-router VPN, is the more widely deployed of the two. This version gives two networks a permanent VPN connection to each other through their VPN gateway routers, allowing devices and servers on either network full-time, on-demand access to each other. The permanent VPN connection can be established over a dial-up or a dedicated ISP access circuit, although dedicated ISP access is more common for the permanent router-to-router VPN. In either case, the same general VPN configuration issues apply, although they may vary depending on the specific implementation of VPN software by specific vendors. For example, the routers' VPN software will tunnel data to each other over the VPN, possibly encrypting the data after each router authenticates itself to its VPN partner router.

The Dial-Up VPN

A remote user who establishes a VPN from a dial-up connection must first connect to an ISP, then create the VPN connection to the VPN gateway in a second, separate step. Each connection—the first dial-up connection and the second VPN connection—may require a separate IP address assignment for the client.

A dial-up client usually has no valid IP address, even though an IP address may have been preconfigured in the client. The client will have to get an IP address from the ISP because the ISP will be responsible for routing data to and from the dial-up user for the duration of its session with the ISP. During the *Point-to-Point Protocol* (PPP) negotiation with the ISP's remote access service, the dial-up VPN client requests and receives an IP address. It's a host address from an IP network address that has been allocated to the ISP. For all intents and purposes, the VPN client, like any ISP client, will become a host on the ISP's network for the duration of its dial-up session.

The dial-up ISP client, however, will use that ISP connection to become a VPN client. When the VPN connection has been established, the VPN client and the VPN gateway will use the IP address assigned by the ISP to pass traffic between the client and the VPN gateway. The client and the gateway will use that connection to tunnel data across the Internet. The destination of the tunneled data originated at the client side will be an IP address on the internal network behind the VPN gateway, as illustrated in Figure 14.4.

With a valid address and a way to connect across the Internet, the VPN client and VPN gateway establish the VPN connection. The address assigned by the ISP to the VPN client is a valid public address, so it is fully routable on the Internet. Once the client and the VPN gateway have completed their negotiations, and once the remote client has been authenticated to the VPN gateway, the gateway assigns a second IP address to the client. This address is from the internal network behind the VPN gateway. It may be assigned from an address pool assigned to the VPN gateway or by DHCP. The address assigned by the VPN gateway may be from either public or private address space, whichever is used on the internal network.

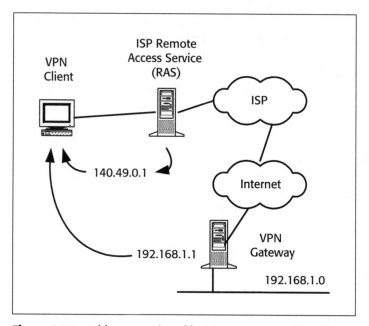

Figure 14.4   Addresses assigned by VPN gateway and by RAS.

The VPN client will use this address, which is the client's *virtual VPN address*, as the source address of the IP datagrams that will be tunneled across the VPN connection on the Internet. In effect, the VPN client will become a host on the internal network, even though it is only "virtually attached" to the internal network through the VPN tunnel. The address from the internal network may not be a routable Internet address, if it is from private address space.

Note that the tunneled datagrams bear internal network source and destination addresses, but they are encapsulated in other IP datagrams that bear public, routable Internet addresses. For example, traffic originating from the VPN client and destined for the VPN gateway use the ISP-assigned address as the source address and the VPN gateway's external address as the destination address. Internet routers see these valid addresses and deliver the datagrams to the external interface of the VPN gateway.

When they arrive at the VPN gateway, the VPN gateway identifies them as VPN traffic. The VPN gateway strips off the outer IP encapsulation and extracts the tunneled datagrams within. This is the real VPN traffic, as its source address is the internal address assigned to the VPN client by the VPN gateway, and its destination address is a host on the internal network.

The data that crosses the VPN connection may be encrypted either by the ISP's RAS or by the VPN client. Which one does the encryption usually depends on how the VPN gateway handles encryption. Some VPN gateways that are also firewalls use their own VPN client software. The client encryption can be decrypted by the VPN gateway in the firewall because that's the only encryption the firewall trusts. Many ISPs offer a VPN service that encrypts data sent across a client-to-gateway VPN. In that case, the termination point of the VPN on the ISP access point to the VPN gateway decrypts the transmission before passing the data in the clear back to the VPN gateway. In this case, the VPN gateway may seek only to authenticate the remote user.

If the ISP does the encryption, a dial-up PC really isn't a VPN client per se. A dial-up PC is only a real VPN "client" if it encrypts the data itself. Otherwise, if the ISP creates the VPN, the remote PC is a client of the service it reaches, but not a VPN client. It's a semantic difference, but a "real" VPN client is the "distant end" of a VPN connection that merely passes through the ISP's network.

The VPN gateway may also employ NAT to change those addresses before it passes the traffic back into the internal network. It would do so if it has assigned the VPN client an external, routable address, as a means to protect whatever addressing system is being used on the internal network.

VPNs and NAT

So where does NAT enter into the VPN environment? First, clients that connect into internal networks through VPN tunnels may become part of networks that use private addressing. When a remote client becomes part of an internal network over a VPN, it uses a host address from the internal network's address range. The intent of the VPN is to allow the remote device to be part of the internal network environment and to give it connectivity to internal network hosts.

The remote client may act like any other internal network host and establish contact to external hosts. For example, a remote VPN client is connected to the internal network over the VPN tunnel set up over the Internet. It already has Internet connectivity through the ISP, but all of its traffic is being tunneled over the VPN tunnel back to the VPN gateway. It's possible, though, that the VPN client may have to communicate with a host on the Internet, at the same time it's using the Internet for its VPN tunnel. The remote client can't have it both ways, using the ISP connection for both VPN and general-purpose Internet connectivity. Its pathway back out to the Internet will be back through the internal network firewall, as illustrated in Figure 14.5.

If the VPN client's virtual address, as assigned by the VPN gateway at tunnel setup time, is a private address, then that address would have to be changed to a routable public address by the firewall. The firewall and the VPN gateway may well be the same device. If so, its NAT function will translate the VPN client's internal private address to a public external address before forwarding that traffic onto the Internet. If the NAT function is configured to translate all internal addresses to a single external address, that's what the VPN client's address will be translated to as well.

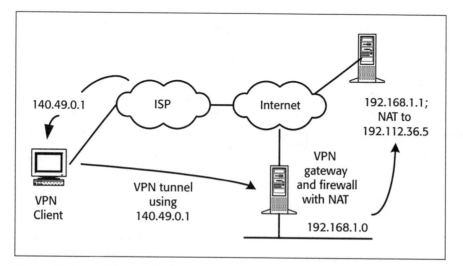

Figure 14.5 VPN bounceback to Internet through VPN gateway.

NAT and VPN Encryption

There are two significant complications for NAT in configuring and maintaining VPNs. Neither, fortunately, is anything new, but while one of the complications can be addressed, the other can't. The two problems are these:

- Embedded IP addresses in IP datagram payloads
- Encrypted data in tunneled datagrams

First, let's deal with the embedded IP addresses. We've seen these embedded addresses before, in the discussion of NAT and applications in Chapter 7, "Making Applications Work with NAT." The FTP PORT command, for example, embeds IP addresses in the data payloads of IP datagrams. Some video applications, such as those that use the H.323 standard, use embedded addresses to set up video and audio session parameters.

The solution to these problems is an application-level gateway (ALG). An ALG is a NAT software solution that has the ability to reach into the data fields of datagrams and change IP addresses and, if necessary, TCP port numbers, checksums, and other fields. In Microsoft Windows terminology, an ALG is referred to as a NAT editor, but it's the same thing.

This sounds like a terrific solution, but there's a catch. The catch is that NAT can't very well play around with addresses in encrypted transmissions of any type unless it is the end-point of the transmission (i.e., the device that encrypts and decrypts the data). The encrypted data issue is always problematic for NAT because the traffic that goes across a VPN tunnel is often encrypted. The fundamental problem is that NAT can't handle encrypted data too well, particularly if it can't read the IP address and TCP port fields it's supposed to translate.

Fortunately, there are ALGs for a few types of encrypted VPN data streams, but not for all of them. Some types of VPN encryption, such as the Point-to-Point Tunneling Protocol (PPTP), can be handled by NAT, as long as it has an appropriate ALG or, in the Windows environment, NAT editor. On the other hand, data encrypted by the Level Two Tunneling Protocol (L2TP), combined with IP Secure (IPsec) encryption, can't readily be translated by NAT. To borrow a concept from the ever-expressive Austin Powers character, the L2TP-IPsec combination causes NAT to lose its mojo, so to speak.

PPTP Traffic

A VPN connection that uses the PPTP protocol encapsulates the data formatted by another protocol, the Point-to-Point Protocol (PPP), into IP datagrams. PPP is a commonly used protocol for a dial-up connection to an ISP. As its name implies, PPTP tunnels PPP within it, for transmission over the VPN. PPTP uses a TCP connection, which is called the PPTP control connection, to create, maintain, and terminate the VPN tunnel. PPTP encapsulates PPP frames as tunneled data. The payloads of the encapsulated PPP frames may be encrypted or compressed, or both.

The PPP frames, which the dial-up ISP client uses to connect to the ISP, can be encrypted and then embedded in PPTP frames for transmission over the Internet VPN. The PPTP framing includes the source IP address of the client, a TCP destination port number, and another identifier, the Call ID, to identify the VPN client session.

This is all good and well, except if there are multiple PPTP clients on the private network side of a NAT device that are tunneling to the same PPTP server. If this happens, NAT translates all of the internal source addresses to the same external address. Consequently, all of the tunneled traffic has the same source address because that's how it was changed by NAT. Furthermore, the PPTP clients don't know about each other, so it's possible that some of them might pick the same Call ID when they establish the PPTP tunnel. As a result, it's possible that tunneled data from several different PPTP clients on the private networks side of the NAT device might have the same Call ID, as well as the NAT-translated source address, when they appear at the other end of the PPTP tunnel.

Obviously, this won't do because the other end of the PPTP tunnel won't be able to tell the data streams apart nor return responses to the correct systems. To prevent this problem, either an ALG or a NAT editor must monitor the PPTP tunnels when they are created. If that's done, the ALG can create separate mappings between the private IP address and Call ID the PPTP client uses, and the public IP address and Call Id that will be seen by the PPTP server on the other end of the VPN.

Fortunately, such an ALG or NAT editor already exists to do just such a task. In the Windows 2000 Routing and Remote Access Service (RRAS), there is a NAT editor for PPTP. The NAT editor translates the Call ID on outgoing PPTP tunnels so that the multiple PPTP tunnels can be distinguished on the private side of the NAT box.

L2TP with IPsec Encryption

As discussed in Chapter 13, "NAT and Security," the Level Two Tunneling Protocol (L2TP) combined PPTP and another protocol, Layer Two Forwarding (L2F). The latter was devised by Cisco Systems, but to avoid having two competing standards in the market, the best features of both PPTP and L2F were combined into one protocol, L2TP.

The standard way to create a VPN with L2TP is to encrypt the data tunneled within it over the VPN connection with another encryption standard, *IP Secure* (IPsec). The data tunneled through L2TP is encrypted with IPsec, making the VPN data secure. That's good because the data is secure. It's also bad because NAT can't translate anything that's been encrypted with IPsec (nor, for that matter, any other encryption algorithm).

The problem is that even if an ALG or a NAT editor could look into the IPsec fields and translate the source and destination addresses, the ALG or NAT gateway wouldn't have the correct cryptographic key to recalculate the cryptographic checksum in the IPsec framing. This would invalidate the encryption because the destination decryption algorithm would not match the checksum. Consequently, IPsec encryption is just as big a problem for NAT in VPN environments as it is in regular encryption scenarios.

VPNs, NAT, and IT Strategy

Among the IT executive set, VPNs have become a fashionable trend, but they also have a practical appeal as well. The idea of using the Internet for more practical purposes than an employees' free-form Web surfing mosh pit holds a strong appeal to IT executives long accustomed to regarding communications costs as an ever-rising, monolithic expense item. Use the Internet as a substitute for those expensive leased lines? Sounds good to me, most IT executives say.

Fortunately, NAT can be thrown into the VPN mix without causing many more complications than address translation normally does. If anything, establishing a VPN into a private addressing domain, which must use NAT anyway to make those private addresses routable on the Internet, helps to preserve the privacy of the virtual private network concept. Encryption on VPNs, particularly IPsec, can pose problems for NAT on VPN gateways, but fortunately, IPsec isn't part of every VPN solution.

IT executives who are considering a wholesale leased line-for-VPN substitution program would be well advised to consider the downside of this idea. It might seem that running large numbers of leased-line circuits over the Internet would be a fabulous way to make the most of that investment in Internet access. If it can reduce leased-line costs, what's the problem?

The answer is that VPNs, like the Internet itself, aren't perfect. Does the Internet seem to have its bad days once in a while? So will your VPNs. Do your globe-trotting road warriors have problems getting Internet access in Sao Paulo? So will their VPN connections. Would you trust a mission-critical application to the Internet? These days, the answer to that question more and more seems to be yes, as businesses move all kinds of applications, even their basic business activities, to the Internet.

IT executives should temper their enthusiasm for VPNs with a measure of caution. There are a number of things about leased lines that still make them more attractive alternatives to VPNs. Leased lines can be less trouble to manage and use, and they make for less complex finger-pointing exercises when something goes wrong.

Summary

In this chapter, we've looked at the use, application, and configuration of VPNs as substitutes for leased lines or as an alternative to long-distance charges for network access. Just like the Internet that forms the underlying structure of VPNs, the concept of using the Internet for all kinds of long-haul communications applications seems well founded. Today, more and more organizations and companies are jumping into VPNs. For many, it's a cost-saving measure. For others, it's a way to maximize the use of that Internet connection. For others, it's a way to tie far-flung operations together without having to provide anything more specific than Internet access from all network points.

In the VPN environment, NAT is either a simple configuration issue or, when certain types of encryption are involved, a profound roadblock that scotches attempts to establish VPNs. It's perfectly acceptable, as we have noted in this chapter, to establish VPNs to or between private addressing domains and to use NAT on the VPN gateway to translate addresses back and forth to public addressing domains. Encryption is the significant stumbling block to NAT in VPN environments, particularly if there's no NAT application-level gateway to read embedded IP addresses and TCP ports in datagram data fields. If the NAT device isn't the end-point of the VPN, encryption may foil any attempt to mix NAT and VPNs.

In the next chapter, we'll look at a new proposal to allow NAT to work in most any network configuration, including ones that deploy IPsec and other techniques that confound NAT. The proposal is called *Realm-Specific IP* (RSIP). It is a technique by which IP addresses do achieve end-to-end significance, even though there may be a NAT device somewhere in the network. It's a way to have the cake of NAT and to eat it, too.

CHAPTER

15

Realm-Specific IP and NAT

One of those nagging problems with NAT that we have mentioned frequently is that applications can have a nasty way of embedding things in data payloads that standard NAT devices can't see. What NAT can't see, it can't translate, and what it can't translate can sometimes hurt its ability to pass application data transparently. For example, as we discussed in Chapter 13, "NAT and Security," NAT, like any external party to encryption, can't tell what's inside the encrypted or signed part of a data payload. Sometimes applications, even simple ones like FTP, embed IP addresses in data payloads that aren't always translated correctly.

In the greater scheme of things, NAT is supposed to be transparent to everything in the network, including routers, applications, and ultimately end users. The trouble is that NAT isn't always quite transparent enough because data payloads aren't completely "clean." As we discussed in Chapter 7, "Making Applications Work with NAT," some day all applications may be designed with the possibility that traffic might go through NAT address translation somewhere in the network. Obviously, they're not all designed that way; although today, many application developers try to accommodate NAT by not embedding IP addresses and applications pointers in data fields. Encrypted data is another matter, but there are solutions to that problem, too.

But even so, and even if it's supposed to be—and, in most cases, is—transparent, NAT can impose barriers that obstruct the flow of data between end applications. It's not as if we can just dispense with NAT and solve all applications problems that way. Solving application issues can be quite complex, particularly if we have to impose an *application-level gateway* (ALG) between two applications. ALGs aren't simple, and they can impose severe performance penalties on application data flow. Furthermore, ALGs aren't available for many applications, and those that are sometimes don't work reliably.

The real world has many examples of networks that use private addressing, not to mention illegal (not officially assigned) addressing, overlapping addressing, and other tactics that network administrators have routed to "liberate" address space for their networks. The simplest way to connect these networks to the Internet is through NAT. It's not rocket science, although it does have to be implemented carefully, and most firewalls and routers incorporate NAT in their basic feature set. For most network administrators, NAT is the most practical solution to making private and public addressing realms interoperable.

The RSIP Solution

But what if there were another way, besides NAT and ALGs, to link applications running on systems in different private and public addressing domains and make applications work transparently? Is there a way to bypass some of the complexities of NAT, particularly for applications that embed IP addresses in data payloads or that use encrypted data fields?

As it turns out, there is such a solution, but it's still in the experimental stage. It hasn't been widely tested, but it has the potential to offer an alternative to NAT and ALGs. The solution is *Realm-Specific IP* (RSIP), which has been proposed as an Internet Draft to the *Internet Engineering Task Force* (IETF).

It is important to note that RSIP is not NAT, although both accomplish much the same end. Both NAT and RSIP divide networks into inside and outside addressing realms. NAT translates addresses between the two, while an RSIP client uses a borrowed external address for outside communications. As we will see, an RSIP client understands the need to use an external address when it communicates outside the network. In a NAT environment, the NAT device does the translation because clients and servers make no distinction between inside and outside addresses. We are examining RSIP because in the future it may be implemented in place of NAT, and RSIP has the potential for circumventing some of the problems that NAT may introduce into networks.

On the surface, RSIP is relatively simple, but it requires two new pieces that aren't part of standard NAT: an RSIP client and an RSIP server. Instead of translating private addresses to public addresses on the NAT device at the entrance point to the network, an RSIP server assigns a routable, public

IETF INTERNET DRAFTS

RSIP is one of a number of networking techniques, protocols, and policies that have been proposed as an "Internet Draft" to the IETF. An Internet Draft is a working document, proposed for consideration by IETF members, to improve, extend, or devise new solutions to Internet communications. The IETF considers the draft documents to be proposals for *Request for Comment* (RFC) status, but they are working documents while they are drafts. IETF members, or anyone else who wants to do so, may comment on the drafts, throw darts at them, or propose new parts to them. The process is meant to be a formalized peer review, as a means to clarify the proposals or specifications in Internet Drafts before they are considered to become formalized documents as RFCs. Internet Drafts may be withdrawn if they're deemed not to be useful, and they're not intended to be permanent. Internet Drafts have a "shelf life" of six months, after which they are either withdrawn or revised.

If they are accepted by the IETF, they may be promoted to RFC status. RFCs are the official publications vehicle for Internet standards documents and other publications of the IETF, which acts on behalf of the Internet community. RFCs cover a wide range of topics and include Internet standards, research results, and documents about the status of the Internet.

RFCs that document Internet standards are usually given an extra designation, such as "STDxxx," but the RFC still keeps its RFC number and place in the RFC sequence. Some RFCs standardize the results of Internet-wide deliberations about statements of principle conclusions about the "best practice" for networking, or some IETF function. RFCs are available at a number of Web sites, including the IETF's Web site, www.ietf.org.

The "standards track" from Internet Draft to Internet Standard is intentionally arduous, progressing through intensive reviews as it moves from Proposed Standard to Draft Standard to Internet Standard. Other documents may move in the "nonstandards track" and be designated RFCs that are Informational, Experimental, or that specify Best Practices. RFCs that are made obsolete by newer RFCs are designated as Historic.

address to an RSIP client temporarily, for use in communicating outside the private networking realm. The RSIP client uses the private address as if it were its own address for the duration of the application session. When the application session ends, the RSIP client returns the public address to the RSIP server, so it can be reassigned to another RSIP client.

When the RSIP client gets a "loaner" public address from the RSIP server, the RSIP client uses that public address in the data payload of its IP datagrams. The RSIP client still uses its private, inside network address in its IP datagrams when it communicates with the RSIP server. IP datagrams that bear the RSIP server-assigned public address are wrapped inside IP datagrams that are addressed to the RSIP server. The leased public address is embedded within the application data fields of the tunneled datagrams, eliminating the need to translate the embedded data. The RSIP server strips off the inside network datagram packaging before the traffic leaves the private network, leaving the tunneled datagrams intact.

RSIP's concept of temporarily lending outside addresses restores the end-to-end significance of IP addresses that traditional NAT removes. In that sense, RSIP is an improvement on NAT because it may truly be transparent to applications that have problems with networks that use NAT. RSIP may be the way to pass embedded IP addresses transparently in applications data or data fields that have been encrypted. If traditional NAT can't read or change those fields, then maybe RSIP can avoid the problem entirely.

Any discussion of RSIP must be prefaced with that "maybe" because, at this writing, RSIP is still in the proposal stage. At this point, there are no products on the market that act as RSIP servers, and there aren't any working RSIP clients. Neither, though, would be all that difficult to implement. Another good thing about RSIP is that like traditional NAT, it would be transparent to all other network components, such as routers, switches, and applications protocols. If the RSIP proposal is elevated to RFC status, we may see RSIP implemented in network clients and RSIP servers embedded in NAT boxes. RSIP is a logical and relatively simple extension to traditional NAT, with relatively few repercussions outside the network that houses the RSIP clients and servers.

You're Preapproved!

In principle, RSIP does the same sort of thing as traditional NAT. RSIP still requires an RSIP server, which does IP address assignment for RSIP clients. The RSIP client is presumably a user's PC, but it could be a multiuser system or a system that runs a specialized application, such as video. The RSIP client negotiates with the RSIP server before initiating the data stream to the external system. Unlike traditional NAT, the RSIP server assigns an external public address to the RSIP client during this up-front negotiation phase. The RSIP server could also function as the NAT box, translating addresses for devices that didn't need RSIP services.

In subsequent communications for the session, the RSIP client would use the assigned external address in the data fields of IP datagrams containing applications data or session setup. The client would use its real private address to communicate back to the RSIP server. The RSIP server, which could also be a NAT box, would strip off the IP address header on the internal network datagram before sending the IP datagrams inside, with its application data, to the external network. If the application data has embedded IP addresses, or if it has encrypted data, with embedded, encrypted IP addresses, they needn't be changed by the RSIP server.

Because the RSIP client knows the external pubic address that will be assigned to it by the RSIP server, the RSIP server doesn't need to make any changes in applications data fields. If the data fields have embedded addresses, they'll be public, routable ones. Furthermore, the RSIP server won't have to map those addresses back to their internal counterparts because that task will be moved back to the RSIP client.

RSIP could be called *presubscribed NAT* because the RSIP client and RSIP server arrange beforehand the IP address and TCP ports that the client will use. Having arranged this beforehand, the RSIP server knows the identity of the RSIP client and strips off the IP wrapper with the inside network address. The RSIP client's tunneled datagrams are already addressed with the pre-arranged external address as the source address.

The process is reversed for return traffic. The RSIP server accepts responses addressed to the RSIP client's outside address and then rewraps them in IP datagrams addressed to the RSIP client's inside network address. The datagrams are delivered over the inside network to the RSIP client, which strips off the IP datagram headers to reveal the "real" datagrams enclosed within. If there are any IP addresses or TCP ports embedded in the data fields or encrypted in the data fields, they won't need to be touched by the RSIP server.

The potential benefit of RSIP is that it offers the internal network the addressing flexibility of NAT, as well as the ability to pass embedded application data field addresses transparently. It's relatively simple, and its manipulations of addresses and data fields is not visible outside the network. RSIP circumvents many of the issues around NAT and ALGs, bypassing both of them.

Making RSIP Work

To illustrate how RSIP might work, let's say that we have a network that uses private addressing from the 10/8 address space, as shown in Figure 15.1. Let's say we also have RSIP client software loaded on selected PCs on this internal network. The RSIP client wouldn't have to be loaded on all clients, but only on those that use applications with embedded IP addresses or that do encryption.

Let's also say that our sample network has an RSIP server configured on a router that connects the network to the Internet through an ISP. The router also runs NAT, translating most internal addresses to a single external address or to a pool of IP addresses. It doesn't matter which way the NAT box does traditional NAT address translation, although the RSIP server software will do things slightly differently for the RSIP clients.

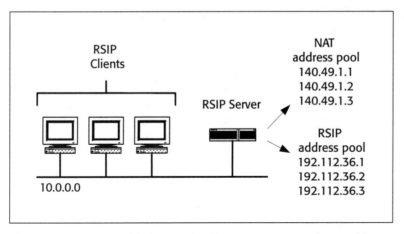

Figure 15.1 RSIP-enabled network with separate RSIP and NAT address pools.

Note that the RSIP server has been configured with two pools of public addresses. The first will be used for traditional NAT and the second for RSIP. There isn't a requirement for the public addresses to come from two different address spaces, but this example will separate them to maintain the distinction between regular NAT and RSIP addresses. The RSIP server will assign public addresses from the RSIP pool to RSIP clients, but it will use the other addresses in the standard NAT pool for standard NAT translation.

The RSIP concept also assumes that the RSIP client and server have a way of negotiating a lease of an RSIP address before the client uses it. Although the details of this client/server protocol have not been spelled out in the RSIP draft specification, it's assumed that this protocol would be part of an RSIP implementation. RSIP also assumes that RSIP clients would be aware of applications that need RSIP, so they might ask for RSIP addresses when they execute applications that need it.

I Want My RSIP

The RSIP process starts when an RSIP client, executing an application that embeds IP addresses in data fields, needs to establish a session with the server or host on an external network. Using its internal network private address, the RSIP client "registers" with the RSIP server. The registration process notifies the RSIP server that the RSIP client, identified by its internal network address, wants to "lease" a public address. The registration process is illustrated in Figure 15.2.

The primary purpose of the RSIP client registration is to establish a session with the RSIP server, making the server aware of the identity (i.e., the source IP address) of the RSIP client. The server also specifies the parameters of the

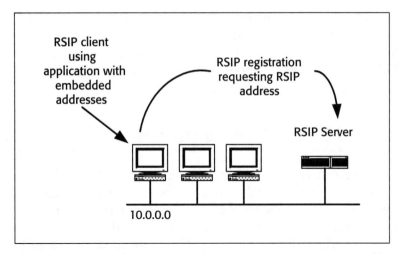

Figure 15.2   RSIP client registers with RSIP server to request RSIP address.

tunneling that the client and server will do to get the embedded data to the RSIP server.

In the RSIP environment, *tunneling* means that the RSIP client encapsulates the IP datagrams that will be sent to the outside network within IP datagrams that can flow across the internal private network. Tunneling is a technique to wrap one type of data within another wrapper. The RSIP client will wrap the datagrams destined for the outside network within IP datagrams addressed to the RSIP server, using its internal address, as illustrated in Figure 15.3.

One of the difficulties foreseen by the designers of RSIP is that routes to the public network addresses maintained by the RSIP server can't be advertised to

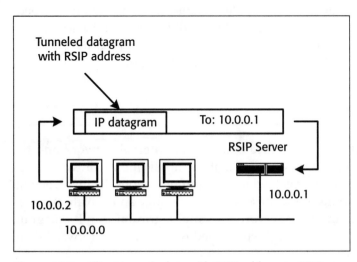

Figure 15.3   Client tunnels data with RSIP address to RSIP server.

the internal network. The datagrams the RSIP client sends to the RSIP server can't use the external network addresses. Those addresses aren't known to the internal network, so there's no route inside the network to those outside addresses. The RSIP server knows about those external networks, but that information is irrelevant to inside network hosts.

Registering and Using RSIP Addresses

Once the RSIP client registers with the RSIP server, the RSIP client asks for a public IP address. The RSIP server takes an address from its public address pool and returns the address to the RSIP client. The RSIP client will use this address as the source address for its IP datagrams, even though it isn't its "real" source address. Those IP datagrams will be embedded as data in IP datagrams that are tunneled across the internal network to the RSIP server.

The RSIP client may also negotiate with the RSIP server for TCP ports that can be used in the tunneled datagrams. Because some applications may require that TCP ports as well as IP source addresses be embedded in data, the RSIP client may request a complete public IP address and TCP source port "package" from the RSP server.

When the RSIP server assigns the address and ports to the RSIP client, the server builds an address-mapping table entry, as depicted in Figure 15.4. The purpose of the table entry will not be to perform address translation at the RSIP server, but to unwrap the IP datagrams that have been tunneled through the internal network to the RSIP server. The RSIP server identifies IP datagrams that will have to be "detunneled" by the source address on the IP header, which is the source address of the RSIP client.

Meanwhile, back inside the tunneled datagrams, the RSIP client has embedded the public address that was assigned by the RSIP server. If the application protocol required it, the RSIP client will have also embedded the public IP address and TCP port within the data field of the datagram.

Breaking It Out

Now the RSIP client can communicate across the internal network and the external network, with some assurance that the application will work properly. The RSIP server will be involved in all communications. Its involvement, however, won't be to translate addresses between public and private addressing domains. Instead, the RSIP server will simply strip off the IP datagram "envelope" around the RSIP client's embedded datagrams and forward them to the external network for delivery.

It doesn't matter if there are embedded addresses and TCP ports in the data

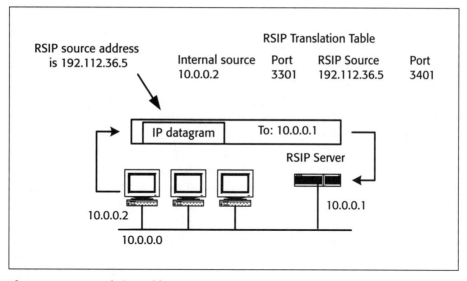

Figure 15.4   Translation table on RSIP server.

fields of the detunneled datagrams because they don't need to be changed by the RSIP server. The data fields may even be encrypted. Even if they are, the encryption is irrelevant and invisible to the RSIP server because it isn't doing traditional address translation. Furthermore, it isn't concerned at all with embedded or encrypted address and ports because they're the client's concern, not the RSIP server's concern.

For the duration of the application session, the RSIP client maintains whatever session parameters it negotiates with the destination application server-side process. The RSIP server needn't be involved in the client/server application session negotiation, nor in conducting the application. Remember that in a standard NAT environment, the NAT box would have to manage address and TCP port translation and maintain application session state. RSIP eliminates both of those complications, throwing all of the application session negotiation back to the RSIP client.

Finishing Up

The RSIP public address "lease" concept has a lot in common with DHCP address leasing. Once the RSIP client has completed its application session, the client must free up the address and the TCP source port, if the RSIP server assigned both. The RSIP server puts the address back in the public address pool, for reassignment to another RSIP client. The RSIP client may also request that the lease on an address and TCP port be extended or that the address and port be reserved for use another time.

Some security systems require the use of the same IP source address, and in some cases, the application session may be simpler if the server "knows" the source address. The RSIP client can request that a public address lease be extended or that the address binding be renewed when it binds a TCP session with the application server in the future.

If the RSIP client gives up the address and doesn't request to extend or renew the lease, the RSIP server deregisters the address and terminates the session with the RSIP client. Once the address has been deregistered and the RSIP session terminated, the RSIP client and server are no longer bound into any type of relationship. There isn't any notion of persistence in the relationship of RSIP clients and servers. Once the RSIP session ends, it's over, and the RSIP client and server no longer have any type of binding between them once the public address and TCP ports have been released.

There's no requirement for RSIP to use TCP either because everything in the tunneled datagrams is transparent to the RSIP server. For that matter, the initial RSIP protocol negotiation between the RSIP client and server over the IP address, lease parameters, and TCP port requirements may also be done over TCP or UDP. TCP will be a more reliable, connection-oriented protocol, but the RSIP draft specification doesn't favor or recommend one over the other.

RSIP on a Single External Interface

One common network configuration that won't work well with RSIP is the single external interface configuration in which all internal addresses are hidden with a single external interface. This is often implemented with a firewall, which represents all internal addresses with a single external interface address. The firewall NATs all internal addresses to the same external address, changing TCP ports and maintaining session state on the fly.

While the RSIP server could be implemented on a firewall or a screening router that translates all internal addresses to a single external address, the RSIP technique won't work properly through a device that represents all internal addresses on a single external address. The problem is that using a single external address requires address translation. That requires NAT to look into and to change the IP and TCP headers. RSIP doesn't work that way. Unlike NAT, RSIP makes no changes to the RSIP client's embedded datagrams except to strip away the tunneling packaging.

Thinking about RSIP

To IT executives who are contemplating various address translation strategies for private networks, RSIP sounds like a great solution. In fact it is, or to put it more accurately, it might be. The problem is that RSIP doesn't exist as a real product yet. Like many of the application-level gateways (ALGs) mentioned in Chapter 7, RSIP is still in the embryonic stage. At the time that this was written, RSIP was still in the Internet Draft specification stage, which means that it's possible that it may never be formally standardized by the IETF. Beyond that, there's the issue of how or if it might be implemented by vendors and how applications would support it.

The concept of RSIP is sound, and for many types of networking environments, it may prove to be an excellent addition to the network manager's toolkit. RSIP stands a good chance of becoming another alternative that IT executives and network managers can deploy to extend the benefits of NAT to applications that otherwise can't use it.

RSIP Advantages

Assuming that it ever appears as a real product, RSIP offers a number of advantages to network managers. Some of those advantages include the following: simplicity, end-to-end extension for NAT, noninvasive manipulation, transparency to embedded applications, higher performance, use for private or public addressing, and extension of the life of IPv4.

Simplicity

Although it does very little address or traffic manipulation at all, RSIP does have one of the most desirable virtues in data communications: simplicity. Note that we didn't necessarily say that it works because it's still a proposed technique. It is a simple, relatively straightforward solution to the problems of linking private addressing domains to the Internet and making address-sensitive applications work across those networks.

End-to-End Extension for NAT

The most significant advantage of RSIP is that it extends the basic operation of NAT all the way from the source client to the destination server process. NAT imposes some limitations on the types of applications that will work with standard address translation. RSIP allows those applications to operate end to end across several types of networks, even the Internet, without changes by NAT.

Noninvasive Manipulation

RSIP doesn't imply any manipulation of any of the fields in the IP datagram, so it's not an invasive technique. Except for stripping away the tunneling envelope around the RSIP client's IP datagram payload, the RSIP server doesn't touch anything in the client's transmission.

Transparency to Embedded Applications

One of the most significant advantages of RSIP is that its noninvasive operation can solve one of the most significant drawbacks to standard NAT. RSIP holds out the hope of working transparently with applications' embedded addresses and ports in data fields. It's also a solution to the encrypted data problem, provided the encryption scheme doesn't encrypt the entire datagram or obscure addressing and TCP port information.

Higher Performance

Without the requirement to change source and destination addresses, map TCP ports, and recalculate checksum fields, RSIP should perform better than traditional NAT software. Once the initial negotiation for an address lease has been completed, the performance of an RSIP server or gateway, measured in the amount of delay that RSIP introduces, compared to what traditional NAT introduces, should be better. Given that RSIP does practically no processing at all, there should be no noticeable effect of running RSIP at all.

Useful for Private or Public Addressing

RSIP doesn't distinguish between public and private address spaces. Except for the requirement that the RSIP server extend a public address lease to an RSIP client, any kind of addressing may be used on the internal network. If there is a requirement to do so, RSIP and traditional NAT may be mixed on the same network gateway to provide alternate ways to map inside and outside networks together.

Extends the Life of IPv4

Like NAT, RSIP is one of those address management techniques that will extend the life of the IPv4 addressing scheme. The same address conservation reasons for using NAT, such as private addressing domains and overlapping address ranges, can be used as the rationale for RSIP. We could argue that techniques that extend the life of IPv4 only delay the inevitable exhaustion of the IPv4 address space and the need to transition to the next version of IP.

RSIP Disadvantages

Lest we get too wrapped up extolling the proposed virtues of RSIP, we should realize that there's also a dark side to RSIP. Try using it in a real product available on the market today, for example. Some of the disadvantages of RSIP are these: it's not real yet, it requires RSIP-aware clients, and it requires tunneling.

It's Not Real Yet

Any discussion of RSIP has to be prefaced by an understanding that it's still only a proposal that hasn't yet been implemented in an actual working piece of commercially available hardware or software. The documents that specify RSIP, the RSIP client/server protocol, and other issues are still only works in progress at this time, not ready for permanent publication. They're works in progress, not FTP. Nonetheless, they're proceeding along toward the standards track, and RSIP does present a practical alternative and extension to NAT.

Requires RSIP-Aware Clients

One of the reasons that RSIP wasn't invented a while ago is that it isn't transparent to clients. There must be a piece of software that executes the RSIP client and another that runs the RSIP server. Until such time as RSIP is a proven technology that is part of a standard operating system package, each must be installed on each of the end systems that is to talk to the outside world. Back in the Pre-Cambrian age, before the invention of the PC, when dumb terminals roamed the earth, there wasn't such a thing as a local client. Traditional NAT was devised as a solution to private addressing domains because it doesn't impose any burden or obligation on the client side. RSIP can't be implemented transparently because of its requirement for client-side software.

Requires Tunneling

Part of that client-side software, as well as the function of the RSIP server, is the ability to do tunneling. That too isn't rocket science, but it is another little complexity thrown into the mix. Tunneling is relatively easy to add to a single network environment, but it's not clear how efficient this might be if traffic from the client crosses more than one private addressing domain before it gets to the RSIP gateway.

Summary

On the surface, RSIP sounds like a simple and elegant solution to making certain types of applications work through a network gateway. It's like NAT, but then, it really isn't NAT although RSIP services could be combined with NAT in the same device. In many networks, each would have a role to play. RSIP isn't completely transparent to clients the way that NAT is (or is supposed to be), but it does have the advantage, in theory at least, of working much more cleanly and more efficiently with some of those troublesome applications.

By far, the biggest problem is that RSIP doesn't really exist yet as working code in any product, but neither do some of the ALG solutions to making some applications work properly through NAT. It seems likely that the RSIP Internet Draft will be promoted into the RFC standards track, and it may eventually become an Internet Standard. It will be up to firewall and router vendors, though, to implement RSIP on their devices and in client software.

One of the things that argues against RSIP becoming as widely used as NAT is that there must be special client software to make RSIP work. The biggest advantage that NAT has is that network clients don't even have to know that it exists. It may exist; then again, it may not. Only your border router knows for sure.

In the next chapter, we will move away from the technology of NAT and on to implementing NAT. Organizations that plan to use NAT as a load-sharing technique, to implement private addressing, or to establish multihomed connections to ISPs must plan the conversion to NAT. The process isn't necessarily complicated, although it can be if NAT is implemented on a large network. Like any type of network reconfiguration, the process must be planned carefully in order to be executed properly.

Planning for NAT

Network managers are usually the first ones to perceive how long a leap it may be from understanding a technology to actually making it work. Understanding network address translation is one thing, but implementing it and configuring it are entirely different matters. Implementing and configuring NAT are no different from implementing most any other type of technology. The exact details of implementing NAT may vary from one vendor's hardware and software to another, but the general principles remain the same. We've focused on the general principles of NAT in this book, rather than a specific vendor's implementation of NAT, for precisely that reason. If the network manager understands the principles of a technology, its implementation will be faster and easier, regardless of the vendor's specific methodology.

In a brand new network, implementing NAT is usually a relatively simple problem because NAT can be integrated into the network design from the start. In an existing network, however, implementing NAT or, for that matter, many other technologies isn't as simple a matter as dropping a NAT box into place and walking away. In fact, in either the new or existing network cases, implementing NAT requires a good deal of planning.

In this chapter, we'll focus on planning for implementing NAT, with a view toward making the result as error-free as possible. To make this example of implementation planning as comprehensive as possible, we will assume that

NAT is being brought into an existing network. Except for determining the network environment into which NAT will be installed and the luxury of starting with a blank sheet of network design paper, the planning process will be the same.

Planning for NAT

Installing NAT is like painting a house. House painters will tell you that the most difficult and time-consuming part of the job isn't the painting. Instead, it's the preparation. Sanding, scraping, cleaning, and priming take more time than applying paint, but if the former aren't done properly, the paint will soon peel or chip. The same principles can apply to networking technology. You plan the installation properly, or it won't work right, or you'll go back and do it again properly.

The steps of planning for NAT aren't necessarily complicated. It's just that the planning must be thorough. In this book, we've examined many of the aspects of NAT, as well as the implications that it may have for other network components and services, such as addressing, routing, DNS, and applications. All of these things may have to be examined and documented, to determine the impact of NAT on network operations.

The approach presented in this chapter isn't necessarily the only approach to planning for NAT that can be taken. Different network environments present different implementation challenges and issues. The objective of this chapter is to present a general-purpose plan for implementing NAT that proceeds in a logical and orderly manner and considers the many repercussions of implementing NAT.

Establish the Objectives

The first step in planning for NAT is to have a clear picture of what will be gained by using NAT. As we have pointed out in previous chapters, there may be several objectives to using NAT, including these:

- Private addressing
- Overlapping address ranges
- Load balancing
- Security
- Multihomed ISP connections

The first step in planning for NAT implementation is to examine the motivation for NAT and the objectives that the network manager or the IT manager hopes to achieve. As with any technology, the objectives should be clear and simple, and so should the benefits of that technology.

For example, the objective of using NAT might be to permit the network to use private addressing. If that's the objective, and it may be a worthwhile one, its benefits should be clear and comprehensible. The benefit of private addressing, for instance, may be that in a large, multilocation network, the network administrator will be able to address everything from the same address space, such as the RFC 1918 10/8 address space, without regard to external routing considerations.

On the other hand, if the objective of using NAT is to enhance network security, the network manager and IT management must recognize that NAT must be only part of a larger, more comprehensive network security plan. In this case, the security shouldn't be the sole objective of installing NAT because hiding network addresses behind NAT is only a subterfuge, not a security defense. If NAT is part of a security system that involves secure Internet transport across a virtual private network, that's another matter. In that case, the benefit is clear, and the objective will be achieved.

Analyze the Alternatives to NAT

As with any network change, someone should play devil's advocate and question whether NAT or, in a larger sense, any new network technology should be introduced at all. Someone—maybe someone in IT management—should also ask what's wrong with not doing this at all. It's a simple exercise of listing the advantages and disadvantages of the change; in this case, it's implementing or not implementing NAT and seeing if the advantages and benefits outweigh the drawbacks.

For example, if the objective is to expand the addressable space on the inside network by converting inside network hosts to private addressing, the network manager or IT management might also consider the alternatives to using private addressing. Is public address space all that constrained that it can't be stretched to cover the inside network's needs? How much would an ISP charge for enough additional public address space to cover everything in the network, plus some room for growth? Is the cost of "leasing" the extra address space from an ISP greater than the cost of implementing NAT?

Because NAT is not without its complications and drawbacks, an organization that is considering using NAT should also consider if there are ways to accomplish the same goals with something other than NAT. In some cases, such as using private address space, that may not be possible. In other cases, such as load balancing, alternative methods may be more expensive or more complicated, or both, but they may do a better job of solving the problem.

Recognize the Drawbacks

As we have discussed in previous chapters, NAT isn't necessarily as transparent as it's often believed to be. For the most part, devices in a NAT environment don't even know that NAT exists. Any addressing and TCP port changes that NAT makes are supposed to be invisible to network clients and servers, whether they're on the network where the NAT device resides or somewhere else on the Internet.

That fabrication falls apart for applications that embed IP addresses in data fields of IP traffic or for applications or systems that encrypt data. The latter is particularly true for systems that use the IP Secure (IPsec) protocol, for encrypting data end-to-end or through a virtual private network tunnel over the Internet. In both of these scenarios, NAT is likely to fail, either because it can't see the addresses to translate or because it doesn't have the cipher key to decrypt the data. In the encryption scenario, even if it did have the cipher key, NAT would interfere with the end-to-end integrity of the data, as the IPsec client and server would detect that some process had changed something in the encrypted datagram.

Some applications just might not work properly through NAT, even though it may seem that they should. Many IT executives have become entranced with the idea of IP telephony, which is routing voice calls over enterprise IP networks and the Internet. In theory and, in some cases, in practice, it works. Firewalls, however, often have a way of shutting off IP telephony access because IP telephony assumes the end-to-end significance of IP addresses, which firewalls can break. And have we heard that line before? NAT does the same thing, and configuring IP telephony through NAT can be complicated, at best.

NAT isn't the only network process that may be guilty of translating or changing addresses. Just as firewalls change addresses, so too do proxy servers, only they're a little more straightforward about it.. Acting on behalf of clients, proxy servers establish completely new sessions between themselves and Internet servers. Consequently, proxy servers don't do address translation per se, but complete session substitution. Proxy server sessions, however, may have the same problems as NAT does with encryption and embedded addressing.

The performance hit that NAT implies may also be another significant stumbling block for high-traffic sites or networks. Generally speaking, there are few ways to avoid performance degradation wherever there's a device that screens or translates traffic. Proxy servers, firewalls, screening routers, encryption devices, and NAT devices, all of which screen, translate, or change some part of the traffic they see, all take their toll on network performance. Some types of NAT impose more delay than others, although router access control lists, encryption and decryption devices, and firewall rulesets usually impose more of a performance barrier than NAT does.

For firewalls and NAT boxes on high-speed circuits, the biggest performance issue isn't so much the time it takes to translate addresses or run through firewall access control lists. Instead, the most significant problem is keeping up with the data rate of a T-3 circuit or a fully loaded 10 Mb or 100 Mb Ethernet. Consequently, NAT performance is related to the data rate. It's one of the reasons that most of the top-level ISPs and big enterprise networks have little interest in running ACLs on traffic entering their networks or in firewalling the top-level connections. First, there's the issue of whether it really would do much good because ACLs and firewalls are best located as closely as possible to the systems that are to be protected. The more pressing practical issue is that the data rate of the connections is so high that no firewall or NAT box could handle traffic rolling in at such a high data rate.

Surveying the Network

NAT will affect everything that passes through it, as a NAT box assumes that all traffic must be modified before it can pass through the NAT box. Unless they are specifically configured to do so, NAT devices don't have "exception modes" that exclude certain types of traffic. Because NAT will affect all network traffic, the next step in planning for NAT will be to get a complete picture of everything on the network that NAT may affect.

This implies that the network manager or the IT organization must do a comprehensive network inventory. It's possible that a network inventory has been done in the past few years, as part of a Y2K project or as part of an ongoing system documentation project. Many IT organizations pay close attention to documenting their communications and information systems, but just as many don't. Frequently, IT organizations document specific parts of their communications systems, such as a security perimeter, but not the entire system. NAT may affect everything that exits the network, so the IT organization and the network manager will need a complete picture of the network.

Assuming that a complete network picture doesn't exist, the network manager may approach the problem piecemeal by inventorying and analyzing specific parts of the network. In a large organization or company, the piece parts of the network may be the responsibility of different groups in the IT organization. Consequently, there may not be one source for a comprehensive view of the network but many sources, whose views will have to be pieced together for a comprehensive view.

Some of the information that the IT organization or the network manager may have to assemble to analyze how NAT will work may include the following: network scope, position of NAT, address ranges, applications, firewalls and screening routers, ISP connections, server pools, proxy servers, VPNs and encryption, routing, network management, and DNS.

Network Scope

The simple view of a corporate network is that everything is contained in a single network "cloud" that creates a nice, neat package. Unfortunately, few networks are constrained to such a simple structure. In reality, most networks have a convoluted, branching structure that doesn't fit into any simple network structure. There may be parts of the network that are owned and operated by subsidiaries, affiliates, or business partners, which really aren't under the control of the main corporate IT organization at all.

The part of the network inventory is to determine the extent of the network that will be affected by NAT. It may be that the interconnected networks of subsidiaries, affiliates, or business partners are held at arm's length and aren't completely integrated into the organization's network. That is, they may connect only to specific systems within the organization's network or simply transfer e-mail or access specific database systems, and nothing else. The inventory must determine if those other networks have full access into the main network and therefore may be affected by NAT. If their traffic goes into the main network and doesn't pass through the main network to another location, then they may not be affected by NAT at all.

The objective of determining the scope of the network is to establish boundaries, if possible, around what will and will not be affected by NAT. For example, the applications, hosts, and traffic from the network of a corporate subsidiary may be excluded from the network inventory if it's not fully routable on the main inside network. The network manager or the IT organization may not have a complete understanding of the connectivity and interconnection requirements between subsidiary, affiliate, and business partner networks. It may be necessary to investigate what types of communications and systems access occurs between autonomous networks, in order to understand the bounds of the organization's own network.

Position of NAT

Once the scope of the network has been determined, the network manager can analyze where NAT might be positioned. NAT will be located at one or more network entrance points to the network. The next thing to determine is where those network entrance points are located. Presumably, they are the points where the internal network connects to external networks. In this case, we'll assume this is the Internet, but in other networks, they may be points where the network connects to other private networks.

In any case, NAT will have to be positioned not necessarily where the internal network connects to the Internet, but wherever NAT is necessary. It's usually on those Internet or exterior network connections, but it could also be on those connections to subsidiary, affiliate, or business partner networks. For example, the objective of the plan for implementing NAT might be to create a private addressing domain and change the internal network from a group of unaggregated public address ranges. Those private addresses may not be routable within the other networks to which the main network is connected. It may be that NAT will be necessary on each of the entrance points to those networks, as well as the ISP connection points.

The main positioning point for NAT is usually at the ISP connection points. This is usually the case because NAT may be used for translating to public address ranges or implementing a load-balancing solution. The primary reason may be that the NAT box is actually a router or a firewall, and its customary location is on the Internet access points to the internal network. Addressing and routing issues may also require that NAT boxes also be positioned on the access points to the subsidiary networks.

Address Ranges

Most network administrators know by heart the IP address ranges assigned to their networks, and they probably think they're aware of every other address range in use on the network. If they're right, that's good, but a complete network inventory, particularly one that will incorporate translating whatever those internal network addresses are to external addresses, must include an inventory of addresses.

In many networks, a single network address space may be subnetworked into some number of smaller subnets, each of which can be of a different size. In most cases, the entire address space will be assigned to the internal network. A number of smaller address spaces, such as /24 subnets, may be used for links to external networks, security subnets, and other special-purpose networks. In any case, all of the address ranges in use must be discovered and analyzed in order to understand what addresses may have to be translated on the NAT box.

The other address range issue is determining the number and ranges of addresses that will be on the NAT address translation pools. For example, should the NAT box do static or dynamic address translation? Will inside addresses be translated to several different outside addresses or just to a single address? If several outside addresses will be used, how big will that address range have to be, and who will provide the addresses? Will these be the outside addresses for the NAT box, and how big an address range does the NAT box need to use?

In some NAT configurations, where the NAT function is in a firewall, there may be another external network onto which all outside traffic flows before it reaches the inside network. This network is called a Demilitarized Zone, or DMZ. It's a separate network unto itself, and it's usually isolated from the inside network. If it's a separate network from the internal network, it too needs its own network address if it doesn't have one already.

The internal addressing plan should be analyzed carefully, so that all of the addressing in use is identified and understood. It may be that when the addressing analysis is completed, some parts of the network may have to be rearranged and isolated from other parts of the network in order to control address translation. It's even possible that the network may have a mixture of public and private addresses on the same network. This type of combination may make for complicated routing schemes, as private addresses should not be propagated out of their addressing realm.

Discovering all of the address ranges in use is another problem. There are a number of automated network discovery tools on the market that can automate the address discovery process. Optimal Explorer is a good example of a software tool that can discover the devices on a network, but they must be manageable by SNMP, and they must use a known SNMP community string. In addition, Cisco also has a device discovery protocol that can be used to find most Cisco devices on a network.

DHCP servers are also another source of reliable addressing information. DHCP servers assign addresses to PCs and network devices dynamically, so their address pools are reliable guides to the addresses in use on a network. Many network administrators leave static addresses in network servers and routers because they must be known by fixed, rather than transient, addresses.

Applications

Application incompatibility has long been the Achilles' heel of NAT. As we discussed in Chapter 7, "Making Applications Work with NAT," there are a number of applications that don't always work properly with NAT. Fortunately, most of them aren't necessarily widely used or used throughout an organization. The most widely used NAT-unfriendly application is FTP, but it's only a problem in the FTP PORT and PASV modes. Other applications, such as DNS, may not work properly with NAT, but that's the reason that there are things like application-level gateways. The application problem is still present in some new, potentially important applications, such as IP telephony. For its part, organizations like the IETF are trying to influence the development of new protocols so that they are NAT-friendly.

To determine if NAT will affect applications, the network manager needs an application survey to determine which applications are in use on the network. Lacking an application survey tool, one indirect way to survey applications on a network that has a firewall is to check out the firewall rulesets. A tightly written set of firewall rules will allow only specific types of applications, based on the TCP ports they use. Some types of applications, such as those that use vendor-specific TCP ports, as well as special client and server programs, may have embedded addresses and therefore may run afoul of NAT. If there is an applications support group with the IT organization, it may be aware of NAT-related issues for those applications. Otherwise, the best source of information is likely to be the vendor, which should be able to advise the network manager on NAT-related issues.

One approach that some network managers take, particularly in networks that have strict procedures to review and approve applications before they are allowed on the network, is to test whichever applications are approved to be on the network and install and configure NAT to support those applications. Anything that's not approved that's in use on the network might still work with NAT. If it doesn't, whoever uses the application will probably open a trouble ticket on it. Then the IT organization can make a decision on whether it wants to support the application.

Firewalls and Screening Routers

The firewall will screen traffic to and from the outside world, and it may also be the system on which NAT will be installed. As such, the firewall may already be doing NAT if it maps all inside addresses to a single outside address or to a small number of addresses on an outside network. Even if the firewall isn't doing address translation, the NAT box will probably be installed in series with the firewall. The operation of one will affect the other.

At a minimum, the network manager must coordinate the NAT implementation with the group that controls the firewall so that any changes that are required in firewall rulesets can be done at the same time that NAT goes into service. For example, the firewall rulesets may screen on inside or outside source or destination addresses, any of which may be changed by NAT. The firewall group may also want to test changes in firewall rulesets that must be made to accommodate NAT.

NAT may also affect screening routers, which use access control lists of IP addresses on which they screen traffic. Screening routers are usually deployed to screen out traffic inbound from the Internet to the inside network. The ACLs may also be configured to work the other way, to filter out traffic from the inside network to the Internet. A screening router may be configured to do either or both, but screening inbound traffic is the more common configuration.

If that is the case and if NAT will be positioned on the inside network side of a screening router, the NAT box should be transparent to the screening router. The NAT device will see only inbound traffic that has already been screened. If the router screens outbound traffic too, its ACLs will have to be changed to screen on the addresses the NAT device uses as its NAT pool addresses. In this case, the screening router may lose some of its ability to screen on addresses. The NAT device may translate source addresses to a small group of addresses, which will obscure the screening router's ability to screen on the real source addresses of inside traffic.

ISP Connections

The number and location of the network's ISP connections are next on the network inventory. There are probably only a few ISP connections, or even just one, so inventorying the ISP connections is not a complicated task. It's possible, however, that the number and location of the ISP connections may have to be changed to accommodate NAT. Internet traffic will go through the NAT box, so the ISP connections may have to be reorganized to pass Internet traffic through the NAT box.

If the ISP connections are to be multihomed, the network manager should contact the ISP or ISPs involved and coordinate routing to the multihomed connections. It's easier to manage multihomed ISP connections if the same ISP controls both connections because only one ISP must configure its routing to support the multihomed connections. Coordinating multiple connections with multiple ISPs can be a difficult task because of different methods that different ISPs may use for announcing BGP routing updates back into the internal network's border routers. Dynamic address assignment in a multihomed environment can compound the problem even more. It's best to explore these issues thoroughly with the ISPs before trying to mix NAT, multihoming, and dynamic address assignment.

Server Pools

If NAT is being installed to support load distribution to a server pool, it's likely that it will replace a simpler method of load distribution, such as round-robin DNS. The other option is that it may be a new server pool using NAT to distribute the load. Identifying the server pool won't be as much of an issue as determining the optimal way to configure NAT to support load distribution. Most firewall or router implementations of NAT support passive load sharing, passing traffic to servers in the pool sequentially. The primary NAT configuration issue may be determining only the appropriate size of the address pool for NAT and coordinating the configuration of the external NAT address in the DNS servers.

Proxy Servers

Dedicated proxy servers are usually located somewhere inside the internal network, so they use internal network addresses as the source address of the proxy connections they establish for inside network clients. In this step, the network manager must identify the proxy servers and their IP addresses. The proxy servers will represent all connections established to them with the proxy server's own address, so individual client sessions won't have to be mapped back to client source addresses.

The NAT box will translate the source address used by the proxy server to whatever external address the NAT box will use. If there are multiple proxy servers, NAT may be configured to use different external addresses for each one, to simply map back internal to external addresses.

VPNs and Encryption

Like some NAT-unfriendly applications, VPNs and applications that use encryption are likely to cause particular difficulties for NAT. The next task is for the network manager to identify where and how encryption is being used on the network. It's unlikely that requirements for secure, encrypted applications will change if NAT is imposed in the path between the inside and outside networks. It is equally unlikely that VPN configurations and connectivity will be changed to accommodate NAT.

The most significant issue for VPNs and encryption will be the use of IPsec, which NAT devices usually can't handle. While it is not a perfect solution, one way to continue to use IPsec in a NAT environment is to install an IPsec gateway system behind the firewall, but in front of the NAT device. This will allow an IPsec-encrypted channel to come through the firewall and into a secure part of the network or IPsec-encrypted traffic to be received and decrypted, thereby avoiding problems with NAT. The IT security organization is not likely to view this configuration enthusiastically, but it is a solution to the problem of NAT and IPsec that brings traffic into a secure part of the network, avoiding NAT issues.

Routing

NAT will affect network routing, particularly if the inside network uses private addressing. Private address ranges can't be announced to the Internet, so NAT may imply changes to network routing. Fortunately, the network manager may have a good understanding of how the network interfaces to the outside world because the border routers may be under the network manager's direct control.

The routing inventory will have to take into consideration the routing announcements that are made to every external network interface, not just those to the Internet. For example, routing announcements to subsidiary, affiliate, and business partner networks will also be affected by changes to the internal addressing and routing structure. In order to control how their customers' networks are advertised, many ISPs are now using static routing to and from customer networks instead of accepting routing advertisements from their customers. That certainly makes routing configuration easier from a firewall or router that does NAT, as the ISP knows exactly what it's going to see from its customers.

Network Management

The systems that manage the organization's internal networks won't necessarily stop working properly once NAT is installed. Changes to the internal addressing plan may interfere with network management systems' ability to collect data and poll devices on the network. Network management systems that use the Simple Network Management Protocol (SNMP) use IP addresses to identify the systems they manage. So too do other network management systems, which poll managed devices by IP address. Consequently, any change to the internal addressing plan, such as converting to a private addressing plan, will imply changes to network management systems.

Changing external addresses, as well as adding NAT devices, will also affect those same network management systems. In a large, complex network, the network manager may not control the network management group, so he or she must coordinate the NAT implementation with them and include them in the network inventory. Uninterrupted operation of the network management systems will be essential in the NAT implementation, in order to monitor system performance and to identify and troubleshoot network problems during the NAT implementation.

Unfortunately, positioning NAT between an SNMP network management system and the systems that the system will manage is not a good idea. The problem is that having a NAT device between a network management system and the systems that it manages currently cannot be supported in any consistent and reliable way. An SNMP ALG would do the trick, but such a device, or one that works reliably, doesn't exist. So, the network management system must be behind the NAT device, not outside it. This is not good news to companies that outsource their network management to a third party and that plan to use NAT between their network and the third-party SNMP system.

DNS

The zone files in the network's DNS services may have to be changed significantly when NAT is installed, only because the outward representation of internal systems may change. If a firewall is already in place at the network entrance points, there may be few changes to DNS because the firewall may already represent internal systems by a few outside addresses. The extent of the changes required in the DNS depends on the types of services that the firewall provides.

If the network administrator isn't thoroughly grounded in DNS operation and maintenance, he or she should coordinate the NAT implementation with the DNS administration group. Instead of surveying the DNS structure, the network administrator might be better off describing the NAT address conversion configuration to the DNS group and letting them figure out how to accommodate NAT.

This has not necessarily been an exhaustive list of devices and systems that must be inventoried before a NAT implementation. A number of other systems and parts of the network infrastructure may be affected by NAT. The purpose of this section has merely been to indicate the breadth of systems and components that NAT might affect. IP addressing is a key element in network communications, and NAT must be implemented with full knowledge of the entire network to work properly.

Preparation

The hardest and most time-consuming part of NAT implementation is preparing for the task. If the preparation has been done properly, installing and configuring NAT should be relatively simple. A number of factors can complicate the actual implementation, such as conversion to private addressing, hardcoded IP addresses, special or unknown applications, multihoming routing issues, and encryption. In this section, we will outline the implementation steps that are applicable to a wide variety of network environments. Network managers and IT executives may use these as they would a large-scale roadmap, to get a general idea of sequencing and a project plan, filling in the details to fit their individual network environments.

Project Management

The NAT project has the potential to affect many parts of the network environment, so it's best to centralize control of the NAT project in a single NAT program group or project team. This group will be responsible for the whole project and will be responsible for coordinating the changes in the DNS, routing, security, and internal network engineering groups. This group will also be responsible for supporting the NAT implementation and for troubleshooting NAT problems.

Testing

In a complicated NAT environment, such as one that involves multihomed ISP connections, the NAT project team should run a test of the NAT configuration on a test network, just to see if the new configuration will work properly. Many organizations don't have the resources to duplicate a full operational environment, particularly if it involves establishing a separate, parallel test environment, complete with firewalls, ISP connections, WAN links, and VPNs. Many organizations settle for a "paper walkthrough," involving representatives of all of the network support groups that will be affected by the change, to scope out any repercussions of the change. Of the two, the operational test is the preferred route, but many organizations don't have the luxury of a test network.

Implementation

Many organizations opt for making network changes incrementally, to try to minimize the negative consequences of a mistake or an unforeseen problem. Because NAT devices sit on the main thoroughfares into and out of a network, the consequences of an unforeseen error can be great. Consequently, many organizations that implement NAT elect to do it in an incremental fashion to minimize the risk.

One approach to the "incrementalism" theory of system implementation is to proceed in a gradual, phased implementation, such as the following:

- Install the NAT device in the network path, but don't configure it to do anything but pass all traffic. This will prove that the device works and that at the default settings, it won't interfere with network traffic.

- Configure address translation on the NAT box for a small number of inside network hosts, translating their inside addresses to one or more outside addresses. This may imply adding DNS records to identify the outside NAT interface, but it leaves unchanged all other aspects of the network.

- Gradually add other operational parts of the network into the NAT configuration, staging the changes incrementally so that only a small number of systems or network functions are affected.

The other approach to implementing NAT is the D-Day approach, in which NAT is brought up everywhere in the network at once, such as over a weekend. The benefit of this approach is that it compresses the implementation phase into a short period of time. This approach implies that the NAT configuration has been thoroughly tested and proven to work properly.

Organizations that don't have the resources for a full test network usually take the incremental approach. It's more complicated, in that it involves staging the changes to the network infrastructure, but it's easier to control. It's also simpler to isolate problems and to troubleshoot network issues because the network changes that may have caused a communications problem can be identified and fixed or rolled back to a previous, working configuration.

Summary

Implementing NAT isn't that much different from making any other network change. The major difference is that when NAT sits at the entrance to the network, it has the potential to affect every transaction that flows into and out of the network. NAT isn't the only part of the network infrastructure that occupies this critical location on the network, as firewalls and routers occupy the same kinds of key network real estate.

Thorough planning and thinking through the implications of NAT will make the implementation process both smoother and more successful. In the next two chapters, we'll examine how the steps of preparing for NAT help in implementing NAT. In the next two chapters, we'll look at two case studies of NAT, each being implemented for a different reason. In each case study, we will assume that the planning and preparation steps have been done, so that we can focus on implementing NAT quickly and successfully.

Case Study: Moving to Private Addressing

The theory of network address translation is one thing, but putting it into practice is another. In this chapter and the next, we will put the theory of NAT into practice in two related but different case studies. In the case study in this chapter, we will look at the implementation steps in creating a private addressing plan for a network, then installing a firewall with NAT to translate those addresses to public addresses. In the case study in the next chapter, we will add a load-balancing capability behind the firewall and use NAT to spread the load among the servers in the server pool.

In both case studies, we will focus on NAT implementation, taking a step-by-step approach to the process of implementing NAT. In the first case study, we will have to convert the entire network to a different addressing plan and bring up NAT at the same time, in order to maintain inside and outside connectivity. The second case study will be less complicated because the network will have already been converted to use NAT, but load sharing will have to be configured on NAT. We'll also have to figure out exactly how the DNS services will be modified to support the NAT load-sharing configuration.

To keep this case study as comprehensible as possible, we'll use a relatively simple network, with only one network access point, connected to a single ISP. Many network environments are much more complex, but in order to make the case study straightforward and comprehensible, we'll keep it simple.

Remember too that the exact circumstances that a network manager uses in implementing NAT may vary somewhat from those described in this case study. Vendor-specific configuration details may necessitate some changes in the plan, but its general form will be the same.

Situation

Longhorn Electric & Gas (LE&G) is an electric generating utility in the southwestern United States. Despite recent changes in the organization of the electric power generation industry, Longhorn is a vertically-integrated electric company. It operates three coal-fired generating plants and owns the transmission lines it uses to distribute electricity to its residential and business customers. At one time, it ran a natural gas pipeline operation to distribute gas to its industrial customers. It sold off the gas operation but retained "gas" as part of the company name.

The company has five major offices, one at each generating plant, one at a maintenance and operations center, and one in its administrative offices. The networks in each of the five offices are numbered from several different /24 network addresses that the company has acquired from ISPs. Several years ago, one of its former ISPs allowed the company to keep three /24 addresses. There are about 1200 computers in use in the company's networks, which are depicted in Figure 17.1.

One of the company's near-term business objectives is to reorganize its IT infrastructure, to prepare it for possible acquisitions or to make the company more valuable as a take-over target. The IT organization wants to standardize addressing in the network, increase security, and give it more flexibility in dealing with ISPs. One of the parts of that plan is changing its internal network addressing structure to use private addressing.

One of the reasons that the company's IT director has decided to consider private addressing is that the company has changed ISPs frequently. The company's main offices are located in a small city, but despite the small size of the city, the company has a choice of several ISPs. One is the local phone company, but most of the rest are small, independent ISPs, two of which are affiliated with local cable TV franchises. The ISPs frequently lower rates or propose different pricing plans to the company, and they'd like to have the flexibility of considering other ISPs—even if they don't actually change providers—as a way to control or lower Internet access costs.

The company installed a firewall last year, as well as an inside router behind the firewall. The company has plans to install an *intrusion detection system* (IDS) and to use this router as a screening router, but the IDS hasn't been installed yet.

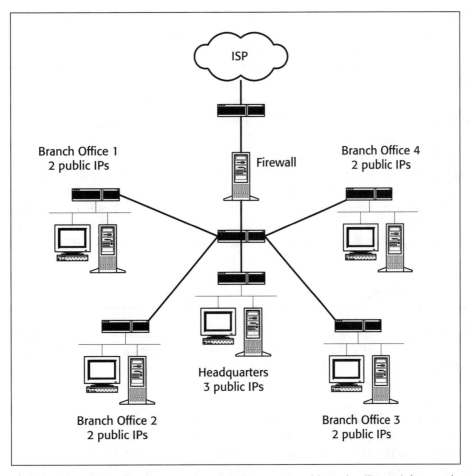

Figure 17.1 Network links connecting headquarters and branch offices of the Longhorn network.

Scoping Out the Project

Because the company plans to convert from a hodgepodge of public addresses to a consistent private addressing plan, there are two parts to this project: renumbering the network and implementing NAT. Of the two parts, renumbering is the more complicated part of the project. It causes the most internal change, in that its effects touch every device on the internal network. Installing and configuring NAT will have to be done at the same time as the network is converted to private addressing.

On the surface, it might seem that the readdressing part of the project might drive the NAT part of the project. The simplest way to conduct the conversion of the addressing plan will be to install NAT first and then readdress the network. By doing NAT first, then changing the addressing on the network, the readdressing project and Internet connectivity for inside hosts will not depend on each other. NAT will have to be implemented in order for hosts with private addresses to reach the Internet. NAT will work for any type of address, so it can be installed and configured first. This will give the readdressing project more time and allow for a more flexible conversion plan because all inside network addresses will be translated by NAT.

At this time, the primary purpose of the firewall is to control access from the Internet into the internal network. The firewall doesn't run NAT, so inside network host addresses, which are public addresses, are visible on the Internet. Routes to the internal networks are advertised to the ISP. As has been depicted in Figure 17.1, there is only one DNS, and it's located at the ISP. LG&E doesn't have its own DNS, as it has outsourced that responsibility to the ISP.

Project Plan

Implementing NAT in this environment means taking the steps listed next. This isn't necessarily the only order in which these steps may be taken, but a suggested order for this type of project. A network manager or IT executive may decide to vary the order, depending on the complexity of each network environment.

The project plan describes the sequence of events of the NAT implementation. The project plan doesn't have to be a written document, but the more extensive the network or the more complicated the network infrastructure, the more smoothly the project will run if there is a written project plan. It can be as simple as a brief document that describes the steps, responsibilities, and timeframes, or as complicated as a project management tool. It's up to the network and project manager and the IT department, which will be responsible for making sure it comes in on time, on budget, and that it works.

The steps of the project plan are as follows:

1. Check the applications.
2. Position NAT.
3. Devise the inside addressing plan.
4. Separate the inside and outside DNSs.
5. Move the Web server outside the network.
6. Configure and test NAT on the firewall.
7. Convert the networks to private addressing.
8. Change the DNS pointers.

9. Return the public addresses.

10. Document the new network.

Check the Applications

The purpose for having a network is so that applications will work, so there's no point in installing NAT if it's going to break applications. One of the first considerations in the project plan is to analyze the applications in use on the network and to determine if NAT will interfere with them. The usual suspects are FTP and H.323 applications like NetMeeting and any type of *Voice over IP* (VoIP) applications, such as IP telephony, or anything that transmits voice over the Internet.

In addition, anything that will try to use the SNMP network management protocol through the NAT device probably won't work properly. Usually the network manager or the IT organization will be aware of network management systems in the network and where they are positioned with respect to the proposed NAT site, so SNMP applications shouldn't be a surprise. Although they are not applications per se, VPNs and applications that use encryption may also not work properly through NAT.

Any applications that may pose a problem must be tested thoroughly before dropping NAT into the network. IT organizations that have stringent application certification or approval policies have a substantial advantage in inventorying applications on the network. Those that do know what applications are certified and supported on their networks can test and plan for supporting those applications under NAT.

Position NAT

In this network, NAT may be done by the firewall or by the inside router. This network is not so large that the firewall would be unduly burdened by doing NAT as well as traffic screening. Besides, all it's configured to do is to screen traffic coming in from the Internet, so its primary responsibility is security. Changing all the internal addresses to a single outside address or to a small group of addresses will help increase security somewhat, so it's a good job for the firewall. Assuming that the firewall has enough horsepower to do both the traffic screening and NAT jobs, the firewall is a good choice for locating NAT. If the firewall is to function as an application-level gateway, NAT won't produce any appreciable extra load.

Another reason for locating NAT on the firewall is an administrative reason. Centralizing NAT and traffic screening in one device makes the firewall administrator the focal point for managing and controlling the network entrance point. Instead of coordinating addressing and rules with another group, the firewall administrator is the top dog at the network entrance point, centralizing administrative control of network access.

Devise the Inside Addressing Plan

The public addresses on the inside network will be replaced with private addresses, so the next step is devising the private addressing plan. The existing addressing plan uses a number of public addresses, all of which are advertised to the ISP. With private addressing behind NAT, there will still be public address space advertised to the ISP and the Internet, but usually not as much of it as is necessary to number everything on the inside networks.

Two addressing plans will have to be established. One will be for the inside private networks and one for the outside public NAT addresses. To keep the conversion simple and to mirror what already exists, for the inside addresses we'll use addresses from the private address range, 192.16/16. There are 255 /24 blocks within this address range, so we have a considerable amount of flexibility in choosing how we're going to use the space. The existing addressing plan uses two public /24 blocks in each remote office and three /24s at the LG&E's headquarters offices, enough addresses for about 3000 hosts. You can never have too much IP address space, and private addressing will give us plenty.

There are several possible ways to conduct the conversion to private addressing on the inside networks, but we will use a gradual transition approach, converting each branch office to private addressing, one at a time. As for the addressing plan, we'll use a total of 16 of the /24 blocks from the 192.168/16 space. We'll assign the first 4 blocks to the headquarters, then 4 of each of the next 12 network addresses to each of the 4 branch offices, as shown in Figure 17.2.

Note that Figure 17.2 also shows two other parts of the addressing plan. There's an address for a new external network, on which will be located the external DNS, the public Web server, and other publicly accessible hosts. They'll be moved outside the firewall for network security reasons. The two public network addresses from the ISP will become the NAT address pool. These will be used only temporarily during the conversion, as they will be returned to the ISP after the conversion has been completed.

The concept of the conversion plan is to proceed from one branch office to the next, finishing at the headquarters office. As the hosts in each branch office are converted to private addresses, the host addresses will use static NAT to map to the two public address ranges from the ISP back to the new private addresses. Using static mapping temporarily will help the network administrator troubleshoot any host connectivity problems. When the new addressing plan works at each branch office, the branch office's inside network addresses will be mapped back to the firewall's single, external address, and

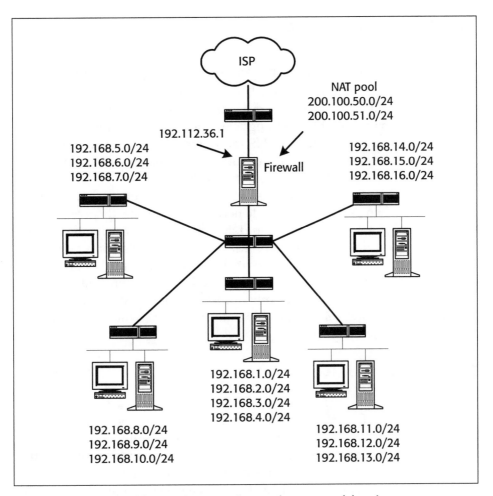

Figure 17.2   Private address assignments for Longhorn network locations.

the temporary address pool can be reused for the conversion of the next branch office.

If it hasn't been used already, a Dynamic Host Configuration Protocol (DHCP) server should be set up on the inside network to distribute addresses to inside network hosts. While a single DHCP server may serve the entire inside network, it may be more reliable to set up one in each location so that hosts can get IP addresses locally.

This transition plan makes more work for the firewall administrator, but it permits an orderly migration from the old addressing plan and brings up NAT progressively on the firewall. The effect of NAT on firewall performance will be gradual, and the firewall administrator will be able to adjust the firewall configuration, if necessary, as the transition proceeds.

Separate the Inside and Outside DNSs

The ISP's DNS is now used as the DNS for the entire corporation. When inside network hosts want to determine the IP address of other inside network hosts, their requests will have to go through the firewall and NAT to reach the ISP's DNS. The company could leave things this way, but it might be better if the company set up its own internal DNS server for inside network hosts. Hosts that are reachable from the outside network, such as the public Web server and a mail relay, would be listed in the external DNS.

The internal DNS could be located on the firewall, but it might be better to put it on its own server on the inside network. We've already given the firewall the tasks of screening traffic and doing NAT. Acting as an internal DNS wouldn't impose much of a burden on the firewall, so it's not a question of overloading the firewall's processing capability. In the future, though, the network administrator may want to set up a VPN through the firewall, have it act as a proxy server, or take on some other processing-intensive task. It might be best if we put the DNS service on a separate, internal network host, instead of throwing that task on the firewall.

Move the Web Server Outside the Network

Positioning the public Web server is a decision that will be influenced by a number of factors. If it's inside the firewall, it will be protected better than it might be if it's outside the firewall. But if it's inside the firewall, then all of that Internet Web server traffic reaches inside the firewall, giving hackers a beachhead from which they can try to launch attacks inside the network itself. If it's outside the firewall, the Web server traffic doesn't burden the firewall, but it can be an easy hacking target if it's not secured properly.

In this case, we've made the decision to put it outside the firewall. Ideally, the network should have two firewalls that bracket the DMZ. The first would screen Internet traffic, allowing it into the DMZ, and the second would backstop the DMZ, securing the inside network. LE&G has only one firewall, so we've put the Web server outside the firewall, with an address on the outside network.

Configure and Test NAT on the Firewall

Because the firewall will be the NAT device, the network administrator should configure the firewall to do NAT, assign the outside firewall interface address, and set up the NAT pool of public addresses. To test the operation of NAT and the address pool, the firewall administrator should set up static mapping from a test system behind the firewall and map it to an address of a host outside the firewall. Once the NAT capabilities have been tested and the NAT options that are available on the firewall have been explored, the conversion can move to the first branch office network.

Convert the Networks to Private Addressing

The transition to the private addressing plan will progress from one branch office network to the next, converting each branch office network to private addressing. Starting in the first branch office, the hosts in the branch office network will be assigned private addresses from the two /24 private addresses (a /23 block) assigned to that branch by the DHCP server. File and print servers and other applications hosts that need fixed addresses may use DHCP's static address assignment, or their addresses may be hard-coded into the host configuration files.

At the same time, the firewall will be configured to map the new private address ranges to the two public address pools on the firewall. For troubleshooting purposes, the network administrator may want to use a static, one-to-one mapping between each inside network, privately addressed host, and a fixed public outside network address. It's more work to do that, but if a particular host can't connect to an outside address, it's easier to troubleshoot the problem if a specific inside address maps back to a specific outside address.

The public address ranges that had been used on the first branch office network should be taken out of any route advertisements going from the inside to the outside network. Instead, the ISP will advertise the /23 "loaner" addresses to the Internet and route traffic for those addresses back to the firewall.

Once the network administrator is satisfied that NAT is working properly and that all of the inside hosts can reach Internet hosts, the network administrator will want to convert the static, one-to-one NAT mapping back to the firewall's single outside address. This implies that NAT will translate TCP port numbers as well. This will be the second and final phase of the conversion of the branch office networks, and it will proceed in this fashion up to the headquarters office network. When the conversion has been completed, all of the networks will use private addressing and the firewall will NAT inside private addresses to a single outside address, translating TCP port numbers as well. The final configuration will be as is depicted in Figure 17.3.

One additional complication that NAT might create is distributing traffic to servers that provide a common service, such as acting as an e-mail relay. Unless NAT is configured to do load distribution, as described in Chapter 11, "Load Balancing and NAT," all of the traffic for any of the servers would arrive on the same address (the external NAT interface) and be destined for the same

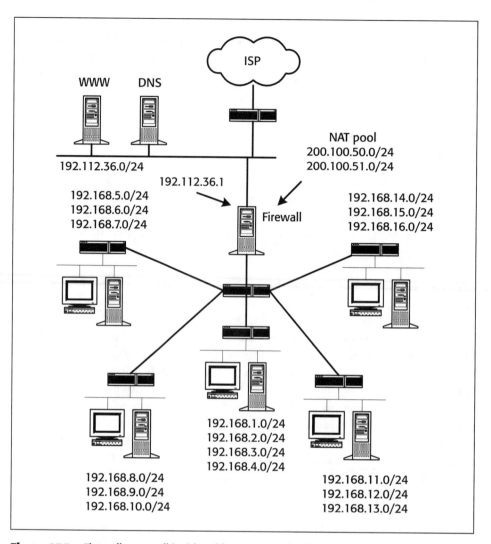

Figure 17.3 Firewall maps all inside addresses to a single external address.

TCP port (port 25 for SMTP, in this example). Without load distribution on the NAT device, it wouldn't know to which of the mail relay servers it should forward the mail. What might happen is that one of the mail relays would get all of the mail and the other would get none. This is why NAT load distribution isn't necessarily an option; in some cases, it's essential.

When the entire inside network has been converted to using private addressing, all inside network addresses will be translated to public outside addresses by the NAT software on the firewall. The inside addresses will translate to a single outside address, but that's not necessarily the only way that could work. The network administrator may want to use a single external address for each of the office locations, as a means to get a rough idea of Internet usage and to give the firewall administrator more flexibility in selecting the port ranges for translating TCP ports.

Change the DNS Pointers

During the conversion, and certainly when it is done, the network administrator will have to make sure that the external DNS records point to the correct outside addresses for the firewall and for the Web server. For example, when the Web server is moved outside the firewall, the A record for the Web server in the external DNS will have to be changed to the Web server's new address. If there are any hosts inside the network that must be reached by hosts on the outside network or on the Internet, the A records for those hosts will have to be changed to specify their address as the outside address of the firewall. For example, the outside DNS will need the address of the inside DNS (but it will see it as the external firewall interface), and the inside DNS will need the real address of the outside DNS.

The inside DNS will have completely new records, but the zone files could be created by modifying the zone files from the ISP's DNS. It may be that the network administrator elects to include relatively few of the PCs and workstations on the inside networks on the internal DNS, listing instead just the servers and applications hosts that inside network users must access.

Because the IP address of the outside DNS will not change, its pointer in the top-level domain (TLD) DNS servers won't have to be changed. If the primary DNS for the company's domain had been moved elsewhere, the TLD pointers would have to have been changed at the same time it was moved, or it would not have been found by other DNSs. The positioning of the mail relay, as well as its IP address, has also been changed, so changes will have to be made in the mail exchanger (MX) record in the external DNS. Note that if several servers act as mail relays, for example, now they will all appear to have a single address. The solution to this problem is NAT load distribution, to prevent all e-mail from going to one server.

Return the Public Addresses

One of the consequences of transitioning to private addressing and NAT is that most of the replaced address space is public address space. In the case of LE&G, three of its public addresses had come from a former ISP that had let the company keep the address space. Presumably, the rest of its public address space had come from its current ISP.

Even though it might be nice to keep that public address space stockpiled, just in case LE&G ever needed it again, the network administrator should really do The Right Thing, which is to give it back. The current ISP, from which two additional /24s had been borrowed for the NAT transition project, is probably aware that most of those addresses won't be used any more. They should be turned back to the ISP when the project has been completed and after a 60-day shakedown period to make sure everything works properly. The company's contract with the ISP probably requires this anyway. Furthermore, the ISP has a contractual responsibility to ARIN to make sure the addresses are used efficiently, so returning them helps the ISP fulfill that commitment.

As for the other three public addresses, the right thing to do is for the network administrator to turn them back to the old ISP. By rights, they belong to the old ISP, which may reissue them to its customers. Furthermore, they're probably part of a larger CIDR block that belongs to that ISP. If they're back in the ISP's address blocks, the ISP can delete the "holes" in its CIDR blocks and advertise the complete block to the Internet. This will help simplify the routing tables in the defaultless core routers at the Internet traffic exchange points and in the backbone ISPs' routers. It will help Internet traffic to flow faster and more freely, and it will help prolong the life of the Internet.

Document the New Network

Once the network and NAT are running properly, the last chore will be the one that is most often left for last and then forgotten—documentation. There's no better time to document changes to the network than when they're fresh in everyone's mind and before everyone rushes off to the next network crisis. Network maps, addressing plans, connectivity diagrams, and the like will be an invaluable help to whoever comes along months or years later and who may need to make sense of the network.

Certainly, by that time, some parts of the network will have changed, but who knows if those changes will have ever been documented? Even outdated network maps and diagrams are better than none, and they can be used to reconstruct the undocumented changes that have been made to the network.

Summary

Transitioning a network with public addressing to private addressing is one of the most common ways that NAT is implemented. It is also common to use NAT as a means to map inside public or private addresses back to a single outside address, such as that on a firewall interface to an outside network. In this case study, we have tried to combine the two implementations, even though using private addressing implies the use of NAT to translate inside addresses to one or several outside addresses.

This case study has not been intended to be an all-inclusive discussion of every step of the conversion and NAT configuration process. The specifics of how NAT is configured depend on the interface and implementation of the software in specific vendors' firewalls or routers. Our objective has simply been to illustrate putting the theory of NAT into practice. The exact details of another network transition to NAT, as they say, may vary.

In the next chapter, we'll look at another NAT case study. This will involve installing NAT for load balancing. It's not necessarily the most widely deployed way to do load balancing, but it will work. It will also allow us to look at a case study where NAT isn't necessarily dictated by other circumstances, such as the use of private addressing, which is something that affects everything in a network.

Case Study: NAT Load Balancing

In the first case study, we dropped NAT and a private addressing plan into an existing network. We did this without making a number of changes to the network infrastructure, and to the organization of the networks, although we could have done so. Often, network administrators will use the switch to using all private addressing as a chance to reorganize the network completely.

For example, changing to private addressing is sometimes just a sideshow to a more fundamental change to the network infrastructure. The network administrator may want to change or update the routing protocols in use on the network, such as changing from a version of the Routing Information Protocol (RIP) or Cisco's proprietary Interior Gateway Routing Protocol (IGRP) to a newer routing protocol, such as Open Shortest Path First (OSPF). OSPF usually implies an extensive route summarization methodology, which is most easily done when the network designer has a consistent block of addresses with which to work. The contiguous addresses in a CIDR block fit the bill, but for a big network, they might not be readily available in the public address space available to the network. Using private address space, translated through NAT, is a reasonable option for a fundamental network infrastructure change.

In this case study, we will look at using NAT to enable more effective use of a network service, specifically access to a group of servers, to balance or share the load on the servers. Load balancing usually doesn't imply massive changes to the network infrastructure or to its addressing structure. Load balancing also doesn't necessarily imply the use of NAT. As we discussed in Chapter 11, "Load Balancing and NAT," NAT is a relatively simple way to balance the load on a group of servers and to scale access to a network, without imposing extra burdens on clients or on other parts of the network.

Situation

The National Association of Mortgage Banking Professionals, a trade association for people in the mortgage banking business, has always had a visibility problem. The trade association was founded shortly after World War II, just when returning GIs started buying homes, fueling the post-war housing boom that created suburbia. Home owners and home buyers have long been aware that there are such things as mortgages and that they make payments on them every month, seemingly forever. Most people think that mortgages have something to do with banks, and somehow those oddly named people like Fannie Mae and Freddie Mac also have something to do with mortgages.

As for mortgage bankers, their titles give people the impression they have something to do with mortgages too, but precisely what they do is never quite clear. Therein lies the problem the *National Association of Mortgage Banking Professionals* (NAMBP), more specifically its Web site, is trying to address. The association knows what its members do, but their customers do not. To promote awareness of the role its members play in the home mortgage business and to raise its own professional standards, NAMBP has set up a Web site.

The Web site started out as an electronic newsletter about the association, but it drew little traffic beyond other mortgage bankers, Web spiders looking for content, and the stray Web surfer who thought it was a gambling site. It took the simplest way to wade into the Web, so the association let its ISP host the Web site on the ISP's own shared Web server. The ISP also ran an intrusion detection system as an extra-cost service. Instead of having its own firewall, the association contracted for a managed router service from the ISP. The ISP has configured screening rules and access control lists on the router, according to data collected by the ISP's *intrusion detection system* (IDS), to protect the association's network. The ISP has also provided a DNS service for all internal and external network hosts.

The Changing of the Guard

Recently, the association hired a new MIS director. He has his own ideas about how networks should be run, and he's not wild about how previous network managers have given the ISP so much control. He plans to take control of more of the network infrastructure, specifically installing a firewall to control network access more closely. He may leave the DNS with the ISP because it's a standard service the ISP provides at no extra charge. The network that was in place when he arrived on the job is depicted in Figure 18.1.

Before he can get too involved in changing the network architecture, the MIS director's first task will be to ramp up the Web servers to handle a terrific increase in traffic to the association's Web site. Last year, the association installed a number of new, consumer-oriented applications on the Web server, such as a mortgage loan calculator, links to mortgage lenders, and a mortgage qualification "agent" service to advise borrowers on mortgage financing qualification. The resulting new traffic has overwhelmed the existing Web site. The new MIS director plans to split the site among three or four Web servers, each of which will be a mirror of the others.

His idea is to put the Web servers behind the firewall and to use NAT on the firewall as a load-sharing mechanism. Having read Chapter 11 of this book, he understands the limitations of using NAT for load balancing. Load balancing

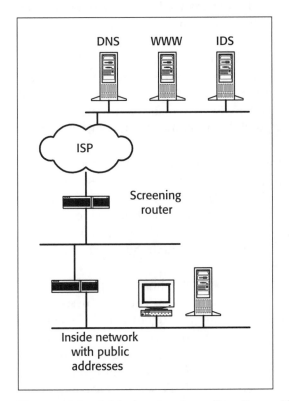

Figure 18.1 Original network configuration, with screening router to shield inside network.

with NAT is a relatively simple solution, and it's one that he will be able to control. The other option he's considered is round-robin DNS, but he may decide to leave DNS with the ISP.

Having seen how popular the consumer-oriented Web site has been, and how much the consumers' impressions of the site and, by extension mortgage bankers in general, depends on how fast the server responds, the MIS director decides to install several Web servers, each a mirror of the other. In addition, he plans to put up a special Web server for association members. The regular public Web site will be accessible through the standard HTTP port 80, but the members-only site will use Secure HTTP, which is port 443.

Scoping Out the Project

In contrast to the case study in the previous chapter, using NAT doesn't imply any IP addressing considerations, such as transitioning from public to private addressing plans, hiding inside addresses, and other considerations. In this case, the public outside address of the Web site may be translated back to a public or a private address. It really doesn't matter because we can assume that the association's network uses public addressing throughout the network.

The bigger tasks in the project will be installing and configuring the firewall, moving the Web servers to their new locations, and configuring NAT for load balancing. Fortunately, the network is relatively small, and it already has a security perimeter of sorts, consisting of the screening router. The proposed new network configuration, depicted in Figure 18.2, leaves the screening router in place and puts the firewall with NAT behind it at the entrance to the network.

With so much of the network infrastructure run and hosted by the ISP, it's as if the MIS director, who is also acting as the network manager, is starting with a relatively clean network configuration. Except for installing new Web servers and moving Web applications to a new server farm, most of the work will be configuring the firewall and NAT. The MIS director will have to make a few other decisions about the role the ISP will play in maintaining the DNS and how it will control the screening router.

The MIS director should also ask some basic questions about the assumptions he's made about load balancing. As we have already discussed, NAT load balancing works, but it's not a terrifically intelligent load balancer. For example, it balances traffic loads based on the number of addresses in the address translation pool, not on the load on each server or even if the server is operating. Once NAT load balancing passes traffic back to an inside host, it doesn't necessarily make any effort to see how well the servers are coping with the load passed to them.

The MIS director should plan to track the performance of the Web servers

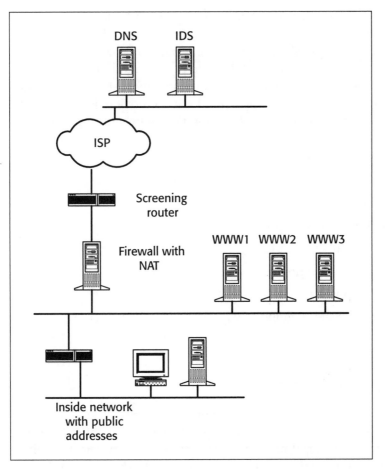

Figure 18.2   Revised network configuration with Web server pool and firewall with NAT.

over time, to determine how well the NAT load-balancing scheme is working. If it's not, or if he has to expand the number of servers in the pool even more, he might have to consider an active load distribution system. Multiserver Web sites that have high traffic loads or that support e-commerce applications frequently can't rely on passive load-balancing mechanisms because they can't measure or compensate for individual server performance.

Project Plan

As was the case with the first case study, the project plan describes the sequence of events in implementing NAT load sharing. In this case, the project is relatively limited, and it won't affect network users. In addition, the networking support staff consists of the MIS director and a few tech support people, so there may not be a need for a written project plan document.

Even so, the MIS manager should have a clear plan for how the project will proceed and the contingencies that will have to be managed in the transition. Fortunately, the new Web site will be configured on new systems on the association's network, so the MIS director won't have to move existing systems. Instead, the old and new systems can (and should) be brought up in parallel until the concept has been proven.

The steps of the project plan are as follows:

1. Review the applications.
2. Position NAT.
3. Determine the addressing pool.
4. Set up the firewall.
5. Configure NAT on the firewall.
6. Reset the DNS pointers.
7. Configure the firewall logging.
8. Document the network.

Review the Applications

The only application that should be affected by installing NAT load balancing should be HTTP because only the Web servers will be moved behind NAT. The Web servers offer a number of other applications, such as the mortgage load calculator, some of which may use other protocols to get to back-end databases or applications. Although it seems that HTTP will be the only application that the NAT device will have to handle, the MIS director will find it useful to determine exactly how that Web server handles all requests sent to it, to make sure that NAT doesn't have to be configured to pass other protocols, too.

More important, NAT will be running on a firewall, and both the firewall and its NAT function will be new. Presumably, the primary purpose of the firewall is to protect the inside network, so the firewall administrator will have to write screening rules for the firewall to use. It's essential to understand the applications that are running on the network and their requirements for outside connectivity, so that the firewall rulesets can be configured to allow the inside traffic out and to screen outside traffic properly.

In addition, the members-only Web site will use *Secure HTTP* (SHTTP). It is a version of HTTP, but it uses a different TCP port, and as far as the firewall is concerned, it's a different protocol. Like the public Web site, this Web site will now be behind NAT as well, so the MIS director must understand how its applications work, too.

Position NAT

In this case, the task of implementing NAT is part of the larger task of installing the firewall. If the MIS director elects to leave the screening router in place, in addition to installing a firewall, NAT could be run on either box. He doesn't control the screening router, though, because it's part of the ISP's managed access service, so the only other position for the NAT service is on the firewall.

The MIS director may be somewhat of a security freak, so it's fair to say that he plans to write some fairly restrictive rules for firewall screening. That's good from a security perspective, and the association's network is not so big, nor are its traffic screening requirements so onerous that the firewall rulesets are likely to affect firewall performance. In a larger network, with thousands of users' traffic undergoing firewall ruleset screening, firewall performance would be an important consideration.

Had firewall performance or traffic volume been a consideration, NAT might have less effect on performance if it's moved to another device, such as a screening router. Only inbound Web server traffic will be modified by NAT, however, so its performance hit should be minimal.

Determine the Addressing Pool

The network addresses on the association's inside network were assigned by the ISP. Unless there's some reason for the firewall to translate all inside addresses, there won't be any need to configure NAT on the firewall for all network devices, nor to map all inside addresses back to a single outside address through NAT. The MIS director doesn't have a problem with inside network host addresses being visible on the Internet. The only thing he wants to translate for now is the group of addresses for the server pool.

In the new network configuration depicted in Figure 18.2, all traffic will go through the firewall, but only the Web server addresses will be translated. To users on the Internet, all of the public Web servers will have the same virtual address, which will be the external address of the firewall. For that matter, Internet users won't know there isn't a single Web server. Any traffic addressed to that interface will be traffic for the Web servers, so it will also be traffic that the firewall's NAT process will translate.

There will be two Web servers reachable through the same address. The public Web server will be reached through that address, but at port 80, and the Web server for the association members will be addressed at port 443. It will be the firewall's job to sort out traffic for those two ports and to readdress it to the correct server. For the time being, there will be three public (HTTP) Web servers and only one members-only Web server, but the MIS director would like the flexibility to change that in the future.

The MIS director thought about asking the ISP for a small number of public addresses for the Web servers, say eight addresses, just enough to cover the four servers, with some room for future expansion. He will need an outside firewall interface address from the ISP. The ISP has assigned him a small subnet, consisting of four host addresses, from one of its /24 addresses, for use on the link from the screening router to the firewall. One of the addresses will be used on the firewall's external interface.

For the inside network on which the Web servers are located, the MIS director has a different idea. Instead of requesting more public space for the address pool for translating the Web server addresses, he's decided to translate the Web server addresses to private address space, using addresses from the first /24 private address block, 192.168.1.0. He'll use the first four addresses (192.168.1.1 through 192.168.1.4, or 192.168.1/30) for the four Web servers, as depicted in Figure 18.3.

The MIS director has two reasons for choosing private addresses for the NAT pool for the Web servers. His reasons have nothing to do with load balancing because the NAT load-balancing function will merely rotate inbound connection requests to a sequence of addresses, and it matters not to NAT if they are public or private addresses.

His rationale in selecting private address space is rooted primarily in flexi-

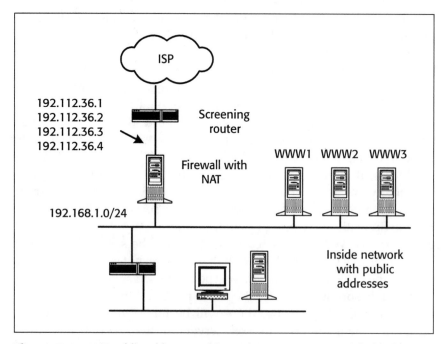

Figure 18.3 NAT public address pool for Web servers on network behind firewall.

bility and secondarily in security. First, choosing private address space will allow him to expand the number of servers on the network without having to ask the ISP for more public address space. The private network need only be advertised to routers on the inside network, so that the webmaster can connect to the Web servers, and the firewall administrator to the firewall's inside interface. That much address space also means that the MIS director could move other services to that inside network in the future, such as the DNS, an e-mail relay, or other network servers.

The second reason is security, although the MIS director realizes that NAT isn't a terrifically effective security measure. With private addresses, it will be difficult for hackers outside the network to connect to the Web servers directly because their addresses will be unroutable private addresses. That's not to say that someone couldn't hack through the firewall, exploiting a vulnerability on the firewall or in its rulesets. After all, NAT changes only addresses, and it relies on other measures, such as a firewall, for real security. Routers on the inside network could also be configured not to allow incoming connection attempts from those addresses. Those access control lists (ACLs) erect another barrier to a hacker who manages to penetrate the firewall, to prevent him or her from roaming deeper inside the network.

Set Up the Firewall

Once he has settled on a Web server deployment strategy, the biggest decision that the MIS director will have to make is to choose, set up, and configure the firewall. Based on previous experience with different vendors' firewalls, he may already have decided on the hardware platform and the firewall software he wants to use.

Whatever that choice is, its NAT software will have to be able to act as a load balancer. In the simplest case, the firewall will have to be able to identify HTTP and SHTTP traffic and pass it to the NAT software process. The NAT software will have to be able to sequence through a set of addresses in an address translation pool, each address of which is the real inside address of one of the Web servers in the address pool. Firewalls will be able to identify traffic by protocol, but not all NAT software will be able to do load balancing.

The firewall will be doing traffic screening as well as NAT, but it's a new device, and it stands squarely in the path between the inside network and the Web servers on one side and the Internet on the other. If it's not set up or configured properly, it could choke off all network access, blocking the path between the inside and the outside networks. The right way to determine that the firewall will pass traffic properly is to set it up, configure its interfaces, and delete any default screening rules. If there was no firewall in the first place, it won't do any harm to have one that doesn't screen any traffic, and it proves that the firewall's interfaces work properly.

Configure NAT on the Firewall

Once the NAT address pool had been determined, and the Web servers have been set up behind the firewall, the MIS director can have the firewall administrator configure firewall screening rules and the firewall's NAT load-balancing process. The firewall will receive all inbound connection requests, but the firewall rulesets will determine which will be accepted and which will be refused. For example, the DNS is on the ISP's network, and there's no internal DNS that any outsider should have to reach, so the rulesets will stop any attempt to connect to DNS port 43.

The NAT load-balancing operation will be relatively simple. Inbound HTTP connection requests sent to the firewall's external interface will be examined by the firewall rulesets, which will determine if they are permitted connection requests. The rulesets could prohibit connection requests from certain addresses, but initially, all inbound requests will be passed through the firewall. Inbound HTTP connection requests will be handed to the NAT process, which will translate the destination IP address to one of the private addresses in its HTTP server pool. The NAT process will also have to translate the source TCP port and create a NAT table entry to map that port to the original source IP address. The NAT process will use this entry to translate the destination address of the traffic, which will be addressed to the firewall's inside interface, to the original source address, before sending it to the ISP.

Inbound connection requests from association members to the Secure HTTP (SHTTP) Web server will also arrive on the firewall's external interface, and they'll be handled the same way. There's only one SHTTP server, so the destination address on inbound traffic will be translated to the SHTTP Web server's private address (192.168.1.4). The NAT process will have to translate the source TCP port, too, and map that back to the original source IP address. As with any application, clients may choose any source port, and the only way to guarantee mapping traffic back to its original source is for the NAT process to map a unique TCP port number back to the source address.

Reset the DNS Pointers

The ISP would also have to change its DNS references as part of the transition process. When the association's Web server was on the ISP's network, the DNS resource record for the Web site, www.nambp.org, pointed to the Web site's IP address on the ISP's network. With the new Web server configuration, the Web server has moved to the association's network, so its IP address, and the DNS reference, must change.

The Web site is really three Web servers, but they will be referenced by a single DNS resource record. The A record for www.nambp.org will point to the firewall's external interface, so all inbound connection requests for the Web site will go to the firewall. The firewall will distribute the connection requests to one of the three Web servers through NAT load balancing.

The special Web site for association members is a new Web site, so it will need its own A record in the DNS. That too will point to the firewall's external interface, but it will use port 442 instead of the standard HTTP port 80. The members' Web site can be given any host name that distinguishes it from the public Web site, such as www1.nambp.org, or members.nambp.org. Because this Web site is for members only, the webmaster may want to configure it to require a user ID and password to get into the site. SHTTP will secure the transmission only through encryption. It doesn't necessarily act as an authentication mechanism, so if the site maintains confidential or sensitive information, it should have an authentication and access control mechanism.

The ISP should also add A records in its DNS for each of the hosts in the Web site server pool. Each host name, such as server1.nambp.org, will map to a private IP address in its DNS record. Users on the Internet won't use these host names as URLs, because they will point their browsers to www.nambp.org. They are in the DNS so that the webmaster can refer to the servers by host name, instead of by IP address, to connect to the servers to administer them. Their addresses will be private network addresses, which will give them some measure of protection from intrusion. The private network addresses will be reachable from the network behind the firewall but not from outside the firewall.

The way the network is configured, all DNS requests, even for inside hosts, must go through the firewall to get to the outside DNS. Because he intends to take control of more of the network infrastructure, the MIS director might want to set up a second inside DNS for use by inside network users. The Web servers' A records on the outside DNS, which would be maintained by the ISP, would point to the firewall external interface. The A records on the inside DNS would contain the Web servers' real host names, as well as their external names (e.g., www.nambp.org) and their private network addresses. Most firewalls can run a DNS service, so the internal DNS could be run on the firewall instead of on a separate server.

Configure the Firewall Logging

When the new network configuration is finished, the firewall will be the only entrance point to the network. It's also the logical place for the MIS director to monitor traffic to and from the Web sites, through logging firewall traffic. He can get statistics on Web site usage, determine usage patterns and trends, and get some idea of where the Web site traffic originates. The latter statistics won't be perfect because users who come through an online service, such as AOL, will be identified by the service, not individually.

The firewall may have the ability to log NAT service statistics as well, such as whether the traffic was distributed evenly over all of the servers in the server pool. These statistics will have to be correlated with the performance statistics logged by each of the servers, to determine that NAT load balancing was actually balancing the load fairly evenly. Because it is a passive load-balancing technique, NAT load balancing distributes only traffic, with the intent of balancing it. Only the servers know for sure.

Document the Network

The MIS director has made a big change in the network infrastructure, so he should document the change. He might take this opportunity to document the whole network, too. He's new on the job, and his own "network discovery" process will help him get a better understanding of the network. He might well discover remote access ports, backdoor connections to other networks, and network services that had been configured but never used. He's interested in network security, so he'll have to understand his network completely in order to secure it properly.

Summary

In this case study, we've looked at how to insert NAT as a point solution to the problem of load balancing. As we have noted, NAT isn't as capable a load balancer as active load-balancing and distribution systems, but for relatively simple load distribution problems, it works well. In addition, it can be positioned in a device like a firewall, centralizing network access control with NAT operation.

It's not a perfect solution, though. Systems that have stringent requirements for uptime and availability, such as financial transaction and e-commerce systems, need more positive control of load distribution. It isn't that NAT load balancing won't work in those situations. It's just that their operational requirements go beyond what NAT load balancing is capable of doing. Those systems also need strict transaction logging, fault tolerance, resource recovery, and backup systems to ensure uptime and performance.

In the next chapter, we'll look forward into the future to see how NAT and the IP protocol it translates may change in the future. Specifically, we'll look at the proposed next version of the IP protocol, IP Version 6, and how its use and implementation may affect NAT. As we'll see, NAT may play a big role in the transition from the current version of the IP protocol to IP Version 6, however that occurs.

CHAPTER 19

The Future of NAT

Back when this thing we call the Internet was first devised, it seemed to its creators that they had developed a solid foundation for whatever growth and change the future might bring. The protocols that they devised decades ago—not just the TCP/IP protocols, but also many of the fundamental applications protocols—have proven to be remarkably flexible and adaptable.

The creators of the internet had no way of knowing, and little reason to anticipate, however, that by the end of the Twentieth Century there would be hundreds of millions of computers in the world, with many more to come, and that apparently, each would someday want one of those IP addresses. Moreover, they had no reason to think that people would want to press the connectionless, best effort delivery mechanisms of the IP protocol into service to deliver telephone calls, radio programming, movies, and video transmissions across the simplest of networks, let alone the worldwide Internet.

As we discussed in Chapter 12, "The Crisis in IP Addressing," the depletion of IP addresses is only one of the reasons why the mechanics of the Internet have been planning to implement a new, improved version of the IP protocol. One of the many problems of implementing anything new is devising a method to transition from the old to the new without making a pit stop along the way. As we will see, NAT is one of the techniques that seems to hold promise as a transition strategy from the old to the new.

The Future Is NAT

For a tool that was originally devised simply to accommodate private addressing, NAT has worked remarkably well. It's been adapted to a number of other uses, such as virtual private networks and load balancing. When combined with firewalls and screening routers, NAT can be one of the components of a comprehensive network security system. It is true that NAT can complicate network connectivity, but it's not uncommon to find NAT being deployed in many different types of network environments.

NAT deployment is becoming more widespread, as network administrators and IT executives see NAT as a solution to new problems. The rapid depletion of IPv4 address space has made private addressing a more attractive option. Frankly, NAT and other technologies that seek to use address space most efficiently, such as CIDR, have pushed out the IPv4 doomsday scenario, when all available IPv4 address space might be exhausted, to 2010 or so.

By a combination of innovation, hard work, coercion, and cooperation, the Internet engineering community has managed to brake the demand for IP address space. New demands, however, may be placed on the IP address space in the near future that could erase the progress made so far to stave off the inevitable address exhaustion scenario. There are already millions of wireless phones, pagers, and personal digital assistants (PDAs) in use. Most have no Internet access, but it's clear that future generations of mobile devices, some of which are already on the market, will have Internet connectivity or a "mobile IP" identity, or both. That identity is likely to be an IP address.

Since the mid-1990s, most of the rapid growth of the Internet has happened in the United States, but that growth—and the corresponding demand for IP address space—has spread to Europe, to Asia, and to other parts of the world. Based on per-capita ISP connections in the most populous nations in the world, India and China, the Internet basically hasn't even happened yet. Their use of the Internet, and their projected demand for billions of IP addresses, has yet to be felt. The IP address space as we know it today won't last long under that kind of demand.

Looking out into the future, it seems that no matter what happens, NAT will be with us for some time to come in one form or another. For one thing, there aren't a whole lot of alternatives for some of the problems that NAT solves. NAT is essential for networks that use private addressing because private addresses have to be converted to public addresses. Firewalls that hide either the public or private addresses of hosts and systems on a protected network use NAT to map internal addresses to a tightly controlled pool of externally visible addresses.

Four trends in networking portend even greater use of NAT in the future. Two of these are current issues, and two are completely new areas. The new trends are more stringent network security, wider use of private addressing, home networking, and mobile IP.

More Stringent Network Security

Security will continue to be an ongoing problem for network managers and IT executives. In response to increasingly sophisticated and troublesome hacker attacks, viruses, and Trojan horse programs, network security will erect even more restrictive barriers between their networks and the outside world. Not only will address translation be part of the network security perimeter, but so will be more complex security procedures, such as security certificates, authentication, and other forms of digital identification. As we have noted, NAT won't work properly with encryption methods like IPsec unless the NAT box is the end-point for the IPsec encryption. Unless it were encrypted a second time, this means the traffic could be sent in the clear behind the NAT box, which might be where more security threats lie.

Wider Use of Private Addressing

The crisis in IP addressing will be with us as long as the Internet continues to grow. At the present rate of address consumption, the available public address space might be exhausted in a few years. Wider use of private addressing behind NAT devices takes some of the pressure off the dwindling supply of public IP addresses, but this trend won't go on forever.

Home Networking

When homes are wired to the Internet through cable TV channels or DSL services, the service providers assign IP addresses to each home. In order to conserve address space, typically a single IP address represents a house, no matter how many individually addressable devices there are in the house. The cable company or ISP assumes there's only one device there because it might want to charge more for service to more devices. Many ISPs see a location that needs more than one IP address as a business and charge business rates, not residential rates, for the service. As the number of Internet-connected devices in a house grows, the cable modem or the DSL interface may be capable of acting as a NAT device, assigning private network addresses to all the PCs in the house. Again, a small business might have the same requirement, but it might be charged different rates because it is a business, not a residential, customer.

Mobile IP

Cellular phones with Internet access, PDAs, such as the Palm Pilot, and other wireless devices will all get IP addresses or be identified as an IP device. Just as the explosive growth of fax machines, cell phones, and pagers has created a huge demand for phone numbers, the growth of wireless devices with Internet access will create a huge new demand for IP addresses. Either these wireless devices will have real IP addresses, or they will have phone numbers or some other identifier that will be proxied into an IP address.

Any way that you look at it, as long as the demand keeps rising for IP addresses, NAT will be here to stay. The other question about the future of NAT is what role it will play if the IP protocol changes. No less an authority than Vint Cerf, who is one of the coinventors of TCP/IP and the Internet, has questioned whether hiding networks behind NAT devices is really a viably long-term solution to the IP addressing crisis. Cerf has pointed out that it is possible that eventually there may be so many networks hidden behind NAT devices that all the available IP address space could be consumed by NAT devices. It's unlikely that would happen, but it's one of those distant clouds on the horizon that could grow to be a real storm.

The rising demand for IP address space has been the impetus for the development of a new version of the IP protocol. It has been proposed as a solution to the IP addressing pinch, as well as to a number of other problems. This new protocol, IP Version 6, would, among other things, expand tremendously the pool of IP addresses. It would also require changing the current version of IP in TCP/IP software. It might become part of a new version of Windows—or whatever PC desktop software is called in the future—and be installed as part of a system upgrade. The change might not be so simple for other systems, especially ones with embedded operating systems and communications software.

What's Wrong with IPv4?

Version 6 of the IP protocol (IPv6), sometimes referred to as *Next Generation IP* (IPng), holds a great deal of potential for solving some of the problems with the current version of IP, which is IP Version 4 (IPv4). But, you might say, IP seems to work just fine just as it is. How can you quibble with a protocol that's been robust enough to handle all of the traffic on the Internet? Not only that, but it has adapted remarkably well to applications and circumstances for which it was never designed, such as streaming audio and video, multicasting, and even IP telephony. If IPv4 is a problem, maybe we should have more problems like it.

IPv4 works, but there are a number of things that IPv4 was not designed to do that would be useful to have in the protocol. That is, the current and future environments in which IP will be used will be different from today's environment. Maybe we would all be better off changing to a new version of IP, to set a surer course for the future.

The Internet networking community is divided on whether these benefits are worth the trouble of converting to IPv6. Most networking professionals would agree that yes, IPv6 is a terrific solution to the IPv4 addressing crunch, and yes, it would be convenient to have a new version of IP that fixes some deficiencies of IPv4. But their support has yet to be matched by a commitment to make the transition. It would be overstating the case to say that there is any widespread enthusiasm for IPv6. In the long run, it's good medicine, but many networking professionals are anticipating that it will have a really bad taste because there would be so much software to change. Let's hope they're wrong.

Some people like the idea of IPv6, particularly if they don't have an installed base of legacy IPv4 systems, and they have much to gain just from the expanded IPv6 address space. People in the cell phone and wireless industries, for example, like the idea of IPv6. Generally speaking, they don't have to convert much of anything because today most cell phones, PDAs, and pagers don't have IP addresses. In the future, though, it seems highly likely that they will. The broad and deep IPv6 address space has a strong appeal for numbering the millions of wireless devices that will need IP addresses in this decade.

Many networking professionals, including some in the Internet engineering community, regard IPv6 with the same respectful distance that they do the metric system. Everyone agrees that the metric system is a terrific system of measurement, it would be much easier to use, it would bring us into conformance with the rest of the world, and so on, but nobody wants to make the conversion. IPv6 garners the same blend of enthusiasm and reticence as the metric system because no one wants to make the change.

Frankly, many networking professionals say that IPv6 is a great idea, but there's no compelling reason to move to IPv6. Many say that despite its flaws, IPv4 works remarkably well. They add that the benefits of IPv6 aren't so significant that it's worth the bother of migrating to IPv6—at least not right now, that is. Besides, they say, the workarounds that have been developed to overcome the shortcomings of IPv4 have been remarkably effective. NAT is one of them, as is CIDR, and conservative and efficient address assignment strategies will keep IPv4 going for some time to come.

The bottom line is that without a killer app for IPv6, it may not go anywhere. There's certainly no industry-wide buzz for IPv6, and nobody's ever done an IPv6 IPO. And all of this is for a protocol that most everyone agrees the Internet will need one of these days—but just not today, or this week, or any time soon. The other side of this issue is that even if there's no IPv6 killer app, the shortcomings of IPv4 may do for IPv6 what the absence of a killer app couldn't do.

But wait, IPv6 proponents say, the killer app is already here. You're holding it in your hand. It's your cell phone, or that Palm Pilot, or your pager. Many of the world's corporate foot soldiers already have two of the three parts of the wireless trifecta, and the cell phone seems to be a new body part for homo sapiens all around the world. Just wait until all of these wireless devices become Internet-enabled. That's the killer app, IPv6 proponents say. As we noted earlier, demand for IP addresses for wireless devices of all types might be the crowning blow to the IPv4 address scheme. If you add the issue of assigning enough addresses for China, you've easily maxed out IPv4 addressing.

IPv4's Problems

What are those problems that everyone says that IPv4 has? And are they so terrible that we need to change the IP software in every Internet computer? That's the nub of the controversy over IPv6, but IPv4 does have some problems, specifically these: address space, security, address configuration, and Quality of Service.

Address Space

When the IP protocol was devised in the later 1970s, its 32-bit address space seemed enormous. Even if it was divided into different classes of addresses, for very large, medium, and small networks, there seemed to be enough individual IP addresses to accommodate practically any kind of IP network growth that could occur for decades.

Two decades later, here we are, staring at the end of what was originally declared Class C address space, and already we're dipping into the trust funds of what was once considered the reserved Class B and A address spaces to make ends meet. Other techniques and technologies, such as CIDR, NAT, and private address usage, have all helped alleviate the IP addressing issue, but none solves the problem permanently. As we have noted, RFC 1715 indicates that at best, the efficiency of our usage of the IPv4 address space is only about 25 percent at best. IPv6, as we will see, expands the address space dramatically, resolving the address space issue maybe not permanently, but for a good while. The IPv4 address space issue gets the most attention, and it is the easiest to understand, but it's only the most visible of the IPv4 problems.

Security

Like the mainstream implementations of DNS, IPv4 was never designed with security in mind. Encryption technologies like IPsec can be introduced to secure IPv4 communications, but there is no native security requirement in IPv4. If we assume that security will be a necessity, not an option, in the future, it might be worthwhile integrating it more completely into the protocol, or at least into its implementation. IPv6 won't necessarily be any more secure than IPv4, but IPv6 hosts will have implemented IPsec.

Address Configuration

Every IP device needs an address, but until the advent of DHCP, there was nothing automatic about assigning IP addresses. In addition, most computers have two different types of addresses—an IP address, which is a software address, and an Ethernet address, which is a hardware address. There isn't necessarily a relationship between the two, forcing routers and other devices to use yet another protocol, the Address Resolution Protocol (ARP), to map one to the other.

Quality of Service

We may regard it as such, but IP isn't intended to provide any guaranteed data delivery service. It's referred to as Quality of Service, or QoS. If the data gets there, it gets there; if it doesn't, it's some other protocol's job (TCP, mostly) to make sure it gets there. Worse, many of the new applications for which IP is being pressed into service, such as IP telephony, require consistent data delivery, guaranteed amounts of bandwidth, and reliable delivery. All of these requirements are news to IPv4, which makes its best effort—and nothing more—for data delivery. There is no easy answer to the QoS issue because IP is now and will probably remain a "connectionless" protocol. Other protocols, such as RSVP, and routing techniques like tag switching and bandwidth management have been used to retrofit IP for QoS.

The IPv6 Solution

The solution to IPv4's problems is IPv6, which offers, among other things, better ways to deal with the addressing issue and at least some accommodation for the security issue. Its alternate name, the Next Generation IP protocol, also hints that IPv6 is intended to be part of the new foundation of the Internet, to make the Internet be all that we want it to be. Not that the Internet isn't more than it was ever intended to be right now, but the intent is that IPv6 will make the Internet a more capable, robust, and comprehensive protocol.

RFC 2373 specifies the details of the IPv6 protocol's addressing architecture, and the protocol itself has been under development and testing for several years. The fundamental RFC for IPv6 is RFC 2460, which describes the specifications of the IPv6 protocol. Microsoft has made available a test version of IPv6 for the Windows 2000 operating system, so that network engineers could test the protocol, even if they didn't use it in Windows networks.

IPv6 expands the IP address space dramatically and adds a number of new features, capabilities, and requirements to support security and automatic address configuration. Specifically, IPv6 will provide these capabilities:

WHAT HAPPENED TO IPV5?

There has never been a Version 5 of the Internet Protocol. The number was skipped because the "5" designation was given to an experimental protocol called the *Internet Stream Protocol, Version 2* (ST-2), which is described in RFC 1819. ST-2 is a connection-oriented protocol for real-time digital audio and video multimedia applications that require Quality of Service and reserved bandwidth across network routes.

ST-2 operated at the same level as the IP protocol (the network level), so it was designed to complement IP. Data applications would use IP, and real-time audio and video would use ST2. Both protocols used the same packet header format, as well as IP addresses. The only difference was that the first field of an IP header had a "4" (for Version 4 of IP), while the first field of an ST-2 header had a "5." ST-2 didn't use TCP or UDP. Instead, it used different upper-level protocols for real-time transmission, such as the Packet Video Protocol or the Network Voice Protocol.

ST-2 was intended to be only an experimental protocol, and it has since gone by the wayside with the advent of the everything-over-IP movement.

increased address space, address types, automatic address configuration, neighbor discovery, and QoS.

Increased Address Space

If we focus only on the change that IPv6 would make in IP addressing, we'd miss most of its other benefits, but we'd see the attraction that most networking professionals find in IPv6. It would expand the IP address size to 128 bits, raising the number of possible IP addresses to 10^{38}. That's a very large number—more than 900 decillion addresses (more than 900 trillion trillion), which should keep us in IP addresses for a while. It's so large a number that there will be enough IP addresses for several quadrillion or so of them to be assigned for every square meter of the earth's surface. It also means that IP addresses will be twelve dotted-decimal digits long, so they'll be even more difficult to remember than they are today.

Address Types

IPv6 doesn't have address classes, which means that its inventors learned something from the experiences with the original, now-outdated classful IPv4 addressing scheme. Instead of classes of addresses based on network size, IPv6 establishes types of addresses that have implications for how routers make routing decisions. For example, there will be "link-local" addresses, which must not be routed to another subnet, and "site-local" addresses, mentioned earlier, which must not be routed to another site.

Automatic Address Configuration

One of the biggest headaches for a network administrator of an IP network is assigning IP addresses. There is no mandatory logic to assigning host addresses, and if it weren't for DHCP, no automatic way to number hosts. As we have noted, a single host may have both IP addresses and Ethernet addresses, but each refers to different processes and hardware. IPv6 will join these two concepts and make it possible for a host to determine its own address automatically, in a plug-and-play type of autoconfiguration. An IPv6 host can take the number of the network it's on and combine it with its Ethernet address to determine its IPv6 address. Another option will be for an IPv6 host to use a random number to create an IPv6 address.

Neighbor Discovery

The IPv4 Address Resolution Protocol will be replaced by the IPv6 *Neighbor Discovery* (ND) protocol. It will be a single protocol, instead of the various, link-specific versions of ARP that exist in the IPv4 world. Neighbor Discovery will be a multicast protocol, targeting specific neighboring hosts, instead of using the ARP broadcast technique. The disadvantage of ARP's broadcast technique is that it can create "broadcast storms" that flood a network with ARP traffic. In addition, network bridges that are "ND-aware" should be able to control ND traffic more carefully.

QoS

As beneficial as it might be, there won't really be anything in IPv6 that will do anything for QoS. Applications that depend on some measure of QoS, such as streaming audio and video and IP telephony, will still have to rely on other protocols and techniques, such as RSVP, and multiprotocol label and tag switching for QoS capabilities. Basically, IPv6 will do QoS the same way that IPv4 does, which is to say that neither version of IP incorporates any QoS capabilities.

There are a number of other features and capabilities to IPv6, but these are the important ones. They're all incorporated into the standard, so they should make it into actual, working implementations of IPv6 when they start to appear.

Transitioning to IPv6

One of the biggest issues in the IPv6 story is how we get from here to there. That is, what are the technical issues in transitioning IPv4 networks to IPv6, and exactly how are they to be carried out? We'll leave for the time being the more problematic issue of whether the Internet community is interested enough in IPv6 to make the change. The differences in the two protocols' IP address sizes is only one of the issues, but it's the first in a number of stumbling blocks along the road to IPv6. Furthermore, the IP address size has implications for other parts of the network infrastructure. DNS records would have to be added to incorporate new types of resource records with IPv6 addresses, and routers would need to be able to route both IPv4 and IPv6 datagrams.

Three basic strategies have been proposed for making the transition to IPv6:

Dual IP stacks. The first approach to transitioning to IPv6 is for systems to run dual IP protocol stacks, one for IPv4, and the other for IPv6. Both versions of IP interface to TCP as the transport protocol, and to the network layer beneath them. An interface at the application level would have to identify traffic intended for IPv4 or IPv6 hosts (differentiated by their DNS addresses) and direct it to the appropriate version of IP. In Microsoft's experimental IPv6 stack, there's a Winsock 2 applications programming interface (API) that does this.

Tunneling IPv4 in IPv6. A second approach assumes that IP network routers convert to IPv6 first and that IPv4 traffic is tunneled through those networks in IPv6 datagrams. Converting backbone networks to use IPv6 is another issue, but if it were done, it would make IPv6 the backbone protocol, and the stub networks could use IPv4 until they were converted to IPv6.

IPv4-to-IPv6 address translation. The last approach, sometimes referred to as "NAT on steroids," focuses on IPv6 addressing as the fundamental transition problem. In this approach, the backbone network would run IPv6. IPv4 addresses in stub networks would be translated to IPv6 addresses, then sent across the backbone network to the destination, where they would be translated back to IPv4 addresses.

One of the difficulties common to the tunneling and NAT approaches is that any nifty new IPv6 features would be lost in the translation. Clients and servers could keep running IPv4 but use the IPv6 backbone until they converted to IPv6. There's the flaw in the transition plan, though, IPv6 critics say. If there's a way to keep using IPv4, what's the incentive to change? It's a valid concern, and it will remain an issue in the IPv6 debate as long as IPv4 persists as a viable option for Internet communications.

Of the three transition scenarios, the tunneling scenario is the one that seems likely to be the most widely used. It will be a lot easier to convert individual networks connected to the Internet to IPv6 than it will be to convert the Internet backbone itself. Individual corporations, organizations, and enterprises control the former, but no one controls the entirety of the latter. Networks that use IPv6 can tunnel across the IPv4 backbone. When their customers say they want IPv6 on the backbone, ISPs can enable it.

IPv6 and NAT

Regardless of which side networking experts line up on the IPv6 controversy, the fact remains that it seems inevitable that IPv6 will happen eventually. When it does, it may not be called IPv6, but whatever it is, it will have to solve the problems of IPv4. The controversy today seems to be about how long "eventually" is, not necessarily whether IPv6 is even necessary.

If IPv6 solves the address space crisis for the foreseeable future, you might think that it would eliminate the need for NAT. After all, one of the justifications for using NAT is to take pressure off the limits of IPv4 addressing, so shouldn't the arrival of IPv6—whenever that is—also put an end to NAT?

Well, not really, despite the fond wishes of NAT opponents, who think that NAT complicates networking unnecessarily. Like it or not, NAT, in one form or another, is most likely here to stay. There are several reasons why NAT, in one form or another, will be around for a while.

IPv6 Transition

For one thing, NAT is one of the transition strategies for moving from IPv4 to IPv6. We will examine the IPv4-to-IPv6 transition scheme, and how NAT fits into it, later in this chapter, but translating addresses between the IPv4 and IPv6 addressing realms is a practical necessity in the IPv6 transition strategy.

IPv6 Private Addressing

IPv6 will expand the IP addressing space so much that limits on IPv6 address space will disappear. Furthermore, there won't be such a thing as private IPv6 addresses. Instead, hosts will have several different types of IPv6 addresses, some of which border routers won't pass outside the network. This will provide the same "self-sealing" effect as IPv4 private addresses, which Internet routers won't route, without setting aside specific address ranges as "private" IPv6 addresses.

Instead of private addresses, IPv6 hosts will use a site-local address when communicating on the local or enterprise network and a global address when communicating outside the network. A host address will be a 64-bit interface ID, and the site-local address will be another 16-bit address on top of that. Network administrators who don't want traffic to escape from an IPv6 network to the Internet can use only the site-local addresses. IPv6 routers won't forward site-local addresses outside the local network, blocking that traffic from escaping to the outside world.

Load Balancing

Changing addressing schemes won't change the need to spread the load of network traffic across a number of servers. There are more sophisticated load-balancing systems available today than NAT devices that do passive load balancing. For example, there are load-balancing systems that track actual load and availability of individual pool servers and maintain active communications with each server in the pool. Whatever the load-balancing scheme, they still use NAT, translating the single, external virtual address of the site to multiple inside pool server addresses. This technique won't change, even if addressing changes to the longer IPv6 format.

Security

In the future, heightened security concerns will drive almost all networks behind firewalls, intrusion detection systems, and other barriers that conceal the extent and existence of most networked systems. Most networks will be represented to the outside world as a small group of externally visible systems, with addresses mapped and translated back to inside addresses. Obviously, this means NAT, even though those internal networks will probably have site-local IPv6 addresses, instead of private IPv6 addresses.

It's the practical justification for NAT that will keep it going, even in an IPv6 environment. The most pressing NAT issue will be how it will help the Internet get from the IPv4 environment of today into the IPv6 world of tomorrow.

Getting to IPv6

Translating addresses is one thing, but translating between different protocols, even if they're both versions of the IP protocol, is rarely a simple and straightforward exercise. In this section, we'll focus on the address translation issues of transitioning from IPv4 to IPv6, ignoring most of the messy and often gory details of the rest of the IPv4-to-IPv6 protocol translation story. Needless to say, getting from IPv4 to IPv6 involves more than translating addresses. As we have already noted, the IPv6 header is different from the IPv4 header, and moving between the two protocols also means modifying the headers between the two protocols. It's no mean feat, but we'll ignore that problem in this discussion.

The RFC that describes IPv4-to-IPv6 NAT, RFC 2766, combines the principles of a traditional network address translator with that of the complex IPv4-to-IPv6 protocol translation. The latter is detailed in RFC 2765, which describes a IPv4-to-IPv6 protocol translator, leaving the operation of the address translator to RFC 2766.

The protocol translation tactic described in RFC 2765 translates the IPv4 address to a replacement IPv6 address, and vice versa, without maintaining the status of the session, or the "state," between the two. In addition to translating the IPv4 address to an IPv6 address, the NAT device also replaces the IPv4 header with an IPv6 header. On the other hand, there will be such things as IPv4-compatible IPv6 addresses that can be translated automatically, eliminating the need for the state table in a one-to-one mapping.

IPV6 ADDRESS FORMAT

There are three types of IPv6 addresses, each used for a different purpose. They are as follows:

Unicast. Sent to a single interface, although, as noted later, there are several different types of unicast addresses.

Multicast. Sent to a number of interfaces and delivered to all of them.

Anycast. Sent to a number of nodes but delivered to what IPv6 routers consider the "nearest" node.

One of the more confusing things about IPv6 addresses is that a single host with a single interface will have several different types of IPv6 addresses. Multiple addresses may be configured on an IPv4 host interface, but they are the rule in IPv6, not the exception. They may be a link-local address, for communications on a nonrouted Ethernet segment, a unicast address, for use across network segments linked by routers (such as the Internet), and a loopback interface address. IPv4 hosts, by contrast, usually have only two addresses, a host address and the loopback address (127.0.0.1), even though many users aren't aware of the latter.

Every IPv6 interface will have a number of addresses, including the following:

■ Link-local address (one)

■ Site-local address (many)

■ Compatible unicast address (none, one, or many)

(continues)

IPV6 ADDRESS FORMAT *(Continued)*

- Global unicast address (none, one, or many)
- Selected-node multicast address (many)
- Link-local all-nodes multicast address (one)
- Anycast address (many)

Just as the 32 bits of an IPv4 address are represented as being divided into 8-bit segments to make them more comprehensible to people, for representation purposes, the 128 bits of the IPv6 address space are divided into eight 16-bit segments. Instead of representing each 16-bit segment in its decimal form, which is how IPv4 represents each 8-bit byte, IPv6 address notation expresses each 16-bit segment as 4 hexadecimal digits, separated by colons. So, an IPv6 address may be expressed as:

21DB:00B6:0000:2F07:000A:00FF:3F2A:9C5E

To shorten the string of hex digits, any leading zeroes in any of the segments may be deleted. The previous IPv6 address may also be expressed as:

21DB:B6:0:2F07:A:FF:3F2A:9C5E

It's not uncommon for IPv6 addresses to have a number of consecutive segments with all zeroes. Another IPv6 addressing notation convention is to use two consecutive colons (::) to represent some number of all-zero segments. This can be done only once in an IPv6 address, so that the segment order isn't lost. This IPv6 address can be shortened even further as:

21DB:B6::2F07:A:FF:3F2A:9C5E

The zero suppression system can shorten some IPv6 addresses dramatically. For example, this address:

F06A:0000:0000:0000:0000:0000:0000:0006

can be expressed as:

F06A::6

Initially, most IPv6 nodes will be running dual stacks, supporting both IPv4 and IPv6. In most of those cases, the node will have one or more IPv4-compatible addresses on each interface. The IPv6 address will be in the first six 16-bit segments, and the IPv4 address will be in the last two 16-bit segments. The last 2 segments are expressed in the IPv4 "dotted quad" form, so that they appear in their native IPv4 format. An IPv4-compatible IPv6 address might look like this:

0:0:0:0:0:0:192.112.36.5

We might assume that because the versions of the IP protocol are different, IPv4 devices and IPv6 devices won't be mixed together on the same network. It is expected, however, that routers that understand both versions of IP should be able to deal with IPv4 and IPv6 devices just fine. After all, routers can route TCP/IP, AppleTalk, and DECnet devices on the same network, so IPv4 and IPv6 shouldn't impose any substantial problems. Clients running dual stacks will make the IPv4-or-IPv6 decision based on the address of the server.

In order to make the RFC 2765 standard work properly, the source and destination addresses that IPv4 devices use to communicate with IPv6 devices would have to be changed to IPv6 addresses. Similarly, IPv6 addresses would have to be translated back to IPv4 addresses. Conveniently, this translation can be done at the border between the IPv4 and IPv6 addressing realms, at a NAT box that separates the two addressing realms and does address translation, as illustrated in Figure 19.1.

Like a traditional NAT device, the NAT box between the IPv4 and IPv6 networks would bind source and destination addresses in one network with those in the other network. The only significant difference between the function of the NAT box in Figure 19.1 and that of a traditional NAT box is that the IPv4-to-IPv6 NAT box may also act as a DNS application-level gateway (ALG) and read DNS resource records when they come back through the NAT device. It should make whatever changes are necessary in the IP addresses in the resource records, to translate IPv6 DNS addresses to IPv4 address, and vice versa. This won't be necessary in all cases because there could just as easily be a IPv6 DNS on the IPv6 network side, and an IPv4 DNS on the IPv4 side, eliminating the ALG issue.

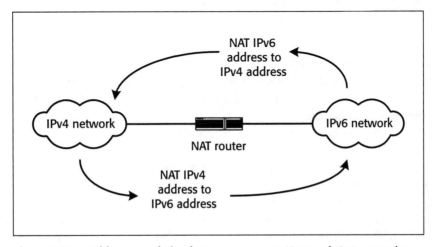

Figure 19.1 Address translation between separate IPv4 and IPv6 networks.

IPV6 DNS RECORDS

In IPv6 networks, DNS will work in much the same way it has under IPv4, but there will be a new type of DNS resource record for IPv6 addresses. The new record is the A6 record, for resolving host names to IPv6 addresses. Host names won't necessarily change under IPv6 because the current system of domain names and subdomains won't change.

The A6 record is similar to the IPv4 A record, in that it maps a host name to an IP address. IPv6 interfaces may have several addresses, and each address may depend on a particular ISP's view of how that network is reachable. There may be several A6 records, each of which creates a linked "chain" of A6 records that identifies a number of addresses for the device. Another IPv6 DNS record will also contain a text domain name, further specifying where the device is located.

For example, a host on a network that is connected to two different ISPs, which are served by different transit ISPs, may have three different host addresses listed in the A6 records in its DNS. Each of the addresses has three parts, all expressed in hexadecimal, which are as follows:

- The ISP's view of the address, called the *Next Level Aggregate*, or NLA (first three octets)

- Local subnet address (fourth octet)

- Local interface address (fifth through eighth octets)

The three addresses listed in the DNS A6 records might look like this:

    2345:00C1:CA11:0001:1234:5678:9ABC:DEF0

    2345:00D2:DA11:0001:1234:5678:9ABC:DEF0

    2345:00D2:EB22:0001:1234:5678:9ABC:DEF0

If an IPv6 device doesn't have a IPv4-compatible address, the NAT device would also have to track the sessions between the two addressing realms. For this reason, as well as for maintaining the IPv4-to-IPv6 address mapping for the sessions, traffic between the two addressing realms would have to pass through the same NAT box, as shown in Figure 19.2. This restriction would be removed for an IPv4-compatible address.

In order to bridge the two network environments, the NAT box would be configured with a block of IPv4 addresses. The NAT box would use these addresses to translate the IPv6 addresses in IPv6 datagrams to IPv4 addresses, replacing the entire IPv6 header with an IPv4 header. The IPv6 host would see the IPv6 side of the NAT box and direct traffic for IPv4 devices either to a single external interface address or to one of several external interface addresses.

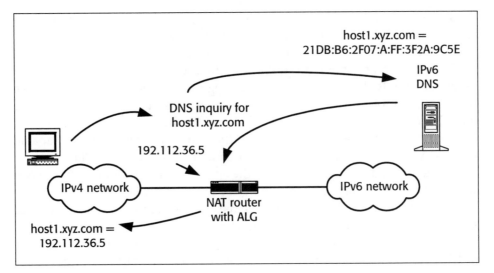

Figure 19.2   DNS ALG translating IPv6 DNS records to IPv4 format.

These would have IPv6 addresses and be resolvable from host names in IPv6 records in the DNS on the IPv6 side of the NAT box. Again, this restriction would not apply for IPv6 interfaces with IPv4-compatible addresses.

Note that the NAT box would replace both the source and the destination address in the IPv6 header with IPv4 addresses. The source address would be the inside interface of the NAT box, and the destination address would be the IPv4 address mapped to the IPv6 destination address.

Is IPv6 Necessary?

Do we really have to go through the trouble of converting everything that runs the IP protocol to IPv6? Or is there some other way around this mess? And is this trip really necessary?

The answers are that yes, we'll probably have to do this sometime, although not necessarily right now. The cell phone and wireless device addressing issue may force the issue eventually, but it may be years in the future. And yes, there is a way around this for the time being. As you might suspect, it's NAT. Even though there are those misguided souls in the networking community who aren't fond of NAT, it works, and it's going to be part of the solution in that it's a viable transition strategy to get from IPv4 to IPv6.

The problems that IPv6 solves are real, and the solutions it proposes, as well as its extra features and capabilities, will be necessary if IP and the Internet are to become ubiquitous networking technologies and networks, respectively. IPv4 has proven itself to be far more flexible, robust, and accommodating than was ever imagined. It's quite remarkable that IP has supported a network of the size, scope, and scale of the Internet, as well as real-time applications, such as streaming video, voice over IP, and multimedia applications.

Host networking professionals will acknowledge that even though those applications are possible with today's Internet technology, they are far from mature. Not only that, but Internet technology as it stands today doesn't give them much hope of improving those applications substantially. Throwing more bandwidth at the problem has led only to the use of applications that demand even more bandwidth. More traffic requires faster and more capable routers. And more IP addressable computers, phones, and Palm Pilots require more and more addresses. It's not that the approaches and solutions have been wrong, it's that we may be approaching the limits of IPv4 technology.

IPv6 is intended to solve these problems. Expanding the size of the address space means only that the crush of IP devices can get exponentially larger, which makes the problem worse, not better. We have left out most of the story of IPv6 addressing, though. It goes far beyond the size of the address space and incorporates various types of addresses, autoconfiguration of host addresses, and other capabilities intended to help the Internet scale tremendously. And Internet routing will be hierarchical, imposing some organization on what is today a deterministic core routing system.

Who's to Decide?

It's not the individual network manager or IT executive who will decide on moving the entire Internet from IPv4 to IPv6. Instead, they will have the power to move their own networks to IPv6 first, then let the rest of the Internet follow when it's ready to do so. As with many network infrastructure changes, most users will be unaware that anything has changed, as they are usually shielded from changes to the Internet's network infrastructure. Unless it leads to a substantial improvement in performance, most users are unaware of any changes that don't affect applications directly.

There are two schools of thought about how the transition to IPv6 will get started. The first is that individual network managers or IT executives will decide to move their networks to IPv6. They will run dual IPv4 and IPv6 protocol stacks on hosts in their networks and configure their DNS servers to handle both IPv4 A records and IPv6 A6 records. IPv6 traffic will be tunneled through the Internet as IPv4 traffic, and then reach an IPv6 host on another IPv6 network on the other side of the Internet. As far as the hosts are concerned, they will talking IPv6 to each other.

Another part of this scenario, and part of the impetus for individual networks making the transition to IPv6, may be the creation of new IPv6 networks for cell phones, PDAs, and other wireless devices. These devices will use IPv6 from the start, and there will be so many of them that they will kick off the move to IPv6.

The other school of thought is that the change to IPv6 isn't a grass-roots kind of thing at all and that network managers and IT executives will be followers, not leaders. According to this school of thought, the move to IPv6, when it occurs, will be initiated by the big, top-level ISPs, who will convert the core of the Internet to IPv6 and then lay out the blueprint for the rest of the Internet and attached networks to follow. The theory in this school of thought is that the big ISPs have the most to gain from IPv6 and that they are in a position to wield enough influence to force such a change.

It will probably take dramatic action by some organization or entity who has the power to force change to make that change occur. Individual corporate or enterprise networks could convert to IPv6, but who would necessarily follow? If the Internet core converted to IPv6, there would be a reason for all of the smaller ISP networks, and the customer networks behind them, to follow suit.

Whether the big, top-level ISPs are interested in converting to IPv6 is another question. Most of them are preoccupied with keeping the Internet running for another day, making sure their routers can keep up with the rising tide of traffic, adding backbone bandwidth, and stabilizing their routing tables. Who can think of orchestrating changing all of their infrastructure for IPv6 and introducing who knows what kinds of interface problems with their customer networks? Like any change, it's fraught with the potential for problems, which is why no one's made the move yet. Admittedly, some of the IPv6 standards are still in flux, so any IPv6 movement may have to wait until all of the necessary standards are in place.

Most people agree that the change to IPv6 is the right thing to do but that it's not practical yet. If the change can be made as transparently as IPv6 proponents claim it will be, then maybe it isn't such a big deal. If the Internet is to continue to grow, and if the demand for IP addresses will not abate, the Internet community will have to devise a transition strategy to leave IPv4 behind.

How practical is that scenario? There are precedents for starting things over "the right way," however that's defined. The Apple iMac, for instance, was the first successful, mass-market, "legacy-free" system. Instead of being preoccupied with backward compatibility with all kinds of older peripherals and interfaces, the iMac abandoned most of them in favor of Ethernet, USB ports, and a CD drive. Some of the interfaces and peripherals to which the iMac had no direct interface included some that were, for a time, unique to Apple, such as the SCSI interface. Apple's view was that things will never change for the better as long as computers and their owners cling to the past.

The IT Executive's View

Moving enterprise networks to IPv6 usually has few champions in the IT executive ranks. Among IT executives, backward compatibility and transitioning to the future are conflicting goals that must be balanced carefully. There is good reason to believe that most major computer systems vendors will pro-vide support for IPv6 in parallel with IPv4, which will make it easier to justify the transition.

For example, Microsoft has an IPv6 protocol stack for Windows, which it makes available as part of the Windows Developers' Toolkit. It isn't embedded in every copy of Windows 2000, but it's available for application developers and network engineers, to test how IPv6 will work. It's reasonable to expect that in the future, Windows (or whatever Microsoft calls it) will ship with both the IPv4 and IPv6 protocol stacks and will support running both protocols at the same time. Cisco has production IPv6 code for many of its routers, and other router manufacturers will soon do so as well.

It's unlikely, however, that many IT executives will be willing to stake their careers on initiating a move to IPv6. There's no industry mandate to do so, and the benefits for an individual network aren't clear. The IP addressing crisis? That's somebody else's problem. And why march to that different drummer if nobody else is? Even though IPv6 will be hidden in the network infrastructure of the Internet, there's no compelling reason today why any customer network should convert to IPv6.

That doesn't mean that network managers and IT executives should ignore it, either. The best advice is to stay aware of how it might be implemented and to prepare for it. Once most network software vendors support IPv6, convert-ing to IPv6 may not be a huge operational undertaking. It will certainly be eas-ier if network managers and IT executives pay attention to regular network upkeep and maintenance. For example, keeping and maintaining current and accurate network documentation are always useful, and they'd be essential in an IPv6 conversion. Staying up to speed on routing policy issues with ISPs and business partners is another. And understanding the issues and operational requirements of NAT is another because the conversion to IPv6 would most likely involve NAT.

Summary

If we were to take a poll of the Internet community today about what the Inter-net needs most, we would find that users want faster response times, more bandwidth, and more reliable communications. A few might say we need a bigger IP address space or more efficient ways to use what we have. Those who are aware of how the Internet operates might say that we need a more robust way to scale the Internet into the future, make the Internet more reli-able, and provide Quality of Service capabilities.

But getting to those desirable goals may be a function of how well we imple-ment changes in the Internet infrastructure, such as CIDR, NAT, route aggre-gation, and IPv6. Maybe the fabulous invalid that is IPv4 isn't such an invalid after all, but most people would agree that the Internet can't keep growing indefinitely and infinitely without some change to its basic plumbing. The problem is that IPv6 is good medicine, but the anticipation of its bad taste is enough to make even the biggest of the ISPs turn away. But someday, something will have to be done.

Today, IPv6 is largely an engineering exercise in setting standards and redefining those standard through the RFC process. There are some experimental IPv6 networks, but they're neither well known nor widely used. Networking people, however, are getting some experience with IPv6 that will be valuable when the Internet does make the change to IPv6.

Bibliography

RFCs

RFC 950   "Internet Standard Subnetting Procedure." J. Mogul, J. Postel. 1985.

RFC 959   "File Transfer Protocol." J. Postel, J. Reynolds. 1985.

RFC 1060   "Assigned Numbers." J. Reynolds, J. Postel. 1990.

RFC 1155   "Structure and Identification of Management Information for TCP/IP-based Internets." M. Rose, K. McCloghrie. 1990.

RFC 1518   "An Architecture for IP Address Allocation with CIDR." Y. Rekhter, T. Li. 1993.

RFC 1519   "Classless Inter-Domain Routing (CIDR): An Address Assignment and Aggregation Strategy." V. Fuller, T. Li, J. Yu, K. Varadhan. 1993.

RFC 1631   "The IP Network Address Translator." K. Egevang, P. Francis. 1994.

RFC 1700   "Assigned Numbers." J. Reynolds, J. Postel. 1994.

RFC 1715   "The H Ratio for Address Assignment Efficiency." C. Huitema. 1994.

RFC 1817   "CIDR and Classful Addressing." Y. Rekhter. 1995.

RFC 1819   "Internet Stream Protocol Version 2 (ST2)." L. Delgrossi, L. Berger, eds. 1995.

RFC 1918   "Address Allocation for Private Internets." Y. Rekhter, B. Moskowitz, D. Karrenberg, G. J. de Groot, E. Lear. 1996.

RFC 2008   "Implications of Various Address Allocation Policies for Internet Routing." Y. Rekhter, T. Li. 1996.

RFC 2026   "The Internet Standards Process." S. Bradner. 1996.

RFC 2050   "Internet Registry IP Allocation Guidelines." K. Hubbard, M. Kosters, D. Conrad, D. Karrenberg, J. Postel. 1996.

RFC 2205   "Resource Reservation Protocol (RSVP)." R. Braden, L. Zhang, S. Berson, S. Herzog, S. Jamin. 1997.

RFC 2260   "Scalable Support for Multi-homed Multi-provider Connectivity." T. Bates, Y. Rekhter, 1998.

RFC 2373   "IP Version 6 Addressing Architecture." R. Hinden, S. Deering. 1998.

RFC 2391   "Load Sharing Using IP Network Address Translation (LSNAT)." P. Srisuresh, D. Gan. 1998.

RFC 2401   "Security Architecture for the Internet Protocol." S. Kent, R. Atkinson. 1998.

RFC 2460   "Internet Protocol, Version 6 (IPv6) Specification." S. Deering, R. Hinden. 1998.

RFC 2543   "SIP: Session Initiation Protocol." R. Handley, H. Schulzrinne, E. Schooler, J. Rosenberg. 1999.

RFC 2661   "Layer Two Tunneling Protocol L2TP." W. Townsley, A. Valencia, A. Rubens, G. Pall, G. Zorn, B. Palter. 1999.

RFC 2663   "IP Network Address Translator (NAT) Terminology and Considerations." P. Srisuresh, M. Holdrege. 1999.

RFC 2694   "DNS Extensions to Network Address Translators (DNS-ALG)." P. Srisuresh, G. Tsirtsis, P. Akkiraju, A Heffernan. 1999.

RFC 2765   "Stateless IP/ICMP Translation Algorithm (SIIT)." E. Nordmark. 2000.

RFC 2766   "Network Address Translation – Protocol Translation (NAT-PT)." G. Tsirtsis, P. Srisuresh. 2000.

RFC 2784   "Generic Routing Encapsulation." D. Farinacci, T. Li, S. Hanks, D. Meyer, P. Traina. 2000.

Internet Drafts

"IP Network Address Translation (NAT) Protocol Issues" (draft-ietf-nat-protocol-issues-00.txt). N. Holdrege and P. Srisuresh. August 1999.

"Security Model with Tunnel-mode IPsec for NAT Domains" (draft-ietf-nat-security-02.txt). P. Srisuresh. 1999.

"Realm Specific IP: Framework" (draft-ietf-nat-rsip-framework-02.txt). M. Borella, J. Lo, D. Grabelsky, G. Montenegro. 2000.

"Realm Specific IP: Protocol Specification" (draft-ietf-nat-rsip-protocol-06.txt). M. Borella, J. Lo, D. Grabelsky, G. Montenegro. 2000.

"RSIP Support for End-to-End IPsec" (draft-ietf-nat-rsip-ipsec-03.txt). G. Montenegro, M. Borella. 2000.

"A Multihoming Solution Using NATs" (draft-akkiraju-nat-multihoming-00.txt). P. Akkiraju, Y. Rekhter. 1998.

"Protocol Complications with the IP Network Address Translation (NAT) (draft-ietf-nat-protocol-complications-02.txt). M. Holdrege, P. Srisuresh. 2000.

"An SNMP Application Level Gateway for Payload Address Translation" (draft-ietf-nat-snmp-alg-02.txt). D. Raz, B. Sugla. 1999.

"DNS Extensions to Support IPv6 Address Aggregation and Renumbering" (draft-ietf-ipngwg-dns-lookups-08.txt). C. Huitema, S. Thomson, M. Crawford. 2000.

Books

Albitz, Paul and Cricket Lu. 1998. *DNS and BIND*, 3rd ed. Sebastapol, CA: O'Reilly & Associates.

Albritton, John. 1999. *Cisco IOS Essentials*. New York: McGraw-Hill.

Berkowitz, Howard C. 1999. *Designing Routing and Switching Architectures for Enterprise Networks*. New York: Macmillan Technical Publishing.

Chapman, Barry and Edward Zwick. 1996. *Building Internet Firewalls*. Sebastapol, CA: O'Reilly & Associates.

Comer, Douglas. 2000. *Internetworking with TCP/IP Volume 1: Principles, Protocols, and Architecture*, 4th ed. Englewood Cliffs, NJ: Prentice-Hall.

Graham, Buck. 1997. *TCP/IP Addressing*. San Diego, CA: Academic Press.

Greenberg, Eric. 1998. *Network Application Frameworks: Design and Architecture*. Reading, MA: Addison-Wesley.

Habraken, Joseph W. 1999. *Practical Cisco Routers*. Indianapolis, IN: Que Corporation.

Held, Gilbert. 1999. *Understanding Data Communications*, 6th ed. Indianapolis, IN: New Riders Publishing.

Huitema, Christian. 1995. *Routing in the Internet*. Englewood Cliffs, NJ: Prentice-Hall.

Hunt, Craig. 1998. *TCP/IP Network Administration*. Sebastapol, CA: O'Reilly & Associates.

Huston, Geoff. 1999. *ISP Survival Guide*. New York: John Wiley & Sons.

Kaufman, Elizabeth and Andrew Newman. 1999. *Implementing IPsec: Making Security Work on VPNs, Intranets, and Extranets*. New York: John Wiley & Sons.

Kosiur, Dave. 1998. *Building and Managing Virtual Private Networks*. New York: John Wiley & Sons.

Lemon, Ted and Ralph Droms. 1999. *The DHCP Handbook: Understanding, Deploying, and Managing Automated Configuration Services*. New York: Macmillan Technical Publishing.

Lewis, Chris. 1999. *Cisco TCP/IP: Routing Professional Reference*, 2nd ed. New York: McGraw-Hill.

Siyan, Karanjit, ed. 1997. *Inside TCP/IP: A Comprehensive Introduction to Protocols and Concepts*. Indianapolis, IN: New Riders Publishing.

Slattery, Terry and Bill Burton. 1998. *Advanced IP Routing with Cisco Networks (Cisco Technical Expert)*. New York: McGraw-Hill.

Sportak, Mark. 1999. *IP Routing Fundamentals*. San Jose, CA: Cisco Press.

Stallings, William. 1998. *SNMP, SNMPv2, SNMPv3, and RMON 1 and 2*, 3rd ed. Reading, MA: Addison-Wesley.

Steward, John W. III. 1998. *BGP4—Inter-Domain Routing on the Internet*. Reading, MA: Addison-Wesley.

Articles

Akkiraju, P., K. Delgadillo, and Y. Rekhter. 1998. "Enabling Enterprise Multihoming with Cisco IOS Network Address Translation (NAT)." (from www.cisco.com/warp/public/cc/cisco/mkt/ios/nat/tech/emios_wp.htm).

Angel, Jonathan. 2000. "Toll Lanes on the Information Superhighway." *Network Magazine*, February.

"Basic Steps in Writing a DirectPlay Application." 2000. Microsoft Developer's Network. msdn.microsoft.com/library/psdk/directx.

Borello, Mike. 2000. "Protocol Helps Stretch IPv4 Addresses."*Network World*, January 17.

"Introduction to IPv6." www.microsoft.com/technet/network/ipvers6.asp.

Loshin, Pete. 2000. "IPv6 –Why Bother. *Boardwatch Magazine*, March.

Mace, Scott. 2000. "Enter IPv6: New Protocol, Not a Root Canal or a Forklift Upgrade." *Boardwatch Magazine*, February.

Salus, Peter H. 1999. "One Byte at a Time: Internet Addressing." *The Internet Protocol Journal*, Vol.2, No. 4, December.

Semeria, Chuck. 1998. "Understanding IP Addressing: Everything You Wanted to Know." 3Com. www.3com.com/nsc/501302.html.

Index

access control lists, 81, 82, 151, 285
acquisitions, NAT's effect on, 55
active load sharing, 171, 179–180
addresses, *see* IP addresses
addressing crisis, *see* IP addressing crisis
Address Resolution Protocol (ARP), 142, 295, 297
Address Resolution Protocol (ARP) table, 21, 22
Address Supporting Organization (ASO), 189
Age of Empires, 98
aggregation, *see* IP address aggregation
ALG, *see* application-level gateway
American Registry of Internet Addresses (ARIN), 7, 41, 53
    address assignment by, 146–148, 189–190
anycast addresses, 301
APNIC, 147, 189
application-layer header, 14, 16
application-level gateway (ALG), 24, 39, 63
    with DNS, 89, 104–106, 129
    and IPsec, 207
    for IP telephony, 95

IPv4–to–IPv6 translation, 303
NAT contrasted, 88–89
NAT routers as, 161
and performance, 40
reliability problems, 234
for SNMP, 99–100
and VPNs, 228
applications. *See also* specific applications
    checking, 258, 282
    considering in planning stage, 254–255
    making safe for NAT, 106–109
    NAT's effect on, 38–39, 87–110
    NAT's effect on new, 47–48
    and static NAT, 63
application weighting, 177
A records, 125
    for load balancing, 166–168
ARIN, *see* American Registry of Internet Addresses
a.root-servers.net, 118
ARP, 142, 295, 297
ARPANET, 139–140, 188
ARP table, 21, 22
Asia-Pacific NIC (APNIC), 147, 189
A6 record, 304
ATM, 15
attackers, *see* hackers
authentication, VPNs, 222

Automatic Private IP Addressing (APIPA), 144–145
Autonomous System Number, 194

balancing, of loads, *see* load balancing
bandwidth, unbalanced, 156
Battlenet, 98
Berkeley Internet Names Distribution (BIND) program, 115
BGP, 102, 139, 157
BigIP devices, 180
BIND program, 115
Border Gateway Protocol (BGP), 102, 139, 157
broadcast storms, 297
business partners, NAT's effect on relationship with, 56–57

cable modems, 291
Call ID field (PPTP), 209–210, 229
Call Signal Address, 96
Canonical Name (CNAME) records, 126
cellular phones, 290, 291
checksum, *see* IP checksum; TCP checksum
CIDR (Classless Inter-Domain Routing), 42, 138–139, 187, 290